GERMAN PAINTING

OF THE 19TH CENTURY

INTRODUCTION AND CATALOGUE

by

KERMIT S. CHAMPA

with

KATE H. CHAMPA

YALE UNIVERSITY ART GALLERY

NEW HAVEN, CONNECTICUT

in collaboration with THE CLEVELAND MUSEUM OF ART

and THE ART INSTITUTE OF CHICAGO

Library of Congress catalog card number: 78–137506

Designed by John O. C. McCrillis.
Set in Baskerville type.
Color plates by Brüder Hartmann, Berlin.
Printed in the United States of America by The Carl Purington
Rollins Printing-Office of the Yale University Press.

FRONTISPIECE   Feuerbach: *Iphigenia*, 1871. 77″ x 56″   Staatsgalerie, Stuttgart   Cat. no. 28

LENDERS TO THE EXHIBITION

Federal Republic of Germany

Berlin, Staatliche Museen, Preussischer Kulturbesitz, Nationalgalerie
Prof. Dr. Werner Haftmann, Director

Bremen, Kunsthalle
Dr. Günter Busch, Director

Cologne, Wallraf-Richartz Museum
Prof. Dr. Gert von der Osten, Director

Darmstadt, Hessisches Landesmuseum
Dr. Gerhard Bott, Director

Duisburg, DEMAG–AG

Düsseldorf, Kunstmuseum
Dr. Wend von Kalnein, Director

Essen, Museum Folkwang
Dr. Paul Vogt, Director

Frankfurt/Main, Städelsches Kunstinstitut
Prof. Dr. Ernst Holzinger, Director

Hamburg, Kunsthalle
Prof. Dr. Werner Hofmann, Director

Hannover, Niedersächsisches Landesmuseum
Dr. Harald Seiler, Director

Heidelberg, Kurpfälzisches Museum der Stadt
Dr. Klaus Mugdan, Director

Karlsruhe, Staatliche Kunsthalle
Prof. Dr. Jan Lauts, Director

Mannheim, Städtisches Kunsthalle
Dr. Heinz Fuchs, Director

Munich, Städtische Galerie (Im Lenbach Haus)
Dr. Hans Konrad Röthel, Director

Nuremberg, City Art Collection

Nuremberg, Germanisches Nationalmuseum
Dr. Wulf Schadendorf, Director

3

Saarbrücken, Saarland Museum
    Dr. Rudolf Bornschein, Director

Schweinfurt, Sammlung Georg Schäfer
    Dr. Konrad Kaiser, Curator

Stuttgart, Staatsgalerie
    Prof. Dr. Peter Beye, Director

Wuppertal, Von der Heydt-Museum der Stadt
    Dr. Günther Aust, Director

4

ACKNOWLEDGMENTS

On behalf of Yale University, the Cleveland Museum of Art and the Art Institute of Chicago, I wish to thank the West German Government, the many West German Museums and the four private collectors whose generosity in lending has made the exhibition possible, and whose names appear on pages 3 and 4.

When Professor Champa first proposed, some four years ago, that the time had come for a comprehensive exhibition of 19th Century German Painting, he wrote to me as follows: "By general agreement among scholars in 19th century art and culture, this particular phase of 19th century art history appears to be both central in importance and unique in its neglect by non-German scholars. Since a great deal of both British and American 19th century art developed on the basis of influences from Germany rather than from France, many important issues remain clouded by an ignorance of German sources. Beyond this, most scholars generally recognize the fact that Germany produced during the 19th century more artists of major international stature than any other country outside of France."

The present exhibition is the result of long planning and careful consideration to achieve as balanced a presentation as possible of the best German painting of the period. While Professor Champa is responsible for the final selection of paintings, he was assisted early in his deliberations by an informal advisory committee consisting of Professor Dr. Gert von der Osten, General Director of the Museums of the City of Cologne; Dr. Werner Haftmann, Director of the Nationalgalerie, Berlin; Dr. Alfred Hentzen, Director Emeritus of the Hamburger Kunsthalle and Professor Dr. Kurt Martin of Munich. Dr. Hasso Freiherr von Maltzahn and Dr. Rowas of the Foreign Office in Bonn were instrumental in making arrangements with the West German Government for the partial financing of the exhibition. To all of these gentlemen go our deepest gratitude for their interest and extraordinary patience as the exhibition was finally brought into being. We are grateful also to the West German Government itself for its assistance and also to Mr. Paul Kurbjuhn, Consul for Information and Cultural Affairs of the German Consulate General in Boston, Massachusetts, for his continued interest and support. Finally, on the German side, we are greatly indebted to Dr. Helmut R. Leppien, Director of the Kunsthalle, Cologne, for supervising all the technical details incident to the collection, packing and transport of paintings from Germany to this country.

On the American side, we are much indebted to the following members of the Yale University Art Gallery staff: Mrs. Anne-Marie Logan, Associate Curator of Drawings and Prints, for extensive assistance in the translation of German correspondence; Mrs. Virginia M. Haggin, Registrar, in charge of all loan forms and shipping arrangements; Mrs. Estelle Miehle, Administrative Assistant and financial accountant for the exhibition; and Miss Dorothy M. Hooker, Secretary to the Director, who has given major assistance in the coordination of loan requests and the correspondence related thereto. In addition, thanks are due to Mrs. V. A. Champa for preliminary typing of Professor Champa's manuscript and, for bibliographical research, Miss Grace Seiberling, Mrs. Marjorie B. Cohn, and Miss Marilyn Friedman.

ANDREW CARNDUFF RITCHIE
Director
Yale University Art Gallery

5

Exhibition Dates:

Yale University Art Gallery, October 15–November 22, 1970
The Cleveland Museum of Art, December 9, 1970–January 24, 1971
The Art Institute of Chicago, February 27–March 28, 1971

INTRODUCTION

It would be inaccurate to say that nineteenth-century German painting is totally unknown beyond the borders of its homeland. Yet such a statement contains at least a degree of polemical truth. For most non-Germans nineteenth-century painting is understood historically and aesthetically in terms of a French tradition beginning with Jacques Louis David and terminating in an open-ended question in the art of Paul Cezanne. Painting in France from David to Cezanne appears in retrospect as a model of coherent development, embracing at once moments of continuity and of revolution and resolving them all into a transcendent artistic achievement. The painting of other lands—England, America, Belgium, or Denmark—is comparatively incoherent in its history and its quality; and much of the interest which nineteenth-century non-French painting exhibits derives from this incoherence, particularly in the minds and hearts of a native audience. As Americans we revel in the individual achievements of a Thomas Cole, a George Caleb Bingham, or a Thomas Eakins. We grant the primacy of French art as a starting point. We then proceed to our own, and with a sense of near surprise find that our achievements, while not perhaps of the same order as those of the French, are not totally without merit. Having discovered merit we quickly forgive either ignorance of, or dependence upon, French art in the work we choose to honor. What we do in this respect is not very different from what the British, the Belgians, and the Danes do with their native traditions; and, furthermore, it is not wrong. We would not under any circumstances presume to devalue French achievement in order to elevate our own; nor would we, as Americans, expect the British, the Belgians, or the Danes to import our enthusiasms. Content with the recognition of French achievement and grateful for our own we cease looking for achievement elsewhere. Rejecting for the moment such American social subpsychoses as anglophilia, we seem actually to resist dealing with more than "ours" and "the French." Fortunately, the facts of history are gradually forcing us to abandon this comfortable stance. No longer can all movements and influences in nineteenth-century painting be traced to Paris. A surprising number of nineteenth-century Americans, Englishmen, and the like chose Munich or Düsseldorf over Paris as the place to study painting abroad; and in Rome, the world capital of artistic pilgrimage, a street, the Via degli Artisti, was named after German, not French, artists. It was the Germans from Asmus Jacob Carstens to Hans von Marées who dominated the contemporary art scene of nineteenth-century Rome.

From Rome and from Germany itself painters and paintings, too long ignored by non-German critics and historians, cast a shadow of influence over the painting of all western countries. The various forms and degrees of German influence upon nineteenth-century painting in general can only be assessed once it is granted and once the painting itself is better known outside of Germany. One can, however, state at the outset that the influence was considerable—so considerable that it represents a definite international "second stream," less clear in its course than that of France, no less comprehensive, and at times equally vital.

Rather than acting as a backwater for French development or as a classically provincial phenomenon, German painting constituted itself as a source—a confused, but powerful, aesthetic source in its own right. It did so in advance of the existence of a real nation to support it and it appears, in contrast to French painting, rather heterogeneous. But in its very heterogeneity German nineteenth-century painting ranged more widely in its pursuit of artistic significance. It was blessed with an enormous reservoir of major talent. This talent both marked out its achievements and frustrated itself in ways particular to Germany. The ratio of achievement to frustration was unfortunately less favorable than that which obtained in French painting and, as a result, the efforts of many important German artists were as prone to end in shipwreck as they were in a successful voyage.

Unlike the French, German artists in the nineteenth century had very little which they could take for granted. To phrase the situation in Hegelian terms, German painters and the society they represented found themselves increasingly "world-historical" as the century developed, without at the same time having either history or institutions capable of defining precisely what this meant. Seen as a whole, and severed from the coattail of the Austrian Empire, Germany began the nineteenth century without significant external history or internal self-definition. The impact of recent political revolutions in France and America was more theoretical than actual in Germany. Most German intellectuals came to realize very quickly that the kind of immediate political freedom and progress which these revolutions promised were remote ideals in a country of nearly eighteen hundred independent or semi-independent political subdivisions. The sheer numerical complexity of these subdivisions effectively threatened to dissolve any potential revolution (and accompanying constitutions, etc.) almost before the fact. Something which worked in Frankfurt would be thwarted in Dresden, or Munich, or Berlin, or in any number of other political subcapitals. German writers, whether poets or philosophers, longed increasingly for a simple, but at the same time prouder and more powerful Germany—the old medieval "Holy Roman Empire of the German Nation." Monuments to the greatness of a distant German past were eulogized as quickly as they were discovered. From the time of Goethe's essay in praise of Erwin von Steinbach, the Master of Strasbourg Cathedral, to Sulpitz Boisserée's successful efforts to collect masterpieces of old German painting and finally to gain publicly subscribed financial support for the completion (after six hundred years) of the Cathedral of Cologne, Germany's Gothic past provided whatever spiritual rallying point there was for incipient pan-German greatness in the arts or anywhere else. That this rallying point was mystical, inaccurate, and in the eyes of the mature Goethe himself seemingly misguided, made very little difference. It was something for a whole generation of Germans to hold onto through the painfully embarrassing years of the Napoleonic occupation of the western and southern parts of their country.

While embarrassing and in many ways humiliating, the Napoleonic occupation actually served to advance the definition of Germany as a cultural and political entity. Having isolated the kingdom of Brandenburg-Prussia, Napoleon provided a generally uniform and streamlined civil service in the remainder of Germany. Further, he encouraged quasi-liberal political institutions based on French prototypes and he permitted considerable freedom of speech, press, and so forth. But, most important, he reduced the number of political subdivisions within the country and created more or less viable states. His "states" survived the Congress of Vienna and became a Germany, partly under Prussian control, partly independent, and partly watched over by Austria, but at least latently "German."

For two-thirds of the century latency was enough. Regional customs barriers fell and industry and population exploded, making for economic interdependency in the country as a whole. At the same time regional autonomy on many social and cultural levels persisted, and to many observers Germany (prior to 1870) possessed an ideal balance between national unity and regional particularity. It contrasted markedly with France, where a single city, namely Paris, executed all of the political, the social, and the cultural functions of government. But if everything in France focused on Paris, everything was at least focused; and this was not, unfortunately, the case in Germany. Bismarck in his role as chancellor of Prussia understood Germany's lack of focus in political and economic terms. He realized that without central control Germany lacked an international stature and a voice commensurate with its productivity and potential military power. With the lever of a short, unnecessary war with France in 1870, Bismarck unified Germany under Prussia. The new Reich was declared and over the next forty-five years Germany became "modern," "federal," and focused with a vengeance.

The diffuseness of nineteenth-century Germany, its lack of cosmopolitan definition, contributed a very distinct character to the painting it produced. To put it differently, this diffuseness prevented nineteenth-century German painting from generating the kind of cumulative force which seems almost abstractly to have directed French painting over the same period. Germany had no central academy. Each major city had its own. The academies differed considerably in terms of their curricula, their exhibition policy, and their staff of professors. Over a twenty- or thirty-year period any one academy was capable of enormous transformation. A new director might reshape an entire school, or artists outside of the faculty who resided, visited, or at times just exhibited in a particular town might influence a school indirectly. Throughout most of the nineteenth century German academies were numerous, changeable in nature, and never unquestionably dominant beyond the bounds of a given town. Neither as individual institutions nor as groups did they provide the highly formalized standards, the elaborate system of rewards and nonrewards for artists characteristic of the French Académie des Beaux-Arts and made public at annual or biennial Salon exhibitions.

In any given period in the nineteenth century one or another local academy would gain a reputation for its emphasis upon a certain aspect or type of painting. For a young artist, whether German or foreign, the prospect of being able to choose his place of study on the basis of his knowledge of the particular values it emphasized must have seemed very attractive. The period 1835–45, for example, offered the following obvious possibilities (mentioning only the largest of the academies): Munich—history painting with a strong emphasis on sixteenth-century Italian style and little stress upon working from nature; Düsseldorf—history and landscape painting with a balanced curriculum of work from nature and work copying elements from sixteenth-century Italian painting; Berlin—portraiture, perspective painting, and a generally strong bias toward the transcription of nature with drawing emphasized; and Dresden—landscape, both

11

intimate and panoramic, stressing a balance of drawing and painting. The academic menu in Germany was different twenty years before 1840 and it would differ again twenty years later, but it remained a menu from which either one school could be chosen or many sampled. The element of potential "freedom" afforded to a young artist by all of this is obvious; the element of potential frustration perhaps less so.

Yet frustration was the most obvious historical result of the number and variety of academies in Germany. The situation had built into it a kind of aesthetic relativism which undercut any possibility of continued artistic development. All artistic values seemed infinitely susceptible to change and to argument. At no time was there anything like a national artistic consensus, nor was there any real possibility of the productive evolution of a given set of artistic ideas. Important artists were for the most part lone figures. Working single-mindedly either from nature or from the art of the past, painters from Caspar David Friedrich to Lovis Corinth marked off their individual paths outside the academies and without any really significant reference to them. The French artist's ability to set his works within or against prevailing academic norms was in fact a luxury, and a great one at that, which the Germans never truly possessed. In exchange for his freedom the German painter was forced into a critical vacuum. Compelled to seek out standards rather than simply to accept or reject them, he ran the risk of constant self-indulgence and self-deception, something which no French artist could risk in precisely the same way.

The tenacity of academic norms in France made their acceptance a matter of course and their rejection a matter of such concern that an artist like Manet or Courbet placed his entire reputation on the firing line in every major work he exhibited. The threat which these norms conveyed could be countered only by the most immense reservoirs of talent and ambition. An innovative work in nineteenth-century France confronted a comparatively firm and academically biased public taste. In order to convert this taste the pioneer works of Edouard Manet and Gustave Courbet, or those of Théodore Géricault and Eugène Delacroix before them, were informed with that kind of unshakable conviction that can only result from absolutely heroic self-confidence in a situation of total vulnerability. No German artist ever faced so definite a firing line. Because of the diversity and inherent relativity of artistic standards in Germany, public taste was self-conscious, ill-informed, and, in the opinion of most non-Germans, uniformly poor. It is doubtful whether the nineteenth-century German art public of any major city ever had a very strong notion of what did or did not constitute an important painting. But the public could hardly be blamed since the artists tended to share their confusion. Unless he appealed directly to a prevailing bourgeois love for storytelling, an artist could be no more certain of broad public approval for painting in the manner of a local academy than he could be were he to follow a different course. The axiom that can be drawn from this is that every German painter began his art from scratch, making his own decisions as to what it should or should not include. He began by choosing where and what to learn and he proceeded, depending upon his talent and his ability to criticize himself, to achieve more or less significant artistic results. No national group of painters in modern art history as we know it have had this almost overwhelming degree of freedom forced upon them. What is then most remarkable about German nine-

12

teenth-century painters is the fact that so many of them succeeded, albeit in frequently perverse and indirect ways, in producing paintings of undeniably high quality under circumstances which had virtually no built-in promise of viable criticism, encouragement, direction, or support.

The early stages of nineteenth-century German painting revealed very clearly the patterns which would dominate it. These patterns were first diagnosed by Johann Wolfgang von Goethe who saw them for what they were—intensely problematic. Granting the fact that German painting entered the nineteenth century without the precedent of having had a viable eighteenth-century tradition of its own, what began to happen in 1797 and thereafter still seems surprising if one maintains as a comparative reference contemporary developments in France. In France between 1784 and 1794 Jacques Louis David produced a succession of major paintings, beginning with his *Oath of the Horatii*. These paintings drew together stylistic and iconographical threads from earlier so-called neoclassic painting, bound them with an unfailing sense of French classical theater, and reinforced them with a profound belief in study (at least of the human figure) from nature. The result was a qualitative point of reference for an entire century —a point of reference so strong and secure that it virtually guaranteed the tradition which it began. In Germany Wilhelm Wackenroder published, in 1797, his *Memoirs of an Art Loving Monk* where, in an essay rather than in a painting, the call for a new German art was sounded. The model of this art lay, as Wackenroder saw it, in Germany's late medieval and early Renaissance past—in the work of Albrecht Dürer, which was now placed polemically on a level with that of Raphael. Dürer was for Wackenroder a demonstration of the fact that Germany's artistic potential had never been in doubt. Even at the moment of Italy's fairest blossom, Raphael, Germany had countered with Dürer, a rougher and less graceful artist than Raphael—but perhaps even more eloquently spiritual and certainly more honest. Wackenroder contrasted the spiritual power and virility of German art in Dürer's hands with the weak, derivative character it had assumed in later centuries. "German art was a pious youth reared among kinsmen, within the walls of a small town; now that he is older, he has become an ordinary man of the world, who has wiped from his soul, together with provincial customs, his feeling and his special character." Yet racially and geographically the promise of German art remained: "Not only under the Italian sky, under majestic domes and Corinthian columns, but also under pointed arches, intricately decorated buildings, and gothic towers true art grows."

13

In actual fact Wackenroder's essay directed itself toward the art of the past, but few readers failed to understand its desire to expose Germany's contemporary artistic weakness and to contrast that weakness with a great and unrealized national artistic destiny. Like so many romantic historians, Wackenroder phrased his polemics of national artistic pride in the distant past of a simpler Germany, but his eulogy of Dürer was so definite and so compelling that it seemed to suggest a real basis for artistic action. The longings of Wackenroder's contemporaries for the proud unity of the old "Holy Roman Empire of the German Nation" can be read as polemic, and were probably intended as such; but Wackenroder, in addressing himself to a specific manifestation of German weakness, threw down a gauntlet and with it a finite exemplar of how the game was played. Wackenroder's words were a splendid emotional tonic for German painting at the turn of the nineteenth century. They implied confidence and belief, and the model they proposed, Dürer, was arguably great; but more important, he was German. Lacking a live David, the Germans had at least a rediscovered Dürer.

Goethe's response to Wackenroder's essay was immediate and comprehensive. Initially troubled by the fact that many believed him to have been the anonymous author of the Wackenroder essay, Goethe moved to size up the situation of German art for himself. His own ideas in the plastic arts were derived from the theories of classical art which Mengs and Winckelmann had put forward in the 1760s. Basically he accepted Winckelmann's belief in the primacy of Greek art—its "noble simplicity and quiet grandeur"—and further, he agreed with Mengs's judgment which cited as the preeminent achievements in painting the works of Raphael and Correggio. Admirably secure in his taste, Goethe quite naturally sympathized with the "classical" aspect of contemporary French painting, its moral ideals, its ordered and measured structure. To Goethe there was nothing unpatriotic in the recognition of the quality and rectitude of French classicism. He did not recognize it because it was French but because it was formed in ways which he could understand and which he respected. To honor Dürer because he was German seemed sheerest folly, and as far as Goethe was concerned German nationality was about the only basis upon which Dürer could conceivably be honored. Dürer's work ran counter in its values to virtually every value which the mature Goethe recognized.

To counter what he felt to be the subversive influence of the Wackenroder essay and its windy echoes in Ludwig Tieck's *Franz Sternbalds Wanderungen,* Goethe founded and maintained a magazine which acted as an organ for his views on the arts. The magazine, *Propyläen,* began in 1798, and in the year following its appearance Goethe established as a second front for himself the so-called *Weimarer Kunstfreunde* which from 1799 to 1805 ran yearly artistic competitions for German artists. Each year a theme from Homer was announced in advance, entries were received and judged by Goethe, and prizes awarded. All of this was Goethe's way to get German painting off on a proper footing. With the combination of the *Propyläen* and the *Kunstfreunde,* Goethe hoped to provide a central source of standards for German art comparable to that which the French had already possessed institutionally for over a century. Goethe's efforts achieved a certain notoriety and acceptance. Many artists submitted to his competitions and many others sent their work for judgment on a less formal basis.

As the most singularly venerated man in Germany in the period, Goethe's success in any enterprise he undertook was guaranteed at least up to a point. Yet in the matter of his judgments on the arts, and painting in particular, he soon met with considerable resistance. Gottfried Schadow, the director of the Berlin Academy, rejected out of hand Goethe's warnings against the overemphasis of realist values in that academy's teaching. Clearly, Goethe's sphere of influence was not destined to be granted much extension in the world of German academies, even in the one nearest to his home in Weimar. Nor were the views expressed in *Propyläen* to go unchallenged for long. From 1803 to 1805 Friedrich Schlegel published his own periodical, *Europa,* in Frankfurt. As the most forceful writer and dialectician of the young German romantics, Schlegel was a worthy opponent for Goethe and a man whose views were psychologically much more attractive to German artists and intellectuals living under the increasingly dark shadow of Napoleon. Without addressing himself directly to Goethe (whom he respected and from whom he had received a certain amount of favorable attention) Schlegel gradually moved in his views of art toward the hyper-Christian, antirational camp of François René de Chateaubriand, whose *Le Génie du Christianisme* appeared in France in 1802 and had been translated into German by 1804. Chateaubriand's resistance to Napoleon and his periodic self-exiles from France made him personally appealing to young cosmopolitan Germans like Schlegel, while his way of evaluating everything in terms of a quite clearly Catholic spirituality, laden with art and nature worshipping melodrama, was enormously seductive—much more so than Goethe's unflinching belief in objective rational standards. Prepared by Wackenroder and Tieck (and Napoleon) Schlegel gradually gave in to Chateaubriand's seduction. His writings began to stress Christian values as preeminent in all forms of art. Like the brothers, Sulpitz and Melchior Boisserée, Schlegel became increasingly enchanted with early German and early Netherlandish painting. His support of Boisserée's campaign to complete Cologne Cathedral came as a matter of course.

The romantics individually and as a group would have liked nothing better than to have been able to communicate their enthusiasms and their new values to Goethe. In person, by letter, with drawings, and with projects they tried to convert him. Hoping to extend his taste, they made no real attempt to contradict his judgments. But these judgments began to carry less and less weight as the years passed, and Goethe finally gave up, realizing that forces substantially different from those he would have chosen had taken command of the early stages of a new German art. Concerned at the predominance of psychological over purely aesthetic values, Goethe nevertheless began in 1805 to withdraw from the scene. Almost one feels with a sense of defeat, he turned to his studies of color and in 1810 published his *Farbenlehre*. Here at least, he hoped to provide some rational and lasting guidance to German painters. But even the *Farbenlehre* came a trifle late. The painter, Philipp Otto Runge, had in his own *Farbenkugel* (also 1810) already subjected the study of color to a psychological, synaesthetic, and subjectively abstruse mode of discussion, which was much more representative of the aspirations of the day.

What must in the final analysis be said of Goethe and his efforts on behalf of the pictorial arts, and in particular painting, in Germany at the turn of the century is that he diagnosed problems with perfect accuracy, while failing to solve them. Goethe saw the need for artistic efforts to be directed, focused, and, for better or worse, judged by secure standards of taste if Germany were to achieve the kind of artistic world-historical destiny which its young artists and critics believed it deserved. Yet the institutions which Goethe himself could provide were incapable of controlling the already wide proliferation of academies and his values were too exacting to compete with the indulgent subjectivity of early romantic criticism. Goethe's failure was ultimately a loss for nineteenth-century German painting. What was gained in freedom and diversity was lost in productive confidence and direction. The diverseness of academies (and their public) and the relativity of critical judgment which romantic criticism brought about stood as a situation to be inherited by every German artist of the century. The limits of German painting remained undefined. It could propose and be whatever

15

and as many things as it was privileged to discover. It could base itself on anything, and it did.

ROME

In desperation the best German artists of the nineteenth century let themselves be guided by one of two beacons—nature or the city of Rome. As the century unfolded, the guidance which either provided was unpredictable—often fickle—and dependent upon a whole range of individual (or group) ambitions and sensibilities. During the first third of the century the choice of nature or Rome appeared more clearly than at any other time. Yet the predominant currents of romanticism with their emphasis upon "spiritual values" made the artistic results of the choice of either one more similar than might seem possible in theory.

In order to understand how and in what forms nature and the city of Rome acted upon nineteenth-century German painting, it is necessary to define historically what a German artist's decision to be guided by one or the other actually meant.

Beginning first with the city of Rome, it is clear that the fact of an artist's visit to or his residence in Rome could vary enormously in its meaning at one or another point in the century according to the particular inclinations of the artist involved. The first generation of German Romans included two major figures, Josef Anton Koch and Gottlieb Schick. Both of these artists were in Rome for the same reasons that painters of all nations had always gravitated there: A period of work in Rome, in the presence of great masterpieces from the art of the past, was quite simply part—and a rather basic part—of becoming an artist. Belief in the importance of work in Rome developed in the minds of Schick and Koch primarily because of strong French influences active upon them early (in the 1790s) in their respective careers. Schick had actually worked for several years in David's atelier in Paris, while Koch had begun his training in Stuttgart under [1]* the direction of another, somewhat earlier, David student, PHILIPP FRIEDRICH VON HETSCH. As a figure, and primarily a portrait, painter, Schick was in Rome during the first decade of the century trying to perfect his David-oriented style on quite literally the same ground that David himself had occupied twenty years earlier. Koch, on the other hand, had ambitions in landscape. His models were Claude Lorraine and Nicholas Poussin. For him the very landscape of Rome stood as the artistic source which he could share most directly with his great French predecessors. What Schick and Koch had in common with the next group of German Romans, the so-called Nazarenes, was the belief that Roman soil was somehow sacred artistically and that to reside upon it virtually guaranteed both sincerity and achievement More than just a "school," Rome was seen as a kind of mythical parent of the spirit, indulgent and ever encouraging, first to the generations of her own children and later to the youth of other lands. In romantic terms,

*In this text the combination of bracketed numbers and capitalized proper names refers the reader to the plate section of the catalogue, identifying the artist whose work is reproduced and locating the reproductions. All paintings included in the exhibition are described separately in the catalogue entries which follow.

Rome as a city (and as history) represented the geographical fact of a place where the unity of art and life, of nature and the spirit (which was the focus of romanticism's and particularly German romanticism's, dream) seemed manifest. While the German enthusiasm for Rome was not without parallel in the minds of artists of other lands, the more obsessional aspects remained uniquely German—so much so that it would hardly be an exaggeration to propose that, for most of the nineteenth century, Rome was artistically a German colony.

[19, 18]   Of the many Germans who individually and in groups colonized [20, 21]   Rome during the nineteenth century, certainly the Nazarenes (in particular FRIEDRICH OVERBECK, FRANZ PFORR and later, PETER CORNELIUS and Julius Schnorr von Carolsfeld did so with the greatest energy and dedication. Beginning as a group of sincere, if arrogant, refugees from the Vienna Academy, the original Nazarenes, or to use their own chosen name, the Brothers of St. Luke, set out for Rome in order to work in the piously primitive Christian spirit of old German and fifteenth-century Italian painting. After they arrived they settled in the abandoned cloister of San Isidoro and established their manner of communal life along traditional monastic lines. Embracing the city of Rome with an enthusiasm comparable to that which they had already begun to direct toward the Roman Church prior to their departure from Vienna, the Nazarenes remained for almost twenty years a permanent fixture in the artistic scene of their adopted home. Yet for all their permanence, the various Nazarenes remained steadfastly German, exaggerating their German manner of dress, while at the same time building in their minds and in their art the bridge between Christian "Italia and Germania" to which their lives and their art were dedicated. Italy, and Rome in particular, freed the Nazarenes to "be German" in a way they felt they could not be in the artistic confusion of their native country. Unlike Koch or Schick, the Nazarene painters saw themselves in one or another way as exiles from Germany and from an impious modern world in general. There was, however, no general agreement among them as to whether or not their exile was to be irrevocable. In most cases it was not. From his position in exile, Peter Cornelius both entertained and encouraged a succession of invitations to reform various academies back in Germany. First Düsseldorf, then Munich, then Berlin requested his services; and by 1840 either Cornelius himself or one of his fellow Nazarenes (Wilhelm Schadow, Schnorr, Philip Viet, JOHANN ANTON RAMBOUX, Johann David Passavent, Joseph Führich, Edward von Steinle, and Joseph Wintergerst) had received responsible academic appointments in Germany. Only Overbeck lived out his life in Rome, but in doing so he provided a point of pilgrimage—almost a live monument—for later generations of both German and non-German artists.

Overbeck's reputation and that of the Nazarenes in general had become increasingly international after 1830. This is quite remarkable when one examines the great variety of styles and ambitions which were eventually maintained by one or another member of the group. In the period prior to Pforr's early death (1812) something like a Nazarene style had begun to develop as a complement to the bonds of close personal friendship which initially held the group together. If Pforr's taste for fifteenth-century German panel painting and manuscript illumination ran a good deal deeper than Overbeck's, and if Overbeck's earliest paintings inevitably stress the Italian side of "Italia and Germania" with their references to Perugino, Francesco Francia, and early Raphael, a shared enthusiasm for graceful linear drawing and flat, bright, primary color, smoothed out for a time smaller differences of taste. As the Nazarene circle expanded, differing and much stronger points of taste expanded correspondingly. Cornelius and Schadow both figured in the great Nazarene fresco commissions for the Casa Bartholdy (Palazzo Zuccari) in 1815 and the Casino Massimo (1817–29 with much confusion and reassignment in between). Dürer, Signorelli, and the late works of Raphael were increasingly persistent influences on the styles of both artists. Their designs tended to be rather complicated and grandiose, while those of Overbeck and other artists like Viet were comparatively feminine in their self-conscious refinement. Increasingly, the burden of stylistic coherence in the Nazarene group rested on the ancient technique of fresco and upon certain conventions which the technique itself forced. Every artist had had to master fresco technique in order to work on the great group projects; but real stylistic coherence was already severely threatened in the Casa Bartholdy project and, by the time of the Casino Massimo, it was almost nonexistent, conclusively so after Cornelius's departure in 1821. Almost inconceivably the major burden of finishing a large portion of work at the Casino Massimo originally assigned to Cornelius fell to Koch, who, though a friend of the Nazarenes, had never participated directly either in their projects or in their circle. Furthermore, Koch had not himself had any experience in fresco painting, or for that matter in large scale figure painting of any sort. However, for reasons not entirely clear, he was drawn into the work of the Casino Massimo and provided several elaborate scenes from Dante. Koch's paintings with their wierdly scaled rhythms and their leathery figural relief, while impressive, demonstrated very effectively the passing of anything resembling a Nazarene style. His contribution was archaic even by Nazarene standards. Elements of his work recall the great fourteenth-century frescoes of Giotto and Ambrogio Lorenzetti, while informing these recollections with a kind of frenzy that is strangely reminiscent of the art of William Blake, although more likely based ultimately on Koch's memory of the tragically incomplete projects of an old friend, long deceased, Asmus Jacob Carstens.

For all of its enormous internal variations in matters of style, the painting of the Nazarenes achieved a considerable degree of influence both in Rome and in Germany itself. The technique of fresco and the selection of at least generically similar models from the art of the early Renaissance produced a characteristically hard and dominantly two-dimensional kind of painting—linear in its essence and rejecting all virtuosity (and interest) in the handling of paint. Subject matter was at first primarily Christian, although later in the works of Cornelius and Schnorr historical, mythological, and folkloric subjects came to the fore. As various members of the Nazarene group infiltrated academies in Germany, the basic values which had been held jointly began to exercise a deep and lasting effect. From roughly 1825 to 1850 Nazarenism provided what was really the only artistic common denominator between academies (and the art public) in various parts of Germany. In the hands of Cornelius, Nazarene values were made to serve the quasi-political, quasi-historical interests of German monarchy, through large, decorative commissions (many of which were never executed) granted him first by the Bavarian Royal House, later by the Prussian. In the hands of Schnorr they became truly popular through wide circulation of his illustrations of the Bible.

It would, however, be a mistake to assume that Nazarenism, for all its influence, represented the preeminent factor in German painting at any historical point. German academies possessed a seemingly infinite capacity to assimilate, and in assimilating, to dissipate. Along with its Nazarene elements each academy sheltered others as well. Exactly what the others were and what they proposed as alternatives to Nazarenism differed according to the histories of particular academies. Düsseldorf, which operated under Wilhelm Schadow's direction for twenty-three years (1825–48) is a perfect case in point. There an arch-Nazarene director headed a school which stressed, increasingly as the years passed, work from nature, becoming finally as much a landscape academy as one fostering Christian or other types of historical subjects. Clearly the fact that Schadow's father had, during his own directorship of the Berlin Academy, stressed the importance of working from nature (to the lasting discontent of Goethe) laid a foundation for the eventually un-Nazarene breadth of Schadow's tolerance. The very existence of such tolerance in what was potentially the most Nazarene of academies (as well as in Schadow's own painting) demonstrates quite forcefully the relativity of Nazarene influence within Germany, whatever its apparent prominence.

From his permanent residence in Rome Overbeck may in the final analysis have been as influential as any of his fellow Nazarenes who had chosen to return to Germany. While his artistic efforts grew less impressive over the years, his position as an exile and as the ur-Nazarene continued to attract younger artists who visited Rome. The sheer force of his personality overwhelmed the young FRIED-[27, 28] RICH WASMANN during his visit to Rome in 1834–35. Guided by Over-[29, 30] beck, Wasmann became first a Roman Catholic and then, in his portrait [31, 32] painting, increasingly responsive to the kind of "primitive" linearity which Overbeck's work, his drawings in particular, developed to such a high degree. The conversion of Wasmann is particularly telling when one considers the staunchly naturalist basis of his work prior to his contact with Overbeck. Beginning in Hamburg in the company of such straightforward naturalist painters [33] as JACOB GENSLER, then continuing in Dresden under the influence of the landscape paintings of Friedrich, Johann Christian Clausen Dahl, and Carl Gustav Carus, Wasmann seemed destined to work out his naturalism in a dominantly painterly direction. Overbeck's influence confused this, and the schizoid character of Wasmann's later work with its loosely painted landscape and figure sketches and its carefully drawn portraits appears to have been the almost inevitable result.

A contemporary of Wasmann, Karl Blechen, brushed against Overbeck at about the same time during his only visit to Italy. The form of his contact with Overbeck is a matter of speculation, but it was clearly less comprehensive (and much less influential) than Wasmann's. Individual figures of monks, hermits, and so forth, either done by Blechen in Italy or based on studies made there, recall Overbeck from a distance without surrendering to Overbeck's particular kind of draftsmanly effects. Blechen remained generally true to his pre-Italian reliance on painted values—values which he had forged for himself in Berlin and which, like those of Wasmann, received support through substantial contact

19

with Dresden landscape painting. What reliance there was upon drawing in Blechen's work, and it exists both before and after his trip to Italy, stems directly from his work as a theatrical scene designer in Berlin where he adopted almost from necessity the inelegant hardness of a particular kind of perspective and panorama painting practiced there by artists like Johann Erdmann Hummel and Edouard Gärtner. While Wasmann emulated Overbeck's kind of draftsmanship, Blechen did not. His drawing remained as clumsy, provisional and searching as it had ever been. His art achieved, as a result, a more definite personality than Wasmann's. The pictorial qualities through which this personality emerged were erratic and, by Nazarene standards, unpredictable; but they were new and self-reliant in a way which the qualities developed by the Nazarenes never were.

Both Blechen and Wasmann were a generation (or more) removed from the members of the Nazarene group. What they accomplished as artists beyond the shadow of Nazarenism placed them more on the side of German painters who, over the century, relied on nature rather than Rome. Their reasons for visiting Rome, or more properly speaking Italy, were different from those of the Nazarenes, and finally closer to those of Koch and Schick. In the same characteristically international way, Blechen and Wasmann traveled south in order to expand their knowledge of the art they practiced. The motives behind their visits were not substantially different from those of their French contemporary, Camille Corot; and like Corot they experienced all of the usual artistic attractions of Italy including the newest—the works of the Nazarenes watched over by their untiring executor, Overbeck. The effect of this attraction upon Wasmann in particular is a lasting testament to its force at this time.

The next (and last) important group of nineteenth-century German painters who traveled to Italy and eventually settled in Rome did so for reasons which, while perhaps not totally unique from those of previous Germans, must at least be viewed in a different perspective. Like the Nazarenes, they saw themselves as exiles from Germany, but they held to their status in exile with more conviction. At times they may have been homesick, at least for certain aspects of their homeland, and certainly they longed to be honored there, but they did not, either individually or as a group, believe that they were necessarily destined to wield any artistic power within Germany itself. Like Koch and Schick this last group of German-Romans was cosmopolitan; and, further, they were, in a quite modern sense, intellectuals.

The two main figures in this group were Anselm Feuerbach and Hans von Marées. Despite the fact that he eventually opted for a villa in Florence as his ultimate residence, Arnold Böcklin can be considered an associate member of the group, while Franz von Lenbach, Adolf von Hildebrand (the sculptor), and Conrad Fiedler (the art theorist), remained more or less dependable "friends" of the group, without at the same time feeling compelled to join it in permanent exile. During the 1860s the group was supported financially by the Bavarian collector, Graf Schack. However, Schack's support demanded in return substantial numbers of the artists' own paintings and numerous "made to order" copies of sixteenth-century Italian works. It proved itself a mixed blessing, and eventually both Feuerbach and von Marées rejected it.

As painters and as personalities Feuerbach and von Marées are enormously sympathetic. From the distance of over a century it is still possible to identify with many of the pressures that drove them to Rome. Looking first at Feuerbach, since he was already well established in Rome by the time von Marées arrived (Feuerbach came in 1856, von Marées in 1864), we are presented with a man of enormous talent, critical acumen, and self-awareness—yet one tragically ill-equipped to deal with the world into which he was born. His particular kind of alienation was as real as that of the Nazarenes was, for the most part, polemical.

[II, 52]   Born in southern Germany (Speyer, 1829) FEUERBACH entered a
[53, 54]   family of great intellectual distinction, numbering among its mem-
[55]   bers jurists, philosophers, politicians, and, in the case of Feuerbach's
father, an archaeologist, whose life's work, a study of the Vatican *Apollo,* was very nearly frustrated by serious illness and a premature death. Shadowed by the achievements and the frustrations of his family, Feuerbach set off for art school in Düsseldorf at the age of fifteen. As a student he was very much a prodigy, but Düsseldorf was only the first of many academic steps on a path seemingly pre-destined to follow that of his father to Rome. Like Johannes Brahms who was his contemporary and later his good friend, Feuerbach spent an enormously long time (almost fifteen years) trying to come to grips with both the complexity and the history of the art form he had chosen to practice. An archetypal victim of the diverse and contradictory artistic standards that characterized the art world of the German academies, Feuerbach found among his teachers (Schadow and Carl Sohn in Düsseldorf, Karl Rahl in Munich, Gustaaf Wappers in Antwerp, and finally Thomas Couture in Paris) an unlimited amount of fatherly encourage-ment and advice, but comparatively few unequivocal demonstrations of what painting could currently achieve. In a huge body of letters to his stepmother, whose affection was as dominating as it was constant, Feuerbach documented the self-doubt that plagued him throughout his life, sometimes eloquently, and sometimes with the most grotesque emotional self-indulgence.

As he moved from one school to another, Feuerbach lamented constantly the fact that he could not determine to his own satisfaction what constituted "paint-ing." This is not to say that he did not paint, because he did, every year and wher-ever he happened to be. Yet his ambitions were never realized by what he man-aged to produce. He recognized in the art of the sixteenth and seventeenth cen-turies qualities which his own works could not achieve, and which were equally lacking in the efforts of his various teachers. As a student Feuerbach came closest to grabbing hold of these qualities, and of new ones, during his tenure (1852–54) in Couture's studio in Paris.

Judging from his effect on Feuerbach and upon the Frenchman Edouard Manet in the same years, Thomas Couture was clearly the most forceful teacher of painting in Europe at the middle of the century. What he lacked in consistent productivity as a painter, he made up for in his perceptiveness as a critic and in his understanding of pictorial achievements of every sort. Couture's stance in the world of French art had been largely determined by his *Romans of the Decadence* (Louvre) shown first in 1848—a painting central to later critical definitions of the so-called juste milieu. In this painting Couture established a rather tenuous stylistic bridge between qualities of "drawing" reflecting the contemporary art of Jean Auguste Dominique Ingres and those of "painting" reflecting that of Delacroix. On the basis of his identification with the juste milieu, Couture at-

21

tracted a large number of students to his atelier. In his teaching and in his own painting subsequent to the *Romans* Couture explored the painterly achievements of the Venetian and Spanish masters without ever abandoning a complementary taste for fine effects of draftsmanship. More than any of his fellow academicians he responded not unfavorably to the contemporary achievements of Gustave Courbet. Couture stressed the making of copies after masterpieces in the Louvre as an important adjunct to the usual French studio practice of working from the nude model. Lastly, he encouraged sketching in color with oil paint, as well as with charcoal.

For Feuerbach and Manet alike, Couture was in some mysterious way able to suggest an artistic direction without forcing the wholesale adoption of his own style, such as it was. He presented his students with a broad basis for personal self-confidence and he seems to have encouraged (or at least permitted) a sense of "national pride" to act as a focus for this. It is, quite clearly, no accident that his two most gifted students became the most emblematically "national" artists of the century in their respective countries—"national" in the sense that their art began from generally similar sources in the past and present of European painting and then developed along cumulatively historical, hence French, lines in Manet's work, and along somewhat random historiographic, hence German, lines in Feuerbach's.

Compared to Manet's, Feuerbach's paintings done in Paris and later in Karlsruhe (1855) are definitely eclectic, drawing upon sources in Venetian painting and in the art of Rubens. It took Feuerbach several more years to correlate his own personality with the history of painting and then to strike a pose within it. Couture's teaching confirmed Feuerbach's preestablished belief in the necessity to proceed artistically from the walls of museums and to project one's own achievements exclusively into that context. However, Couture did not, and could not, determine for Feuerbach the precise form which these achievements might take. Having left Paris and returned to Germany, Feuerbach effectively removed himself from the highly competitive, yet vital and intrinsically supportive, world of contemporary French painting. Back in Germany, Feuerbach faced the very different aspects of contemporary German art which in the mid-1850s maintained its characteristic indirection of taste and focus. At that moment Germany possessed no artist or institution capable of guiding Feuerbach beyond the rather open-ended critique of painting past and present that constituted his legacy from Couture. Manet was able, on the other hand, to move from Couture's teaching to confront the very real painted achievements of Courbet and Corot. For a while he would be guided by them. Eventually he emerged with an art of his own, one which considered his contemporaries, the history of painting, and increasingly the particularity of his own sensibility.

Lacking an artistic present in Germany upon which to build, Feuerbach moved to Italy—first to Venice in late 1855 and in 1856, to Rome. As he did so he committed himself once and for all to the dominion of art history, never confronting again, or for that matter even considering, contemporary developments either in Germany or elsewhere. Subsequent contacts with Böcklin and von Marées served simply to reinforce his dedicated occupation of the past. When, many years later, in the mid-1870s, Feuerbach gave in to pressure and flattery and accepted a chair at the Vienna Academy he found himself completely out of place in a world he did not understand and among people whose values and ambitions seemed to him almost subhuman. After much agony he beat a hasty, almost desperate, retreat back to Italy and died in Venice in 1880.

Yet, somehow, for all of the searching and seeming indirection of his career, Feuerbach began, once in Rome, to become a major painter. His way of doing so depended very directly upon two elements; first, his persistent preoccupation (exemplified by the making of copies) with sixteenth-century Venetian painting, focusing finally upon the Italian works of van Dyke; and, second, his long liaison with the Roman model, Nanna Risi (1861–67). The first of these factors provided an armature of monumental form—painterly in essence, but rhythmical in its general conception; the second, the actual substance which Feuerbach would make this armature support. His objectified, historiographical identification with prototypically Venetian aspects of style and figural conception combined with the overwhelming (almost Medean) physical presence of Nanna were to lead Feuerbach finally to his own juste milieu. Whether in the guise of a bacchante, the Virgin, some mythical woman, or simply herself, Nanna confronted Feuerbach at once with the classically sculpturesque female image of a distant race of Greco-Roman heroes and with the unclassically threatening sexual presence of a "tarnished" and demonstrably amoral woman. In the very tenseness of his relationship with Nanna, the fear and the guilt which accompanied it, Feuerbach came alive as a painter and for a while the tenuous historiographic foundation of his art held fast. In the years following Nanna's abrupt and unceremonious departure, whatever firmness remained did so largely in the form of an echo of her presence, etched permanently in Feuerbach's memory. The distinctness of the features of Feuerbach's later models was persistently blurred by Nanna's lasting impression; the memory of her sexual domination of him, and the particular ways which he found to express this domination pictorially, appear even in portraits of Feuerbach's stepmother, to such a degree that those portraits have the feeling, if not the actual fact, of incest about them.

In a very real sense Feuerbach built both his art and his life style in Rome around Nanna. To those who knew them, Feuerbach and Nanna had the aspect of fine marmoreal pendants—aristocratic in their appearance and demeanor, impressive from a distance, yet somehow bloodless and unapproachable. This aspect appears to describe at least some of the qualities of the painting which they mutually generated. Heavy, often nearly stillborn, rhythms of contour; modeling which knows neither true lights nor darks; color which fades into the most somber and stately tones of blues, lavenders, greens, and grays juxtaposed in close values —all of these qualities set the predominantly erotic genesis of the works at a sufficient sensuous distance to make it expressible pictorially. Reinforcing these qualities, the literal iconography of most of Feuerbach's work tends toward figural emblems of such abstractions as longing, isolation, inspiration, redemption, and contemplative pleasure. Like the music of Brahms which it parallels in so many ways, Feuerbach's best work seems slightly tired, but nobly and beautifully so. While frequently turgid, the painting remains alive almost in spite of itself. One suspects that in the final analysis the source of what life there is may be bound inextricably to the very fear which threatened to overwhelm Feuerbach— the repressed terror of being dominated sexually and spiritually by a woman who could not be fully attained, either physically or morally. The situation was prob-

23

ably not much different in the case of Brahms. The women, Nanna Risi and Clara Schumann, were distinct, but their effect was remarkably similar. Early in the century Goethe explored this kind of domination in his characters of Faust and Gretchen. Having objectified it to his own satisfaction, he set it to rest poetically. Feuerbach read *Faust* many times, both in German and in an Italian translation; but the domination he felt was too real to be resolved by Goethe's formulation. For him, and for Brahms as well, this domination remained the most powerful sensation of reality they were ever privileged to experience, and the one which for better or worse steadfastly refused to be objectified in a single work of art. Instead it spawned an unending series of circumlocutions and finally constituted the actual substance of two pervasively melancholic artistic personalities.

It is virtually impossible to isolate Feuerbach's exile in Rome from the impact and domination of Nanna. The city and the woman together provided a context and a focus for his painting. Prior to his arrival in Rome, Feuerbach's work was sorely lacking in both. Unlike most of his German predecessors in Rome, Feuerbach maintained his position in exile because the position served increasingly to keep him intact both as an artist and a person. Rome, the home of so much of the past of painting and the home of Nanna as well, became his home, or to use his own words, "his fate." Feuerbach's friend, Hans von Marées, saw his own position there in very much the same terms: "Rome is . . . the place where I feel most myself, since here, my being comes most into its own." Yet, despite their rather similar resignation to a life of exile in Rome, Marées and Feuerbach held little else in common. Their differences of personality, ambition, and accomplishment demonstrate just how much the motivation (and the ideals) of the last German-Romans differed from those of the guildlike, generally group-oriented and essentially "Christian" Nazarenes. Rome was now an intensely personal artistic commitment. Residence there was directed less by actual choice than by existential necessity.

The most basic distinction between Feuerbach and Marées derives from their respective careers prior to their arrival in Rome. Feuerbach's, as we have seen, involved many years of academic study in a whole host of schools in Germany, Belgium, and France. His determination to form himself on the basis of past art and in this way to guarantee the qualitative success of his own efforts inclined him to exaggerate the need for rigorous academic training of every description. In turn the enormous quantity, diversity, and duration of this training, culminating in his years with Couture, reinforced this determination to such a degree that there remained no real alternatives to the art of the past. Couture's influence had the salutary effect of introducing into Feuerbach's work at least some respect for a more open-minded and critical examination of conventions from past art with reference to sketches made directly from nature. This influence notwithstanding, Feuerbach never became a realist even in the most general sense of the term. His oil sketches suggest that nature was in fact maintained as a point of reference, but his large-scale works invariably make major formal and technical adjustments and readjustments in specifically eclectic terms. These adjustments may reflect sources as distant as the sixteenth century or as recent as Couture himself; but they remain steadfastly eclectic. What remains of nature in Feuerbach's works is, in the final analysis, as likely to derive from the residue of nature in Couture's own work as from Feuerbach's own direct observation; so even it possesses an aura of borrowed legitimization and secondhandedness. The reality of Nanna, and to a lesser degree, his stepmother and himself, was as much first-hand contact with nature as Feuerbach could sustain.

With Marées the situation was completely different. His painting began with nature and only after many years of struggling to make nature relevant pictorially did he manage to formulate his ambition and proceed to develop it on a large scale. Where Rome had served to provide Feuerbach with a particular, namely Nanna, upon which to hang his stylistic universals, it served through its treasury of past art to divert Marées's sights from the particulars of nature to the abstract plane of, to use Benedetto Croce's term, "pure visibility."

[60, 61] MARÉES was born in Elberfeld in 1837. He spent most of his child-
[62, 63] hood there, later moving (in 1847) to Koblenz, where his father had been appointed the judge of a local court by the governing Prussian authorities. Marées's artistic training took place in Berlin, first in the elementary class at the Berlin Academy (1853) and subsequently in the studio of the academician, Karl Steffeck, who specialized in the painting of horse subjects. Berlin painting at the time Marées experienced it was still oriented toward the same dry and hard-driven naturalism (and protorealism) that had characterized it for nearly forty years. As in Blechen's time, portraiture, panorama, and "fact" painting prevailed, as a compliment to the rather militaristic order and literalness that characterized nearly all aspects of Prussian taste and demeanor. When Marées was in Berlin, the early works of Adolf von Menzel, insofar as they were known, were just beginning to precipitate some changes in the direction of so-called Berlin realism, causing it to yield some of its dryness in favor of looser, more painterly technical procedures capable of giving pictorial definition to increasingly informal effects of light and increasingly incidental views of visible reality. Menzel had in his own way continued the tendency which Blechen began, but failed (largely as a result of his premature death in 1840) to develop very fully.

When he left his studies in Berlin for two years of service in the Prussian army in 1855, Marées may or may not have carried with him a respect for Menzel's accomplishments as of that date. His later references to Menzel were, at any rate, rather neutral in tone, noting, characteristically, that Menzel was a very competent painter. Marées's works done in Munich, where he lived following his release from the army, are, in their predominantly military subject matter, reminiscent of Berlin painting generally, while reflecting even more directly a personal element of pride in the military service just completed. Stylistically, however, there are many factors which suggest that Marées had begun to take cognizance of at least some aspects of painting in Munich. He was not particularly interested in the work of the local academicians, but Carl Spitzweg's paintings seem to have exerted a rather considerable influence upon him, at least for a time.

[64, 65] For all of his often cloying folkishness, SPITZWEG was by contemporary German standards a cosmopolitan painter. This was due, oddly enough, to the fact that he was largely self-taught, relying from the beginning of his career upon French models of the 1820s and 1830s. His real progress as an artist began when he copied a painting by Eugene Isabey which had found its way to Munich. Spitzweg traveled to Paris in 1851, studying in particular the

works of Narcisse Diaz and Camille Corot. His style, as it developed in the 1860s, reflected the French sources that had formed it. Anecdotal subjects, usually in the form of gentle caricatures of provincial village life, appear in small-scale paintings, where everything is first carefully drawn and then overlaid with richly orchestrated passages of contrasting as well as close-valued colors. Whether tending toward a prevailing tonality in the manner of Corot or featuring the somewhat more opulent effects of Diaz, Spitzweg's work always maintains the quite seductive appearance of being "natural."

Marées seems in many of his works from the early 1860s to have adopted one or another of Spitzweg's characteristic conventions for the organization of color without, however, giving in to the specifically anecdotal qualities of Spitzweg's subjects. At the same time, Marées looked carefully at the many examples of Dutch and Flemish painting available to him in the Bavarian Royal Collections. As a result of this looking, Spitzweg's influence was diluted with an admixture of stylistic elements from seventeenth-century genre painting; in particular, from such military pictures as those of Philips Wouverman. But more important than his interest in either Spitzweg or Wouverman was his growing respect for the more monumental achievements in the pictorialization of nature that appeared in the great sixteenth- and seventeenth-century masterpieces of Titian, Tintoretto, Rembrandt, Ribera, and Velasquez. Marées found in their work nature and pictorial style operating on a grand scale, and in ways more oriented toward vision itself than anything he had so far been able to achieve.

When Graf Schack presented him in 1864 with the opportunity to travel to Italy in the company of Lenbach for the purpose of making copies of "old master paintings," particularly Venetian painting, Marées seized it. Arriving in Rome via Florence in 1865, he cast off immediately all residue of small-scale genre painting from his work and began in earnest on the enormously demanding commissions which Schack set out for him. He took the making of copies very seriously. Largely unaccustomed to work of this sort, his copies were produced with considerable difficulty. Not content simply with achieving a good copy per se, Marées focused his increasingly critical eyes upon the models with which he was presented. Before attempting to make a copy he tried to understand through detailed visual analysis precisely how a given painter had evolved plasticity in his figures—how he dealt with contours and the distribution of light in order to do so. Marées's growing predisposition toward critical analysis was aided and abetted by two friends whom he met shortly after his arrival in Rome, the sculptor Hildebrand and the art theorist Conrad Fiedler. Both of them encouraged Marées's desire to understand and to formulate in terms (both specific and abstract) the complex phenomenology of pictorial vision. Over the next thirty years all three men attempted, within the areas of their particular interest and competence, to explore the coincidence and the interaction between reality and pictorial vision. Behind their separate attempts lay the shared desire to express as purely as possible both the manner and the necessity of the visual arts' age-old dependence upon the perception of nature.

Marées's preoccupation with analyzing pictures rather than with the production of copies on a regular schedule very quickly set him at odds with his patron, Graf Schack. In 1868 the patronage ceased and the following year Marées left Rome in order to travel with Fiedler to Spain, France, Belgium, and Holland.

For both men this trip was instrumental in broadening their knowledge of the kind of painting and the painters they most respected. While neither learned anything exactly new, at least the trip served to give forceful confirmation to tastes already formed. Nothing "modern" managed to penetrate the tastes of either Marées or Fiedler. In France, for example, Delacroix was approved up to a point, but all subsequent French art (although here their knowledge was limited to those works which had already found their way into public collections) was condemned in the most forceful terms. Before leaving Paris (in 1869) Marées lamented that not only were there no masterpieces in modern French painting, but there did not even seem to be an apparent basis for the hope that such might appear.

Marées had intended to take up residence in Rome directly following his trip with Fiedler and to proceed with his work on the basis of aesthetic predilections which the trip had reinforced. However, the outbreak of the Franco-Prussian War brought about his recall into the Prussian army and forced him to return to Germany. After his discharge in 1871 he worked briefly in Berlin with Hildebrand and the following year moved to Dresden. There he taught painting privately for a short time and made several portraits, where for the first time elements of his mature work begin to define themselves. Generally speaking, this work is characterized by a rather somber range of colors with scattered, light-toned accents. A highly flexible manner of drawing with paint acts to establish the disposition of various parts of figures and then to maintain this disposition, while broader passages of paint (often enormously varied in actual density and in the focus given to descriptive detail) simultaneously inflect plastic and planimetric coherence over the whole of a painting. At one point or another, and depending upon the particular sort of coherence Marées is seeking, the drawing with paint and the painting which occurs within the boundaries of the drawing either stand in opposition or blend imperceptibly.

In the images which result, nature is broadly served in the sense that a considerable degree of illusion obtains. Yet "paintedness" is equally, if not predominantly, apparent, particularly so in passages where Marées leaves his image ambiguously incomplete (from a purely illusionistic point of view). Balancing at every point in the making of a picture the effect of each drawn or painted stress against the final desired unity of the picture as well as the completeness of its illusion, Marées's procedural options remain almost frighteningly open. While certain conventions gradually emerge and recur in one painting after another, actual style of the secure, personal sort which Titian, Rembrandt, Velasquez, or for that matter Feuerbach, achieved was something Marées was compelled to deny himself both in principle and in practice. Each of his mature paintings had a complete life cycle of its own. That of a sketch was necessarily shorter and less complete than that of a completed painting. In point of fact the difference between a Marées sketch (either drawn or painted) and a complete work is largely one of duration. In the former Marées pushed himself as far as he felt he needed to in order to solve a limited pictorial problem; in the latter he tried to persist until the painting no longer needed him but stood instead as a visual organism, complete and wholly resolved in all of the terms it presented during the process of its own creation.

The development apparent in Marées's work from the time of his large fresco project in the German Zoological Station in Naples, which he undertook shortly after leaving Dresden with Hildebrand in 1873, to the group of huge polyptychs from the last decade of his life (1877–87) in Rome, is enormously complicated to follow in detail. It can, however, be summarized. In general the Neapolitan frescoes and their preliminary studies represent a moment of balance in the focus of Marées's painting. The perception of particular things in nature, as well as the act of perception itself, guides Marées's efforts to create pictorially relevant images of human figures in an archetypal natural setting at the side of the sea. Illusion and the mode which Marées develops to achieve it stand in a moment of total harmony. Later on in Marées's career, modes of illusion themselves become increasingly liberated from particular perceptual sources. Mythical images, like those of the *Hesperides* or the *Golden Age* (Munich), derive increasingly from processes of illusionism and pictorialization per se. Human figures become wholly anonymous. They are posed and shaped according to nearly undecipherable complexities of formal counterpoint in natural settings which are comprehensible only because they are painted as if they were. The paint surface itself seems patinated with age, and somehow impersonally abstract, through the impenetrable incrustation of layer after layer of both oil and tempera paint.

Unfortunately, Marées's late works can only be partly seen today, since their unstable pigment chemistry (poetically rather like the artist's own well-known hypochondria) has caused them quite literally to consume themselves. Yet what remains of them demonstrates quite clearly the degree to which the last decade of Marées's life was dominated increasingly by the desire to produce painted monuments of a distinctly "old master" sort. Living permanently in Rome, after having undergone a painful severing of relations with Hildebrand (for personal rather than artistic reasons), Marées looked to Feuerbach and to Böcklin for guidance in working out the ultimate phase of his art. Fiedler remained available to him, but from a distance, and really only accessible through letters.

While neither Feuerbach nor Böcklin could offer specific support—as artists and as personalities, both remained problematic in Marées's eyes—they did reinforce his inclinations toward the grandiose and the mythic. Their influence acted in combination with that of Rome itself. The city, as a living museum of ambitiously large-scale painting by so many masters of the art of the past, finally exerted its spell over Marées, as it had over Feuerbach many years before. However, it did so in ways which remained peculiar to Marées.

Feuerbach's submission to Rome was conditioned both in degree and in form by the eclectic and essentially historiographic tenor of his art as a whole. The art history of Rome, as the city of painting and of Nanna, who became for Feuerbach the sole objective correlative for his work in the world of visible reality, together established the character and limits of his art without really changing its essential direction or substantially modifying its ambition. Marées's submission was in many ways more radical in nature. Having begun as a confirmed realist, he found it necessary at first to reject only the specificity of anecdote in order to make visual reality yield to significant pictorialization. In Rome during the last decade of his life he found it necessary to reject the specificity of visual reality itself in order to develop the abstract universals of purely pictorial vision which he had discovered through years of analyzing the art form he practiced. Feuerbach had based his painting on definite historical precedents from the beginning of his artistic career, relying upon this to legitimatize as well as to guide his ambitions. His mature works achieve their "historical" look almost as a matter of course. Marées's, on the other hand, become "historical" only after their direct sources in the world of visible reality have been totally stripped away through continuous analysis and self-criticism. Eventually the processes of pictorializing were completely liberated from whatever sources had, either in reality or in art, produced them. Marées's late works present in distilled, yet monumental form, the accumulated critical essence of a lifetime of perception—perception made concrete in his own work over the years or reconstructed analytically from the work of others. Rome, which had supported spiritually so many summations of artistic achievement in the past, served finally to support Marées's as well.

[56, 57] Moving one's attention from the intensely serious and intrinsically
[58, 59] difficult accomplishments of Feuerbach and Marées to those of
ARNOLD BÖCKLIN, one experiences quite genuine visual and intellectual relief. It is not, however, lacking a distinct sense of anticlimax. The combined powers of art and intellect that drove the painting of both Feuerbach and Marées to the qualitative heights it reached found little, if any, echo in Böcklin, whose level of ambition was of a distinctly less elevated sort; despite, and partly because of, the incredible degree of personal pretense and self-adulation that accompanied it.

Böcklin saw himself as a kind of "Wagner of painting" and his art as a vehicle for the entertainment as well as the enlightenment of an essentially bourgeois audience. At the same time he saw himself as a kind of Nietzschean superman, contemptuous of middle-class values and generally superior to them. Both artistically and literally (via the flying machine he designed) Böcklin desired above all things to fly high over the everyday squalor of a prudish, unimaginative modern world. Yet in the very degree of his reaction to this modern world and to the middle class which controlled it, there existed a considerable dependence as well. In order to carry out the role which his self-image increasingly demanded, painting and a polemic of egotism merged and together relied for direction upon moves which were made to define a position against the middle class rather than to achieve art. As a result Böcklin's painting comes in its most characteristic moments to depend upon the middle class—and the middle class of a particular moment in particular German-speaking countries—as a foil against which its own values are both to be seen and appreciated. Böcklin creates his images with an eye to the forces of frustration, insecurity, and self-hatred within the middle class. He flaunts his apparent ability as an artist to transcend these forces, hoping to capitalize on the envy which results.

Seen against the background of his own personality, Böcklin's periods of residence in one or another part of Italy eventually take on an aspect of inevitability in public, rather than in strictly artistic, terms. At first he worked in Italy for reasons not unlike those of Feuerbach. He, too, began his studies at the Düsseldorf Academy (1845–47), working mostly with J. W. Schirmer and, as a result, receiving an early introduction to landscape painting. He continued his studies in Belgium in 1847, working both in Brussels and Antwerp. After a brief interlude in Geneva, he went to Paris for several months in 1848 and then returned to his hometown, Basel, for the year and a half prior to his first journey to Rome, where he remained for seven years until 1857. Böcklin's work in Rome during this

29

period, like that of Feuerbach, was essentially the last phase of his academic training, carried out on the proverbial home ground of great art. However, in contrast to Feuerbach, Böcklin spent a good deal of time during the following decade in Germany and Switzerland. He succeeded in selling his paintings to such important collectors as the king of Bavaria and Graf Schack. For a short while he held the post of professor of painting in the academy in Weimar (after 1860). At various points in the 1860s he accepted commissions in Germany and in Switzerland; and, despite the fact of a second four-year stint in Rome from 1862 to 1866, residence there seems hardly to have been as uniquely supportive from an artistic point of view as it was for Feuerbach and later for Marées.

To state the matter differently, Böcklin seems after 1858 to have had very little difficulty manufacturing paintings at virtually any point on the German, Swiss, or Italian map. Furthermore, his artistic tastes had taken on a distinctly old German turn in the years following his first trip to Rome. These tastes were confirmed after the return from his second trip. In his memoirs the painter Hans Thoma recalls having spent much time with Böcklin in Munich around 1870, looking at fifteenth- and sixteenth-century German paintings in the collection of the Alte Pinakothek. By the time of his meeting with Thoma, Böcklin had become something of an expert in matters of technique in the painting of the so-called Northern Renaissance, and Thoma was quite content simply to listen. Without ever severing his ties with Italian art completely, Böcklin had, nevertheless, by 1870 given in to a wholly different set of pictorial attractions, so that the degree of artistic urgency evident in subsequent journeys to Italy was relatively insignificant. His Italian wife, the former Angelica Pascucci, kept Böcklin's memories of Italy alive, but it is quite possible that the simple domestic fact of marriage to an Italian woman (in 1853) dissipated almost immediately the potential artistic effect of Italy upon Böcklin. For Feuerbach and Marées exile in Rome, while inevitable and in their own minds determined almost by fate, was never completely comfortable; but the discomfort was more than adequately compensated by the aesthetic achievements which resulted. Since there was never for Böcklin any real personal discomfort in his situation in Italy, there was no compulsion to provide unequivocal aesthetic justification for it.

For the advantages of a more objective, and presumably more balanced, view of the accomplishments of Italian art, Böcklin gave up what might in the long run have been beneficial to him. Incapable of being humbled by the experience of Italy and of Italian art, Böcklin rejected precisely the sort of qualitative exemplars which his painting, even more than that of Feuerbach and Marées, needed. Gifted with enormous technical facility, Böcklin was prone neither to question himself nor to criticize his own work with any consistent rigor. The uninterrupted process of aesthetic refinement that marks the efforts of Feuerbach and Marées finds no reflection in Böcklin. Instead there is a perpetually expanding vocabulary of technical effects, guided in their usage only by the comparative consistency of Böcklin's half-natural, half-mythological imagery.

In public terms, Böcklin's option to live and to work in Italy remained significant. His role as an antibourgeois superman gained considerable stature through the fact of periodic, and frequently prolonged, exile. By moving to Italy he removed himself quite literally from the industrial materialism of contemporary German society and lived instead in a land of nature and poetry—an existence which the middle class could not but admire.

Much, but not all, of the character of Böcklin's art can be explained with reference to his personality and to the particulars of his relationship with both Italy and the German middle class. What remains at issue is the actual appearance of the work itself. Painting is never totally predetermined by factors of personality and circumstances, and it seems at least conceivable that a very different kind of work might have issued from premises identical to those upon which Böcklin's art was based. Böcklin shared, in principle at least, many of the theoretical interests (pseudoscientific color theory and the psychological aspects of composition) of his much younger contemporaries in France—Odilon Redon and Georges Seurat, to name only the most obvious. Further, he shared the polemically antitraditional stance of the French avant-garde. But for all of this, Böcklin's painting per se has very little in common with the art of Impressionism and post-Impressionism in France; and this fact serves to emphasize once again the very different artistic conditions existing in the two countries—France and Germany.

We have already seen the way in which the pattern of Feuerbach's art diverged from that of the Frenchman Edouard Manet, even though both were profoundly influenced by the teachings of Couture. The radically different traditions and institutions of art in Germany and France were seen to have at least encouraged, if not actually to have caused, that particular divergence. The gulf, in spite of interests held in common, between Böcklin's art and later French developments can be described in essentially similar terms. The antitraditionalism of the French avant-garde had the benefit of a powerful and unified adversary—French academic painting. That Böcklin did not have, so he set himself against traditions and values in general, represented as they were in the rather vague formulation of German middle-class taste and supported as they were in various ways by the academicians of a given German city. In order to provide his ego with worthy adversaries, he gave to these traditions and values, via his own polemic of surprising and frequently grotesque images, a force and solidarity they did not in fact possess. Having spent so much effort in the process of determining the negative of which his own style was to be the positive, there remained comparatively little room within that style for the coherent and systematic development of his genuinely original attitudes toward such purely artistic considerations as color and composition.

Much, if not most, of Böcklin's effort in the making of his pictures is spent in conjuring and elaborating his highly imaginative images. The end goal of his work is to make his presentation of these images as arresting in the character of their form and substance as possible. Using at times illusionistic devices of a quite literal sort and at other times featuring emblem-like simplifications of shape, space, and color, Böcklin picks and chooses his way through a painting. In most instances his decisions about what to stress pictorially and how to stress it are made in favor of the image itself. Rarely do these decisions yield to more general demands for overall pictorial coherence. This is not to say that Böcklin's work is dominantly incoherent from a formal viewpoint, but rather that formal coherence is not, properly speaking, its chief ambition. As a result, Böcklin's acidly bright, pure colors, and his tendency to compose his pictures in both two and three dimensions in a manner that permits often jarring oppositions of scale or shape, never achieve a truly pictorial life of their own, even though they seem always to possess the promise of such achievement.

Böcklin's paintings ask in quite unequivocal terms to be accepted or rejected on the basis of their imagistic self-conviction. His life's work, seen as a whole, is quite acceptable in these terms. It is at least arguable that no other painter has ever managed to give birth and nourishment to quite so varied a cast of characters —both human and animal, as well as both in combination. The case of Böcklin, as the great German critic, Julius Meier-Graefe saw it, rests on just this achievement. Böcklin's assorted old German, mythically Greek, or conventionally Christian troupe is invariably entertaining, but it is difficult not to lament the increasingly formidable vacuum of truly artistic quality which "entertainment" is made to fill.

Confronted by the kind of paintings for which Böcklin is best known—those produced from the mid-1870s until his death in 1901—it is often difficult to believe that there had been, somewhat earlier in his career, at least a residual interest in painting as a pure form of expression rather than simply as a vehicle for something else. Yet this was in fact the case, and Böcklin's friends, Feuerbach, Marées, and Hans Thoma, to name only a few, held fast to their memories of the young Böcklin. They refused to believe that the comparatively straightforward artistic efforts that marked Böcklin's work in the period roughly 1855 to 1875, could have been totally abandoned, even though Marées, at least, gradually came to suspect that perhaps they had. Summarizing his views, Marées remarked that Böcklin's work seemed increasingly inside out. To his eyes there was more art in one of Böcklin's paintings just after it had been begun than remained at the time of its completion.

In Böcklin's pre–1875 portraits and landscapes (and even in his early subject pictures) there are moments of undeniable pictorial achievement. Working more directly from nature than either Feuerbach or Marées, Böcklin's style remains open to quite a wide, but as yet unforced, range of coloristic, graphic, and painterly effects. His images emerge from a tapestrylike weave of paint. The scale of successive brushstrokes and of intervals between colors constantly shifts in response to the particular aspect of the image being described. Yet there remains a kind of pictorial consistency in the finished picture, resulting largely from the bristling, arhythmical nervousness of the paint surface itself. Echoes of Corot (whose work Böcklin had seen in Paris in 1848) and of early German and Netherlandish masters exist in great profusion. These echoes lend alternately a diaphanous openness, or a congested two-dimensionality to the pictorial space of Böcklin's paintings. In the best of them, both spatial possibilities are entertained simultaneously, reinforcing the nervous intensity already generated within the paint surface itself.

While none of the qualities evident in Böcklin's work prior to 1875 are totally excluded from his later efforts, they move farther and farther from the sources in both art and nature that were initially responsible for their generation. As this happens, pictorial qualities achieved in a particular context are removed from that context, combined with others from other contexts, and forced into the service of a quasi-literary theme. More often than not, the theme and the emblem Böcklin devises to carry it predominate in completed pictures after 1875 and pictorial qualities (which become increasingly technical effects) are reduced to the role of providing attributive rather than strictly inherent visual meaning.

If one accepts the usefulness of the parallel already drawn between the work of Feuerbach and that of the composer Johannes Brahms, it is tempting to propose another parallel of a quite similar sort in order to summarize Böcklin's achievements. The music of Richard Strauss, who was by many years Böcklin's junior, proceeds along a similar path from enormously creative originality in its early phase to a subsequent career of mannered self-adulation based, as Böcklin's, on the increasingly distant reserve of quality achieved at the beginning of a long career. For both Böcklin and Strauss ego finally triumphed over the making of art.

With Böcklin that side of nineteenth-century German painting which looked to Italy, in general, and the city of Rome, in particular, for guidance and spiritual support ends. In fact, one might almost say that it disintegrates, since Böcklin's usage of exile became as his career unfolded increasingly one of personal polemic. By the time of Marées's death in 1888, Germany—a new, unified Prussian Germany—had begun to develop its own national center of art in the city of Berlin. Gradually provincial art centers such as Munich, Dresden, Stuttgart, Karlsruhe, Düsseldorf, Hannover, and Cologne waned in their importance, even though they have not to this day lost their regional identity completely.

As a focal point for German artistic ambition, Berlin definitively replaced Rome and, over the space of three decades (1870–1900), became nearly as cosmopolitan in matters of art as Paris. Max Liebermann, Max Slevogt, and Lovis Corinth, the most important German artists in the latter part of the nineteenth century, all eventually gravitated to Berlin. As a group they dominated the city artistically with their work, their teaching, and their organization of exhibitions of modern art. They gave contemporary German painting at the turn of the century its particular character, while the National Gallery of Berlin began, through individual and group exhibitions and through the enlightened development of its permanent collection, to put together the fragments of the century of German art which had just passed. Many of these fragments issued from German Rome; many others from Germany itself. It is to the latter of these, which for the most part founded their artistic pursuits on the direct experience of nature, that we must now turn our attention.

NATURE

The decision of so many important German painters of the nineteenth century to work in Rome gives to German painting of this period a genuinely unique aspect. The decision of many others to work from nature is, in general European terms, a much more characteristic phenomenon. Naturalism as it manifests itself in two archetypes of subject matter—portraiture and landscape—is by all definitions the most reliable characteristic of nineteenth-century painting. Yet in every country with an important nineteenth-century tradition naturalism appears and develops in different ways; so that which, in principle, might seem to unite the efforts of artists working in different countries frequently does the opposite.

Nature, more than any other point of reference for painting, exerts forces which are subject to modes of interpretation that vary enormously in both form and number. Like painting itself, nature is a prime source of visual sensation; but, unlike painting, nature is already there—"completely written art," as the French Impressionist Claude Monet expressed it early in his career. In the dichotomy between the preexistence of nature and the need for painting to be made in order to manifest itself visually lies both the challenge to achieve some sort of meaningful cross-reference between the two and the inevitable recognition of the limited means available to do this that drives naturalist painting at all times and in all places.

Within the confines of a relatively focused and coherent tradition of painting such as that which existed in nineteenth-century France, naturalism eventually disclosed a relatively wide range of pictorial options; and in the works of one painter after another conventions of representation appear in order to express certain of these options. Or, to put it differently, certain aspects of nature are seized by a given artist or a generation of artists; they are formulated pictorially and then handed on for rejection or acceptance by subsequent artists working similarly from nature. In the French naturalist tradition which runs, in the broadest sense, from Watteau through the late works of Monet there is, at least from the perspective of history, a kind of deductive logic in process as various aspects of nature which are found capable of significant pictorial expression are proposed, one after another, until color, the most abstract of these, is granted license to dominate all others. At every point in the development of naturalist painting in France, qualitative assessments of the achievements of a given "naturalist" painter were made both by sympathetic and hostile arbiters. The former were usually free-lance art critics, the latter the jurists for the official Salon exhibitions who, in company with their own journalistic apologists, held firmly to the so-called classical standards of contemporary academic painting. In this situation of critical checks and balances, naturalism was able to flourish so long as it remained secure in its own qualities—confident in its past traditions as well as in its continuing achievements.

The particular condition of French naturalist painting prevailed in no other country. In Germany the situation was completely different. There naturalism had a frequency rather than a tradition in the proper sense of the term. During the whole of the century and in every part of Germany artists painted nature, yet naturalist painting of a sort which can be exclusively described as "German" never appeared, even though artists who worked in Munich from the mid-1860s on began to proceed along comparatively common lines. The primary characteristics of German naturalist painting (using the term German geographically) are those of solitary effort, local reputation, and, generally speaking, the historical inconsequence of any achievements beyond the life span of the painter realizing them. The various accomplishments of a given painter never derive so directly from those of a predecessor as they do in France, nor do they preordain in any predictable way those which follow chronologically in the work of other painters active elsewhere in the country, or for that matter, even in the same town. Granting this peculiarity of naturalism in Germany, it is not surprising to find that, in contrast to the situation in France, no single factor except for reliance upon nature unites the work of painters active at any point during the century. Every naturalist painter in Germany worked out his position in relation to nature in ways peculiar to himself. As a result there was a good deal of repetition of effort and a distinct absence of "progress," in the French sense. Not until the final decades of the century when cross-influences between Germany and France increased to the point of becoming a veritable rule does German naturalism generate a momentum even remotely comparable to that which French naturalism had had for well over a century.

What all of this means in principle is that German naturalism seen as the phenomenon of an entire century, appears erratic, nondevelopmental, and, at times, wildly misguided. In fact, however, many individual achievements are substantial, to say the very least. In spite of, and partly because of, the circumstances under which various painters were forced to work, particular manifestations of style and sensibility were often maintained with a kind of unshakable and uncritical desperation that never appears in quite the same way in the work of contemporary painters in France. Operating without national institutions to condemn or praise their efforts, naturalist painters in Germany had to rely to an almost overwhelming degree upon themselves. Not only did they have to make paintings, but having made them, they had to believe in them unequivocally. The encouragements of close friends or provincial critics notwithstanding, individual German painters were forced to provide for themselves ultimate judgments of quality. While it is arguable that all painters, regardless of time or place, make procedural decisions for themselves and, having made them, evaluate the results, nonetheless very few painters, if any at all, have been compelled to a position of such complete self-reliance as they were in Germany at this time.

A surprising number of German painters managed to work productively under these undeniably precarious conditions for greater or lesser periods of time. Unlike those of their contemporaries who opted to work in Rome under at least the passive guidance of masterpieces of past art, the Germans who stayed at home and worked from nature recognized the problematic conditions of their artistic existence for what they were, and confronted them directly. As a result their achievements have in the final analysis a clearer ring of truth, both because they derive from nature itself and because their derivation is accomplished within the reality of the existing social and psychological order (or disorder) of Germany itself. Of course, not every painter who stayed at home and painted nature was successful in attaining consistent or even infrequent artistic quality in his work; nor were the guarantees of success ultimately any more certain for him than for those who worked in exile.

Before proceeding to a discussion of the achievements of the most important exponents of naturalism in Germany, it will be helpful to isolate a basic predisposition which continues in one form or another throughout the century, in spite of the generally heterogeneous character that the works of various artists assume when surveyed from a historical viewpoint. Naturalism in Germany more than anywhere else in the world seems aware of the common ground it shares with other means of emulating the strictly visual aspects of nature. From the beginning of the nineteenth century, even prior to the final invention of photography, German artists were attentive to all forms of scientific and quasi-scientific attempts to show how nature really looked. The camera obscura, the diorama, and the shadowgraph all seem in one way or another to have conditioned the ways in which German painters saw nature. Later on, photography, when it was finally perfected, exerted an influence as well, but a much less direct one.

One may reasonably ask why German naturalism in particular was so responsive to the influence of other reproductive media. The most likely explanation seems to be that, here too, German nineteenth-century painting was, in yet another sense, dominated by the absence of a viable and definable eighteenth century. While France and England developed various eighteenth-century forms of landscape and portraiture, Germany for the most part languished artistically. Faced with a new sense of artistic destiny around the turn of the century German painters looked in all directions for guidance in matters of both procedure and definition. Those who looked to the past ended up for the most part in Rome where they could live in it. Those who looked to nature had to begin by learning how to look. Having learned this, they had yet to learn how to select from what they saw that which could be represented and, finally, how to represent what they had selected. Lacking artistic exemplars of a dependably vital and contemporary sort they turned to nonartistic ones, especially those which, like painting, dealt with the reduction of nature from three into two dimensions.

As they surrendered to influences more scientific than artistic in origin, German naturalist painters found themselves able to do without (or in many cases to remain ignorant of) many of the devices of style that had developed in the naturalist painting of France and England, and which had their ultimate source either in seventeenth-century Dutch painting or in the landscapes of Claude Lorraine. Relatively few of the characteristics (or conventions) of surface organization and of spatial illusion that characterize French and English naturalism take hold in Germany after 1800. The Germans did not share in the "artistic" origins of these conventions and they were not, in most cases, impelled to adopt them. Far more compelling for the Germans was the need to make art from raw and relatively artless optical experiences of nature; while for the British and the French, the progress of naturalism continued for many years to remain encompassed within the continuously expanding membrane of a centuries old "European" naturalist tradition.

The most obvious result of the particular frame of reference within which German naturalism occurred can be described as follows: German artists came up against the problem of painting nature, particularly during the first half of the century, more abruptly than the artists of any other country. Their decisions to paint from nature were for the most part born of desire, rather than based on a knowledge of any manifest achievements of naturalist painting. The principle either of painting from nature or of making art somehow on the model of nature preceded in almost every individual case any knowledge of how to go about doing it. This meant that, on the one hand, the works of the Germans were bound almost by definition to be rather odd quantities in the general context of European naturalism. At the same time, however, it meant that the problems of self-definition which German painters faced were, without intending to be so, prototypical of those which would later face such revolutionary naturalists as the Impressionists in France.

By the measure of cumulative artistic quality the French Impressionists succeeded where the Germans often failed. They did so largely because they were more certain of what they could reject from naturalist tradition and, from the beginning, they were more aware of both the optical and the poetical qualities which could be developed to replace those which they rejected. Lacking this assurance, as they lacked so many other kinds, the Germans proceeded with virtually nothing determined in advance. Developing their poetics and their optics simultaneously, they made many indecisive and finally unproductive moves. Sometimes they relied on theoretical speculation to guide their efforts; at other times they indulged in one or another form of mysticism. But at their best they focused their attention on the production of pictures, relying upon the pictures themselves to justify, through their own particular qualities whatever sources, either in nature or in personal feeling, informed them.

[4, 5]   The ambitious heights toward which German naturalist painters reached as well as the difficulties inherent in the process of reaching became evident at the very beginning of the century in the brief but hectic career of PHILIPP OTTO RUNGE. His art, along with that of his contemporaries Caspar David Friedrich and Wilhelm von Kobell, sets the tone for the diffuseness and nonconsolidation of effort that characterizes German naturalism throughout most of the nineteenth century, while at the same time giving promise and substance to the search for artistic quality.

In a working life that spanned only a decade Runge produced comparatively few paintings, yet he managed in the best of these to explore several ways of making art derive from nature and exist in a metaphoric emulation of natural processes of growth. His manner of exploration remains absolutely unique. Born in Wolgast (Northern Germany) in 1777 Runge, like Friedrich, enrolled as a student at the Copenhagen Academy, where the curriculum was strongly neoclassic and archaeological in emphasis. Working there between 1799 and 1801, Runge was trained as a draftsman and had almost no exposure to painting per se. Engravings of recently excavated fragments of Roman decoration and the tersely linear works of the English neoclassic illustrator John Flaxman were among the more powerful outside influences Runge experienced to reinforce the bias of his Danish mentor, Jens Juel, toward linear effects. Following his work in Copenhagen, Runge returned to Germany and moved to Dresden in 1801, remaining there until 1804. His friendship with the early romantic novelist, Ludwig Tieck, and with the Dresden portrait painter, ANTON GRAFF, together served to bring his personal ideas about art into focus.

[2, 3]   Without rejecting all of the values proposed by his neoclassic training, Runge began to consider others as well. The painterly and coloristic freshness of Graff's portraiture (which represented Germany's closest look at the combined eighteenth-century portrait traditions of France and England) impressed Runge enormously, and much of his own portraiture, particularly his self-portraits, bears out this impression. While formulating his responses to Graff's work in Dresden he began to look as well at the masterpieces of Italian, Dutch, and Flemish painting available to him in the substantial Dresden collections of the Saxon monarchy.

Stimulated by the writings of Tieck and Wackenroder, Runge saw the masterpieces of the Dresden collections both as painting in the strictest sense of the term and as successive expressions of fundamentally Christian ideals—ideals made manifest concretely in specifically Christian images and abstractly in expansive,

37

synaesthetic harmonies of color. A Protestant both in background and conviction, Runge was unable to accept in detail the increasingly emphatic neo-Catholic bent of Tieck and of other romantic writers of the period, such as Friedrich Schlegel. Yet his own kind of Protestantism, which was rooted in the writings of the seventeenth-century German mystic Jacob Böhme and had been nurtured by his youthful (pre-Dresden) contact with the poet-theologian Kosegarten, made him receptive in more general terms to speculations on the philosophy of art that were predominantly romantic, hence "spiritual" in tenor. But while Runge responded to and even took some part in the development of early romantic aesthetics, he also established personal contact with Goethe, whose views on art basically reinforced the classical-archaeological aesthetic which had guided his early work in Copenhagen. Inevitably Runge disagreed with the rational elaboration of details, if not with many of the general trends of Goethe's views on art, so that by the middle of the first decade of the century he found himself alone on a kind of philosophical middle ground between Goethe and early romanticism; respecting both sides of a highly polarized dialectic, he was forced to make a resolution of his own.

Granting the complexity of ideological forces which Runge took it upon himself to resolve, the fact that he chose to do so simultaneously in writing and painting is perhaps not so surprising. We have already noted the general character of his *Farbenkugel,* an essay which represents probably the most coherent written formulation of his artistic philosophy, even though it restricts itself primarily to the issue of color. In what little remains from the painted efforts of Runge's short life as a mature and comparatively productive artist (1805–10) one can at least attempt to give an account of the particular artistic formulations he provided.

In contrast to the highly abstract and quasi-mystical character of the *Farbenkugel* and the many other extant fragments of Runge's writing, much of his painting is relatively down-to-earth. Although he produced two important pictures of a conventionally religious Christian sort, a *Rest on the Flight to Egypt* and a *Christ Walking on the Water* (both Hamburger Kunsthalle) and projected others from the pseudomythology of Macpherson's *Ossian,* most of Runge's mature production centers either specifically or emblematically upon nature. While many Runge scholars prefer to see the forthrightly naturalist side of the artist's work as being largely preparatory, in the sense that it provided him with an arena in which he could, between 1805 and 1808, learn the rudiments of painting that his Copenhagen background failed to provide, any ultimate knowledge of what Runge's art "might have become had he lived" remains an open question. Perhaps the essentially synthetic ambitions of his projected *Four Times of Day* would finally have prevailed, producing a highly symbolic form of monumental decoration; but perhaps not. It is certainly not inconceivable that the visual world, stripped of symbolic machinations, might eventually have taken hold of Runge once the need to justify his efforts dialectically had passed.

Given the intensity of his initial fix on nature, and coupling this with the very real and quite revolutionary pictorial success which he experienced in his great family portraits and in his one heroic attempt to weld together group portraiture and a real landscape setting, *The Hulsenbeck Children* (Hamburger Kunsthalle), it seems quite possible that Runge might have chosen finally to pursue nature in a relatively straightforward fashion, having accepted its fecundity. The other option, that of symbolic decoration drawing freely upon nature both visually and metaphorically, seems in principle a more elevated path, but it was one which Runge could not himself follow productively within the brief lifetime he was granted.

Working strictly as a draftsman Runge was able to devise complicated decorative emblems that follow out this second option with considerable success. Even Goethe respected Runge's black and white designs for the *Four Times of Day;* in fact, he hung them in his own music room at Weimar, thereby recognizing in a way which Runge would have appreciated the undeniably successful evocation of synaesthesia that emerges from Runge's complex harmonies of line and which gestures in some indefinable way toward comparably complex harmonies of music. Runge believed that he could translate all of this into painting, and the penultimate frustration of his life (the ultimate being his early death) derived from his inability to do so. The reasons for this inability stand revealed in the unfinished large version of *Morning,* the only one of the *Four Times of Day* that ever even approached realization in paint. In what remains of this painting one can see the titanic battle that waged between a preestablished armature of line—symmetrical and two-dimensional in its pictorial character; botanical, astrological, and even Pompeian in the origin of its illustrative content—and a development of color that is at some points heraldic in its force and simplicity and at others intensely complicated by small-scale intervals which seem charged with reproducing (almost microscopically) as precise a degree of naturalistic illusion as was humanly conceivable prior to the invention of the color photograph.

Runge clearly hoped that the painted elaboration of his symbolical idea would give to *Morning* some form of half-pictorial, half-psychological unity. Larger units of form and color strive to contain and resolve smaller more disparate ones, as the basic emblems of birth, awakening, and sunrise gradually reveal themselves. The painting, if one can really call it a painting, stands somewhere in the midst of a process of self-disclosure, the termination of which remained beyond the artist's grasp, and perhaps even beyond his intention. Believing as he did that "landscape was the art of the future" and that only in landscape could modern artists guarantee the genuine spirituality of their efforts, Runge tried in *Morning* to give landscape a universal, nonparticularized form by simultaneously rendering actual nature (statically and in the process of growth) and representing it generally in the form of symbolic decorative emblems. However, the abstractness of his ambition, coupled with the definiteness of many of his means of pursuing it, produces an image finally more ambiguous than universal. In the last analysis the viewer is undeniably impressed, yet baffled. He cannot "read" *Morning* and "see" it at the same time in an experience of visual and intellectual resolution. The visual and the symbolic information which Runge provides are too diversified, too reliant upon oppositions to stimulate any mutually complementary processes of comprehension.

In the portraits which he produced in the years immediately preceding his work of the painted version of *Morning* Runge proved, as we have already noted, that he could quite literally see things with a unique clarity and definiteness and, in so doing, make paintings of a resolutely pictorial sort. When working directly from nature Runge did not feel the need either to predetermine his linear design along decorative lines or to elaborate his subjects symbolically. Instead he worked in two distinct steps to bring about as complete a realization of what he saw as he possibly could. Choosing as subjects members of his immediate family or close friends, he began via drawings to get down in black and white as much descriptive information as possible. He surveyed his subjects straight on and from close range so that the edges of his forms were as exact as the details of physiognomy they contained. Having seized as much as he could with line drawing, he enlarged his drawing and transferred it (sometimes after a preliminary oil sketch) to canvas. He then returned to the subject and attempted to render its non-linear aspects in terms of the most careful calibration of painted colors.

The portraits in their finished form assault the viewer with an almost unbearable intensity. Their subjects are almost too present; as a result, first, of the closeness and fixedness of Runge's point of view and, second, because of the artist's instinctive tendency to stress one or another element of line or to alter, usually upward, the values of his already harsh bright colors. Working from such close range on subjects to whom he cannot help responding personally, Runge holds desperately to what he sees, while at the same time yielding to feeling when the pressure of confrontation mounts. Out of the tenseness of his particular portrait situations, with their combined pressures for personal and technical resolution, Runge makes great art in a form that is completely his own. Viewing the paintings one experiences a sensation not unlike that which the poet Heinrich von Kleist described so well when referring not to the work of Runge but that of his contemporary Caspar David Friedrich: "It is as though one's eyelids have been cut away."

While one can invoke Kleist's statement to bridge the very distinct achievements of Runge and Friedrich it is far more important to concede the differences. The gulf which separates the work of these two artists is so great that it defies description in any but the most general terms of romantic criticism. Seen strictly as personalities Runge and Friedrich stand in complete opposition to one another, even though as artists they received basically similar training and, during the first decade of the century, moved within the same "early romantic" circles in Dresden. In both instances their personalities are implicit in the modes and in the tempo of their respective careers. Runge's sheer quantitative productivity in terms of art, writing, and children between 1800 and 1810 is remarkable. Driven to justify his chosen career in the forthrightly Calvinist terms of his merchant family he worked constantly and with a kind of grim determination that seems almost to contradict the highly subjective, mystical goals he pursued. Inactivity whether for reasons of failure or indecision was unacceptable to Runge. With it came, inevitably, feelings of guilt which only more work could assuage. If able to paint, he painted; if unable, he wrote, but under no circumstances could be sit and wait for the resolution of a difficulty to emerge through materially unproductive contemplation.

[6, 7]   Friedrich's personality insofar as it emerges from his work is of an-
[8, 9]   other order altogether. Never driven by the urge to produce great
[10, 11]   quantities of work, FRIEDRICH proceeded carefully, forming each painting in his mind before committing it to canvas. While honoring nature, in the form of particular views of landscape, as a source for ideas around which

paintings could be made, Friedrich never felt compelled to reproduce it in any detail. Instead he spent a good deal of time simply taking in what nature had to offer.

Over his lifetime he made several journeys on foot through all of the various types of landscape that were available to him. Starting either from his hometown Greifswald (on the north German coast adjacent to the island of Rügen) or from Dresden where he spent most of his professional life, Friedrich set off, usually alone, with a sketchbook, but without any felt obligation to fill it. As he walked he immersed himself in nature physically and spiritually, in a way more characteristic of the polemical longings than the actual experiences of German romantic writers. If and when a particular aspect of nature held his attention, Friedrich recorded it in his sketchbook, sometimes stenographically, sometimes in beautifully finished line drawings.

It is difficult to imagine in many instances why Friedrich decided to draw one particular aspect and not some other. Whether a panorama or a small bit of vegetation, each element which Friedrich singles out seems to have been selected as a metaphor, either complete or incomplete, for an experience of nature (as psychological as it was visual in essence) in response to which he could conceive the broad outlines of some future painting. Friedrich learned both the basic moods and the small unexpected incidents of nature firsthand. They constituted a large portion of his memory. What he needed in order to paint were keys to unlock this memory, and to do so in a particular way. It was precisely these keys which his sketches provided.

The actual experience of life in nature was basic to Friedrich's art and personality—much more so than it was to Runge. The act of contemplating natural phenomena and conjuring painted images responsive to the memory of this contemplation absorbed a good deal of Friedrich's time and formed much of the actual creative process from which his painting emerged. Production for the sake of production was a drive Friedrich never felt. Fortunately his creative life was quite long (forty years roughly speaking) so he had time to indulge his quietism and to paint only after an image had gradually been felt into being. Technical difficulties never plagued him in any notable way, and he discovered quite early in his career the compositional means through which the particular qualities of his sensibility and his vision could be expressed most cogently.

While constitutionally incapable of matching or even understanding the sheer existential urgency of Runge's struggle in his portraits to pictorialize nature by confronting it and holding on until the picture was complete, Friedrich quite likely sympathized with Runge's ambitions for the *Four Times of Day*. The type of nature emblems which Runge longed to create have a distinct echo in Friedrich's work. However, Friedrich managed in a way Runge never did to assure that the primarily visual aspect of his emblems remained dominant. He rejected symbolism of the sort which requires "reading" in favor of visual metaphors of the life of nature which succeed for the most part in exposing their message with a psychological directness that is both consistent and highly ingenious. In fact one might almost say that the emotional impact which Friedrich's emblems of nature generate is so direct and unfailing that it seems somehow bonded to the very core of human response to nature, where it strips bare all the truisms of mankind's nature sentiment.

The ur-typical quality of Friedrich's achievements was recognized almost immediately by his contemporaries. His friend and follower, the painter-natural scientist, Dr. Carl Gustav Carus, tried to offer an explanation of this in his *Nine Letters on Landscape Painting* and, in particular, in his discussions of the *"Erdlebensbildnis"*—the painting of the life of the earth. Basing his ideas upon the philosopher Schelling's proposed derivation of a universal world soul from the examination of microcosmic particulars of nature, Carus saw the *"Erdlebensbildnis"* as a metaphoric formulation of essential qualities of the spirit of the earth itself. However, as a scientist, Carus was inclined to stress the specifically informative quality of the *"Erdlebensbildnis"* in a way which seems slightly inappropriate to the actual effect of Friedrich's work, where the resonances of sentiment rather than the reassurances of knowledge (whether universal or particular) seem to predominate.

Carus provided another, more revealing documentation of Friedrich's ambitions (as the artist himself conceived them) in a memorial pamphlet published after Friedrich's death in 1840. There Carus recorded a selection of Friedrich's aphoristic statements about art. These statements provide a remarkably clear (if general) indication of Friedrich's beliefs. They grant the unequivocally spiritual character of Friedrich's self-image and the visionary aspect of his conception of the artist's task. The following is an abbreviated extract from these aphorisms set into the form of a sequential statement:

> The painter should not just paint what he sees before him but also what he sees within himself. However, if he does not see anything within himself he should abstain from painting. Painters [in general] practice inventing, composing, or whatever they call it. Does that not mean in so many words that they practice patching and mending? A picture must not be devised but perceived. Shut your corporeal eyes so that you see your picture first with your spiritual eye. Then bring to light that which you saw in darkness so that it [the forms of your image] may act upon others from the outside [their visual sensations before the picture] to the inside [of their spirit]. The artist's feeling is his law. Pure perception can never violate nature, it can only *be* natural.

A considerable factor in Friedrich's success as a painter resides in the quite fortuitous selection of the motifs which he charged with carrying out visually one or another form of nature sentiment. His gothic ruins, his cemeteries, his moments of sunrise and sunset, his rainbows and full moons, his abysses, his fog, and his distant ships all possess such predictable psychological connotations that their appearance alone guarantees at least the beginning of a communicable emotional experience. With the primary emotional effects of his imagery assured, Friedrich's efforts are directed for the most part toward retaining the full power of these effects as a particular image is translated into the form of an actual picture. He is at his best as a painter when he makes this translation most simply. He is at his worst when the translation appears forced, either by too much emphasis upon secondary images or by the overelaboration of illustrative rather than strictly visual connections between various components of a picture.

Friedrich was able to find within his immediate cultural and artistic milieu most of the stylistic conventions and many of the currents of imagery that eventually became virtual trademarks of his works. The sources for his imagery are numerous and generally literary. Recent scholarship has stressed English eighteenth-century nature poetry, in particular Thomas Gray's *Elegy in a Country Churchyard*, as a source for Friedrich's gothic ruins and cemeteries; but there are more contemporary and available sources for these and other of his motifs as well. In Ludwig Tieck's *Franz Sternbalds Wanderungen* certain of the descriptions of characters immersed in contemplation of nature seem to prefigure Friedrich directly, while in the enormously popular writings of Chateaubriand (in particular *Le Génie du Christianisme*) connections are made almost constantly between the most picturesque scenes and moments of nature, including those involving traces of Christianity in the form of ruins, and so forth, and the origins of specifically religious sentiments. Friedrich, in fact, adopts much of the combined imagery of Tieck and Chateaubriand without substantially modifying it, although he would not have done so had this imagery not corresponded so precisely with his own experiences of nature. Nothing bound him to invoke particular images simply because of their currency and, conversely, the fact of currency did not in any sense obviate for Friedrich the power of a given image. If an image "felt" right and if he could formulate it pictorially he used it.

A similar kind of subjectively based pragmatism appears in Friedrich's stylistic development. Much of his early painting (that done between 1806 and 1816) relies on the same neoclassic conventions of design that inform Runge's work. In the case of both men this is due to the combined influences of Copenhagen and Weimar. For as long as he found it necessary, Friedrich used the geometrically derived and generally symmetrical design armature of neoclassicism. At times he pursued geometry to a point where it provided the total decorative organization of a picture. At other times he used basic geometrical props (center lines, diagonals drawn from corners, etc.) simply as guides in the placement of the various elements he chose to portray. When geometry dominates Friedrich's paintings display forceful nature emblems, related in type, but far simpler in development than those which Runge envisioned for his *Four Times of Day*. When working less rigidly Friedrich relies upon the effect of his decisions to alter, either by stress or by purposeful ambiguity, anticipated relationships between the components of his images, to produce a more mysterious and unpredictable psychological presence.

As his work develops Friedrich cultivates a definite pictorial language of stresses and ambiguities. First of all he rejects the possibility of continuous pictorial space. His paintings pack their imagery into an immeasurable middleground which the viewer must somehow reach visually without the support of an accessible foreground and without the prospect of a literally distant background. The relative location of elements which are set in the middle ground is made intentionally unclear so that Friedrich can, via contrasts of scale, color, or silhouette against light, emphasize whatever psychological cross-references or disjointures he chooses. Alternately, he can isolate a single element irrevocably—a person or a tree, for example—detach it from nearness and distance, and by so doing remove it from the phenomenal world which the viewer necessarily comprehends in terms of space and time. Then, with his color which tends either to stress contrasts, and in so doing to emphasize the separateness of individual parts of an image, or to make, through repetitions of similar intervals of color, no separation at all, Friedrich alters whatever connections he has drawn between pictured elements or introduces them where they have not been. The result of all this is that Friedrich's pictures seen as a group stand like so many apparitions, guided by a few common laws and rephrasing themselves endlessly in both formal and psychological particulars. The range of commonness and variation is evident both in the macrocosm of Friedrich's total production and in its many subgroupings of subject cycles like those dealing with the four seasons or times of day. Friedrich's frequent reliance upon cyclical groups, combined with the cultivated impersonality of his actual process of making a picture once he had formed it in his mind, demonstrates very clearly his desire to remain a neutral medium for the expression of universal statements about the life of nature.

His "neutrality" notwithstanding, Friedrich succeeded in producing pictures which are, from a strictly visual point of view, incredibly modern. Whether intending to or not, Friedrich achieved a directness and lucidity in painted images of nature for which there was no tradition and from which there was no qualitatively significant consequence. Without actually working specifically from nature in any very systematic way Friedrich nevertheless sought to pictorialize it. His methods of doing so were self-reliant in the extreme, and they were effective. Artists working much later in the century in Germany and elsewhere confirmed many of Friedrich's achievements without even knowing about them. Their bias toward nature was of a wholly different and essentially positivistic order, but the unconventional ways they developed to express this bias frequently echo those of Friedrich.

[14, 15] The revolutionary qualities of Friedrich's art emerge most clearly [16, 17] when seen in contrast to those cultivated by such of his contemporaries as KOCH and Ferdinand Olivier, both of whom relied on more traditional formulation of landscape painting. We have already noted Koch's adherence to conventions gleaned from the work of Poussin and Claude Lorraine. This is apparent in the conglomerate aspect of his images—in their tendency to be built from many pieces of "ideal" landscape like mountains, waterfalls, Italianate buildings, and small-scale figures garbed in timeless peasant costumes. Poussin and Claude also are recalled in the way Koch distributes the masses of his landscapes in both two and three dimensions, subsequently weaving them together with rhythmically articulated zones of vegetation. Koch's work, like that of his masters, is predictable and consistent in its development of color, tending to cool greens, blues, and grays with occasional accents of more primary tones. In the harsh, somewhat abrupt aspect of Koch's drawing and in his relatively greater emphasis upon two- rather than three-dimensional organization there is a form of departure from precedent, but a comparatively mild one. When left to his own devices and inspired to deal with "romantic" themes from the narratives of Dante (in the Casino Massimo) or Shakespeare, Koch is inventive but pictorially insecure. Relying on hectic and invariably self-dissipating rhythms of line to convey the drama of his subjects, he usually ends by producing images which, instead of being exciting in any way peculiar to themselves, seem simply overwrought. Friedrich, in images comparably dramatic, if less literal in their drama, is more certain of his pictorial means and more aware of the values they are capable of conveying. Having always conceived of his painting and his im-

agery as an indissoluble unit, Friedrich learned to express through the smallest pictorial adjustments an enormous range of emotion and drama, all of which transpired at a predetermined and totally controlled optical and psychological distance from the viewer. Built to encompass—if not actually built from—the comprehended totality of his capacity for experience, Friedrich's painting rarely oversteps its limits. Koch's painting was less a product of his experience than a result of his artistic taste. This meant that it could break down under the force of ambition and it frequently did.

[22] While usually more "natural" in details of landscape than Koch's, the paintings of OLIVIER are equally the product of taste. Like Koch's, they look toward Italianate sources, including the contemporary Italianism of the Nazarenes. Both Koch and Olivier retained contacts of a more or less regular sort with Overbeck's circle, but while Koch actually resided in Rome for a considerable part of his life, it is not absolutely certain that Olivier visited Rome at all. Nevertheless the Nazarenes considered Olivier a co-worker with ideals comparable to their own and made him an honorary member of the Brotherhood of St. Luke. Working from a position which was, generally speaking, midway between the art of Koch and the practice of pure classical landscape and the strictly Christian ambitions of the Nazarene group proper, Olivier arrived at the quite literal solution of combining Christian storytelling and Italianate landscape settings. His landscape settings are invariably more responsive to observable qualities of light, atmosphere, and color than are Koch's, and his imagery is less overbearing than that, for example, of Overbeck. However, his paintings ultimately yield a composite and quite self-conscious appearance. The disjointure between Olivier's pictorial sensitivity to landscape effects and his drive to produce specific illustrations never resolves itself. His inability to bring the two elements harmoniously together underlines once again the magnitude of Friedrich's achievement. By holding to a more selective and a psychologically more integrated conception of both landscape and quasi-religious imagery, Friedrich consistently managed to convey a unified pictorial presence wherein visual and illustrative elements were mutually complementary.

We have already noted that Friedrich's influence beyond his lifetime was slight. In fact his work was, like that of many other German painters, lost for all practical purposes from the time of his death until the great exhibition of German painting from 1775–1875 organized by Hugo von Tschudi in Berlin in 1906. However, during his lifetime Friedrich was highly influential in the regional art world of Dresden. Although the only official position he ever held was that of ordinary professor of landscape painting at the Dresden Academy, his preeminence among Dresden painters was virtually unchallenged.

45

Two of Friedrich's associates, Carus and the Norwegian painter Dahl were instrumental in propagating Friedrich's achievements, even though their own work represented these achievements in one or another form of dilution. Because of his reputation as a scientist and art theorist, Carus gained a larger audience for his efforts than he could ever have managed had he remained simply a painter. Dahl as a ranking professor at the Dresden Academy enjoyed an officially sanctioned public stature equally beyond the intrinsic merits of his work—if these (and Carus's too) are measured against Friedrich's very formidable standards. The paintings of Carus and Dahl, for all their differences, represent an essentially similar alteration of Friedrich's precedents. The balance of emphasis worked out by Friedrich between naturalism on the one hand and imagistic sentiment on the other is rarely duplicated by either Carus or Dahl, both of whom tend to upset the balance either in the direction of naturalism or in the direction of more overtly melodramatic qualities of imagery. They do so even while painting within Friedrich's canonical domain of subject matter and in direct response to his actual manner of portrayal.

[I, 34] Looking first at CARUS, it is evident that his "romantic" subject
[35]   pictures are far more theatrical in their effects, more resolutely illustrative in their evocation of picturesque narrative, than Friedrich's. Technically looser and more varied in their composition than comparable Friedrich's, Carus's pictures demonstrate a pictorial psychology which is superficially immediate, but ultimately unfocused and controlled by a personality far less integrated than Friedrich's. What Carus's images gain in their greater elaboration of illustrative detail and in their more evidently illusionistic treatment of space, color, and light, they lose in cogency. The particular cogency of Friedrich's work derives from the strictest, most decisive pictorial selectivity, from an instinctive knowledge of what that selectivity is intended to express and, finally, what it is capable of expressing. Carus is most successful as an artist with subjects that are least "romantic" in the narrative sense of the term. His paintings of relatively everyday incidents are invariably straightforward in conception. They are painted with a technical confidence that derives from a real understanding of visual appearances and with a directness of design and presentation that relies in a very positive way upon Friedrich for direction.

[36, 37]   While the balance of Carus's effort (along with that of other Friedrich
            followers like Ernst Ferdinand Oehme and Georg Friedrich Kersting) tends to follow that side of Friedrich's work which is most overtly symbolic and laden with the emotions of romantic naturalism, Dahl's work is dominantly topographical (usually identifiably so). As a result, Friedrich's precedents tend to weigh less heavily upon DAHL than upon Carus, but they are evident nonetheless. Most of Dahl's background prior to his residence in Dresden (temporarily in 1818–20, then more permanently from 1824 until his death in 1857) shows a strong inclination toward panoramic scene painting. Throughout his career in Dresden this inclination persisted and developed. He found two primary exemplars upon which to base an artistic personality already partly formed along those lines. The first was Friedrich, the second was the work of the eighteenth-century Venetian painter of many famous views of the city of Dresden, Bernardo Bellotto. From Bellotto, Dahl adopted the wide angle of vision typical of eighteenth-century Venetian *vedute*. Then in his own free oil sketches, both of topographical sites and of meteorological phenomena, he tried to extend his own awareness of the true (optically scientific) appearance of nature, even beyond that of the Venetians. From Friedrich, Dahl adopted the mood-inducing devices of sharply contrasting colors (and of black and white), while at the same time he began to appreciate the kind of visual presence Friedrich achieved with his starkly projected silhouettes and his planimetric compressions of space. Since the origins of many of the devices in Friedrich's art that Dahl found attractive are, at least indirectly, traceable to pseudoscientific (but prephotographic) reproduc-

46

tive media like shadowgraphs and diorama, it was almost preordained that Dahl with his scientific bent would have been attentive to them. Yet it was Friedrich's actual usage and development of such devices that proved their pictorial viability and their potential.

The ultimate appearance of Dahl's paintings derives almost equally from its two exemplars. By the prevailing contemporary standards of Dresden painting Dahl's subject matter (usually an identifiable view of a particular bit of the city or countryside) is highly specific. Dahl's presentations of his subjects encompass an even wider range of observable natural effects than are evident in his Venetian models, and he is successful in heightening the emotional force of his effects through the use of pictorial devices drawn from Friedrich. However, Dahl's resolution of his two exemplars finally fails to be convincing or truly significant artistically. The particular form of resolution which Dahl arrives at is essentially academic. Holding simultaneously to two exemplars, radically different in their origins and their intentions, Dahl succeeds in forcing them to walk side by side rather than in integrating them. There is a process of practical (and essentially technical) dialectic at work. We do not sense, either theoretically or in the pictures themselves, a single, self-informing creative awareness guiding the artist from within.

[38] Dahl's students, like CHRISTIAN FRIEDRICH GILLE, adopt the external effects of a style already lacking in any directness of conviction. The result is a kind of half-natural, half-mannered, and essentially theatrical "scene painting" which tries to hide its absence of real pictorial and emotional content under a wealth of contrived illusionism and a comparable quantity of picturesque genre detail. Gille's work as it develops in the 1850s and thereafter parallels in its fundamental dishonesty the contemporary efforts, fashionable and equally vacuous, of the Achenbach brothers (Andreas and Oswald) in Düsseldorf and of Felix Ziem in France.

While both Dahl and Carus were inclined at least part of the time to alter the ratio of apparent to specific naturalism in Friedrich's painting in favor of the latter, they failed ultimately to make of their inclination a body of consistently successful work. Each relied on his great painterly sensitivity to incidental effects of light and color to convey his naturalistic inclinations, but neither really discovered nor set out to explore the minor, but basic, adjustment of Friedrich's manner of pictorial construction which his new mode of emphasis demanded.

[12, 13] The only painter of Friedrich's generation who managed even to approach the successful combination of a manner of pictorial construction similar to Friedrich's with an optically more specific species of image did so without any knowledge whatsoever of Friedrich's work. This painter, the Mannheim-born WILHELM VON KOBELL, spent most of his working life in Munich, first as a military painter to the Bavarian Court during the Napoleonic occupation, then as a professor of landscape painting at the Munich Academy (until fired by Cornelius as part of a largely successful campaign to purge that academy of all non-Nazarene elements), and finally as an independent artist until his death in 1853.

As a result of artistic currents active within his own family, Kobell seems to have become a landscape painter almost by preordination. However, the particular manner of landscape painting which he eventually developed owes a good deal to the fact of his residence in Munich and to the influences of the kind of landscape painting which was practiced in Munich at the time of his arrival. Kobell's father, Ferdinand Kobell, and his uncle Franz, were both landscape painters with considerable reputation at the turn of the century. Their work featured either variants of seventeenth-century Dutch (or Italianate-Dutch) landscape conventions, or looked to the more recent decorative landscape manner of the French, as represented, for example, by the work of François Boucher. Wilhelm von Kobell continued the family interest in seventeenth-century Dutch painting by adopting many technical devices for the rendering of light and many of the aspects of quasi-military subject matter that he found in the work of Philips Wouverman, who was well represented in the Bavarian Royal Collections in Munich. Kobell discovered at about the same time the very free landscape sketches of the Munich academician Georg von Dillis. Dillis's sketches emphasized effects of light rendered directly from nature, which were less mannered in their pictorial development than those apparent in Wouverman. The most important aspect of Dillis's work and that which affected Kobell most strongly was its enormous sensitivity to spatial and atmospheric alterations of light and color. In his great series of Napoleonic battle pictures (Munich Stadt Museum) done for the Bavarian Crown Prince Ludwig, between 1808 and 1815, Kobell responded to Dillis's atmospheric effects, while constructing his pictures generally on the basis of contemporary French battle paintings, such as those of Horace Vernet. He developed individual figures and groups of figures with a quite free reference to Wouverman. A brief visit to France in 1809 had served to acquaint Kobell with current French conventions of geometrically obtained neoclassical landscape design. Kobell employed these conventions and expanded them with figural and atmospheric details deriving from sources available to him in Munich.

What sets Kobell's battle paintings above their combined Dutch, French, and German sources is a totally new sense of optical, almost stereoptical, preciseness, evident both in the way pictorial space is organized into discrete, coherent lateral zones, and in the sharply defined, hyperluminous clarity of figures set in the most forward of these zones. In the battle pictures the zones undeniably dominate the figures they contain, and in their rigorously parallel lateral extensions they force the viewer's field of vision beyond comfortable limits in a way which recalls the particular visual impact of diorama. However, in work subsequent to these pictures Kobell presses for a more focused (and usually centered) presentation of large-scale figure groups and comparatively less-encompassing lateral zones of space. As he formulates this latter ambition, many of the characteristic aspects of his pictures begin to parallel those of Friedrich.

Like Friedrich, Kobell sets up his cast of autographic figures—men standing beside or mounted upon horses, and sheep or cattle herders—on the basis of a simple system of intersecting geometrical axes. These involve center lines, diagonals drawn from the four corners of the picture, and regular parallel lines deriving from the bottom edge of the picture and moving upward across its surface. In the images which result, figures inhabit a distinctly limited middle-ground space. The viewer confronts them abruptly because Kobell's foregrounds remain vacant and largely inarticulate. Pictorial distance behind the figures seems immense, yet because of the invariably low level of Kobell's viewpoint and the corresponding appearance of the horizon at the center of the picture, or even lower, the distance remains enormously distant, never competing with the figures for attention. Kobell's figures, like the more varied inhabitants of Friedrich's pictures, seem finally suspended, hanging ambiguously within and simultaneously against their setting. They seem almost supernaturally real. In spite of their apparent removal from the viewer (their habitation of the picture's middle ground) they feel somehow projected out at the viewer in a way which makes his comprehension of the painted image intensely problematic. He is finally unable to exclude either of two phenomenological possibilities—that of the painting as a receding or as an advancing organism of illusion.

From roughly 1814 to 1830 Kobell kept the pictorial tension of his images alive. He reinforced it with his crisp, but highly flexible and naturalistically sensitive, handling of light. Local colors in their definiteness or indefiniteness help to secure the alternately recessive and projective possibilities of his pictures, while at the same time providing what is certainly one of the most pictorially complete and convincing forms of descriptive visual illusionism which the nineteenth century had so far managed to produce. Without denying the mannerisms which inevitably crept into Kobell's work as he repeated his most successful images again and again with minor alterations, it is nevertheless clear that his pictures, more than those of any other single painter active in Germany at the time, gave promise of the quality which naturalist painting of an even more rigorous and thoroughgoing sort would subsequently achieve. This promise was not fulfilled in any of the work which derives most directly from Kobell's—that of the group of landscape painters active around 1830 in Austria (in the *Salzkammergut*) or that of Ferdinand Waldmüller—but in the work of Menzel, and even later in paintings by the so-called German Impressionists.

[40, 39] To continue to the next phase in the halting, diffuse, development of naturalist painting in Germany we shift our attention to the city of Berlin where, as we have already noted, a strong bias toward painting from nature appeared at the very beginning of the nineteenth century. We find it first in the sculpture and in the teaching philosophy of Gottfried Schadow. In painting, the cityscapes of JOHANN ERDMANN HUMMEL and EDOUARD GÄRTNER, and the portraits of Franz Krüger translated this inclination into the most formal and circumscribed stylistic terms. Compared with Kobell's achievements in Munich, the work of Berlin painters seems preeminently literal in its hard, basically linear descriptiveness. The Berliners' obsession with rule-bearing exactitude is evident in their reliance on complex linear perspective in their city views and in the graphic stiffness of their figure drawing. Yet, despite many limitations, there remains a species of visual, if apictorial, impact in much of Hummel's, Gärtner's, and Krüger's work. A quirkish, quasi-photographic presence informs Hummel's paintings, particularly his series depicting various stages in the production and installation of the huge, highly polished granite, bowl-shaped monument which was the featured novelty in one of the new Berlin parks in the early 1830s. Gärtner's extensive (in coverage and frequently in scale) panoramas of one or another Berlin prospect succeed often in overwhelming the viewer visually as a result of the sheer quantity of descriptive information they provide, while Krüger's portraits convey an inelegant, but highly particularized image of actual

49

human beings predictive of that which is later produced photomechanically by the daguerreotype.

[41, 42]   What was prominently lacking in Berlin naturalism during the
[43, 44]   first thirty years of the century was any forthrightly pictorial justification for its existence. This justification begins to appear first in the works of KARL BLECHEN. Blechen's painting is in many ways a rather odd quantity. We have already discussed its reliance upon sketches from nature in both pencil and oil, its contacts with Dresden painting, and its parallels with the art of Friedrich Wasmann. Two factors still to be stressed are Blechen's highly original manner of handling oil paint, both in sketches and large-scale "finished" pictures, and the markedly realist bent of many of his subjects. By Berlin standards of the time Blechen's technique (and, in fact, his whole pictorial approach) seems very painterly. He uses the relative looseness or tightness of his brushwork along with changes in the density of his actual buildup of oil pigment to achieve an extremely wide range of pictorial emphasis. The extent and effect of this is most evident in his larger pictures where bold, pictorial contrasts in the manner of painting successive elements can be so extreme as to threaten the implied visual coherence of the image as a whole. While seeming to paint nature, and in many cases nature of a highly specific contemporary sort, Blechen attempts simultaneously to give his paintings a very definite life of their own. He challenges his viewers to comprehend the only partially resolved alternatives, or multiple possibilities, which result from his decision to deploy pictorial effects in sequence rather than to derive them from a single hierarchical idea of style. His tendency to propose pictorial situations which become relevant in spite of, and often because of, their apparent tenuousness literally tears up the general complacency of more conventional Berlin painting. Even more important in the long run is that he supported, through the undeniable quality of his work, the ambitions of later Berlin painters to pursue naturalism with all of the possibilities inherent in their medium rather than with a few devices determined arbitrarily by some pre-existent set of formal restrictions. Along with apparent license, however, Blechen's work conveyed a sense of risk and a substantial challenge. The kind of open-ended exploratory naturalism he proposed depended for its successful realization upon the ability of a given painter to make productive selections of what to paint from nature and, having done so, to forge pictorial solutions relevant to his selections.

50

Blechen's imagery, or at any rate one facet of it, began to stake out many of the domains of subject matter upon which naturalist painting in Germany, and particularly in Berlin, would rely most productively. His sketches from open windows, looking out over the rooftops of his neighborhood, and his views of literally new aspects of contemporary life—factories, pleasure pavilions, and so forth—served to focus general ambitions to paint from nature on real facts of everyday visual experience. In some respects the increasing specificity and reality of his subjects seems a quite logical extension of the straightforwardly scenic aspirations of earlier Berlin painting, but they are actually much more than this. Ideally Blechen's view of reality remains unimpressed by the self-evidently (and predictably) important, unusual, and imposing aspects of nature. The somewhat random quality of his realism supports his pictorial intentions directly, standing as the most reliable vehicle for their eventual realization. But randomness is also the greatest potential threat to this realization. Alone his subjects are often meaningless and uninteresting. They depend almost wholly upon Blechen's ability to generate meaning and interest pictorially, in terms of the way a painting finally looks.

The shift in emphasis from the generically natural to the real and everyday stands as a turning point of naturalist painting in the nineteenth-century art of every European country, and in every instance it seems to appear almost simultaneously (in the early 1840s) with the first successful achievements in the science of photography. The ideal of deriving images from direct and specific exposure to a single aspect of the visible world is one which painters and early photographers held unequivocally in common, at least for a time, and it is virtually impossible to sort out the relative priorities of their shared ambitions. The drive to get at, and then to work specifically from, discovered, rather than assembled, aspects of nature was implicit in various kinds of naturalist painting practiced in Germany prior to the 1840s, and much the same was true in other European countries as well. In Germany, as we have already seen, much naturalist painting made use of effects parallel to those achieved about the same time by prephotographic techniques of optical-mechanical representation. It is, therefore, possible to propose that quasi-photographic intentions were jointly explored by painting and science as part of a predominantly positivistic "Weltanschauung" which prevailed during the first half of the century, despite a wide variety of intellectual subcurrents many of which seem almost antithetical to positivism. Runge's painting is perhaps the most obvious demonstration in Germany itself of the seemingly self-contradictory, but undeniable, truth of this proposition.

When photography finally happened, it confirmed much of what painting had in one form or another already proposed. There was a moment of concord between the two media. Concord is apparent in many initial parallels of subject matter and viewpoint. In psychological terms, the self-satisfaction of having achieved reality supported this concord at least for a time; but progressively, through the 1850s and 1860s, realist painting and photography both became aware of the differences inherent in the fact that by definition one was an active, the other a passive, medium and that, as a result, their greatest potential qualities were mutually exclusive.

The eventual departure of realist painting from photography (and vice versa) was virtually predestined in Germany and elsewhere by an obvious, but nonetheless historically crucial, factor. At the very moment when photography produced its first successful images realist painting had already taken as its pictorial foundation the sketch—the most evidently free form of its mediological self-definition. The sketch was adopted and honored for its ability to convey the quickness and immediacy of observed effects which it first transcribed and then organized in such a way as to communicate them visually to the viewer with a minimum of imposed formality. Photography, on the other hand (and particularly early photography), presented, pictorially speaking, an absolutely opposite version of reality. Its images possessed a hand-etched stillness—an almost frozen appearance, expressed in resolute black and white tones. While demonstrably, even scientifically, accurate in the effects it was capable of rendering, it looked oddly like certain forms of neoclassical painting. Compared to realist painting of the sort produced by an artist like Blechen, photographic images seem archaic and decidedly removed from the visual realities producing them. An artist of the next generation, Adolf von Menzel for example, might accompany, figuratively speaking, the photographer in his search for real subjects, but having found them, the painter and the photographer realized the fractions of actual vision which either could express were vastly different. Each was in his own way limited by the medium he practiced; either, in order to do well that which he did, had first to accept the limitations of his medium, then to explore the potential that remained. Photography's precision of detail and tone was ultimately beyond the domain of painting, while the painter's ability to select and emphasize even when working from real motifs was outside the limits of photography and was most readily expressible in the form of the sketch.

Because of its obvious usefulness for the making of what are in both the broadest and narrowest sense visual documents, photography passed through the early stages of its history without becoming overly concerned with the meaning or intention of its images. It simply set about the business of making records of the way the world and its people looked—at least, the way they appeared photographically. Patrons of photography knew what they wanted photographs to portray, and photographers let themselves be guided by the demands of the market, using their ingenuity to propose as wide a variety of potentially salable images as possible. Strictly speaking, the value of a photograph depended upon the marketability of its subject either in mass or private terms. It sold because of what it represented, and because of the predictable and scientifically reassuring way it achieved representation. The general public learned very quickly what photographs looked like, and people were in general pleased with their appearance. All that remained for photographers to do was supply photographic images of things people wanted to see. Photographers found that their work was both most satisfying visually and most marketable when it relied on the simplest, "straightest" deployment of the photographic technique itself. They discovered that the photographic image invariably suffered from quasi-artistic manipulations. By the late 1850s and early 1860s it was clear in every European country that realist painting and photography, their common ground notwithstanding, were destined to pursue different and, in most respects, opposed causes. It became clear that realist painting could not hope to provide its potential viewers with circumscribed reassurances comparable to those of photography without losing its unique powers of pictorialization and its identity as art. Granting this fact, realist painters confronted abruptly something which photography had never been forced to consider, namely the problem of what a given image or type of imagery meant. For, as long as realist painters restricted themselves to portraiture and to self-evidently interesting landscape views and painted these in a relatively impersonal manner, the problem of meaning did not become overly acute. But, as soon as realist painting began either to suppress the literal interest of its subjects or to exaggerate particular modes of pictorialization, whatever values it proposed became, from a public point of view, unclear. Increasingly, realist painting came to rely on the very factors which seemed most to obscure its purpose and its worth. It did so because it found that strictly artistic values could only be realized (proposed and developed) in this way. Like the photographers, realist painters discovered their greatest guarantees of quality in the purest deployment of their medium, and clearly painting, unlike photography, could not conceivably define itself by "aiming and shooting." Painting had no mechanical essence; it had instead a history during the course of which proposals rather than solutions had been marked out. In the process of rendering what they saw, realist painters continuously tested the self-definitional possibilities which the history of painting suggested, rejecting some and adding more than a few new ones in an unending quest for the kind of self-certainty that photography possessed as a basic technological fact.

The various successive achievements of realist painting finally rest on any given painter's ability to pursue a single course of painterly self-definition to its purest, most meaningful, and least referential conclusion. His success is ideally dependent upon his discovery of self-evidently expressive ways of painting reality rather than upon the comprehensive representational truth of his portrayal. He is, in other words, seeking out pictorial conventions as painters have always done, but he is doing so at the risk of having these conventions exposed unmercifully as a result of the cross-references he encourages his viewers to make between his images and their direct sources in empirical reality. He finally risks the viewer's puzzlement over what is left unexpressed in order to force him to concentrate upon what is, through a process of selection and exclusion, expressed to a very high degree.

The realist painter's search for subjects is inevitably bound up with his desire, first to discover pictorial conventions, and then to explore their efficiency in successive picture-making efforts. If a certain painter's conventions are primarily optical in inclination, his subjects tend to be simple and relatively free of psychological overtones. If his conventions tend to infer mood or substance, his subjects are usually more definite in their imagery and correspondingly more complicated in their realization. Realist painting of both sorts, and of the two in combination, happens in Germany in steadily increasing quantities from the mid-1840s until long after the turn into the twentieth century. As it increases in quantity and in importance, the highly regionalized, noncumulative tendencies of German naturalism disappear before broader national forms of ambition, stemming at first from both Munich and Berlin, then finally in the 1890s taking up residence solely in Berlin. At this juncture it is appropriate to speak in terms of "German realism" rather than of realism in Germany. Further, it is appropriate to see German realist painting as an increasingly international phenomenon in the sense that it both looks for ideas and parallels beyond its national boundaries and begins to export at least some of its many achievements.

German realist painters from Menzel to Lovis Corinth came, either by choice, or by force of fact, to realize that the pictorial values they pursued were not exclusively personal, national, or even international. By virtue of his historically and qualitatively prodigious development of realism in the 1840s, Menzel clearly deserved at that point a position of international preeminence. However, his later work, like that of many later German realists, tends to fall back into the mainstreams of broader European currents. Artists from subsequent generations, Thoma, Leibl (and his followers), Liebermann, Fritz von Uhde, Corinth, and Slevogt, began working with an awareness of both national and international realism and proceeded to incorporate this awareness into their painting in whatever form (or forms) seemed most productive.

[46, 47]   In order to discover, first of all, how realist pictorialization developed
[48, 49]   generally and, secondly, how it gradually achieved a particularly
[50]   German inflection, it is necessary to look in some detail at the ambitious and promising, if finally inconclusive, art of MENZEL. Born in 1815, the son of a schoolteacher later turned printer, Menzel came into the profession of art as a result of largely practical circumstances. After his father's death in 1833 (when Menzel was himself seventeen years old), he took over his father's small printing business in Berlin. He very quickly learned the printing trade and, as well, became an accomplished commercial lithographer. His need to support the family which his father had left forced him to develop his enormous natural talent as rapidly as he could. His pen, his pencil, and his lithographic crayon were the only tools he had with which to pursue the commercial success and profit which he needed simply to feed himself and his family. The need to draw skillfully and to practice drawing continuously developed under these conditions and persisted relentlessly throughout his long life (he died in 1905) even after the economic struggles of the early years had passed. By the end of the 1840s Menzel had become one of the most accomplished and best-known designer-illustrators in Germany. The most singular vehicle for his success was the large group of illustrations (printed as wood engravings) he provided for Franz Kugler's popular *Life of Friedrich the Great,* first published in Germany in 1842 and soon thereafter republished in English and French editions. As he worked on this project, Menzel gradually emerged as an artist of major stature. More specifically, he became the most forceful exponent of fundamentally realist art that Europe had yet produced. He did so by interpreting his project in a very special way—a way which led him to produce images which were nothing short of revolutionary in their character.

The project called for illustrations of a decidedly historical sort, depicting the life, times, and achievements of Germany's most venerated modern king. However, Menzel's way of forming his illustrations was to try to conceive of his subject as though he were part of the visual present. This meant that (historical costumes, architecture, and furnishings aside) each vignette was developed with a graphic and compositional freedom that seemed to suggest that the artist had experienced each episode firsthand, and recorded it rapidly (but completely) with his pen, from whatever viewpoint presented itself. Menzel's almost unbelievable success in formulating images so consistently disarming in their unpredictable emulation of a fictive reality had no basis in the history of illustration, even though the typology of the project itself echoes very clearly contemporary, and slightly earlier, popular eulogies of Napoleon in France. The style of the illustrations, while consistent in some illusive way, seems enormously varied and capable of responding graphically to whatever degree of formality, informality, or decorativeness seems most to reinforce the simultaneously visual and psychological essence of a particular vignette. If the project as a whole stands finally as a kind of apotheosis of draftsmanship, it does so in a way which emphasizes equally the enormous variety of ways in which visual reality presses the draftsman as its moods shift according to the incidence of light and the correspondingly enormous variety of responses which the ur-draftsman has at his disposal.

What remained for Menzel to do in the many years which lay ahead of him was to accomplish in terms of an actually contemporary reality that kind of convincing and pictorially self-assured presence which he had already achieved in the fictional reality of his *Friedrich the Great* illustrations. He set out to do this, beginning in the mid-1840s, both as a draftsman and, increasingly, as a painter. While remaining more sure of himself in the former role, it was finally painting rather than drawing which led Menzel to the most substantial heights of quality that he reached after the completion of his illustrations for *Friedrich the Great*. Drawing became finally too much habit, too definitely a tool; its solutions came so quickly and easily that very little emerged which was either unexpected or capable of development. Painting, on the other hand, resisted Menzel's mastery, at least for a time. For as long as it did so, Menzel experienced the same order of intuitively based success that emanated from his *Friedrich the Great* cycle, and it did so just long enough for Menzel to produce the first truly important and extended group of realist paintings in Germany. The scope of realist ambition which his paintings from roughly 1845 to 1875 display is so far beyond that previously marked out by Dahl and Carus in Dresden, Kobell in Munich, and Blechen in Berlin, that grounds for comparison are difficult if not almost impossible to propose. At the same time Menzel's paintings assert their otherness from the realism of photography in terms as definite as those achieved at any time by any realist painter. Yet many of Menzel's most successful paintings —in particular his small-scale works of the later 1840s and early 1850s—remained under his most jealous personal guard until the time of his death. Comparatively few of the paintings which today carry Menzel's reputation were permitted outside the walls of his studio during his lifetime. One suspects that his initial hesitation in showing these works resulted from quite genuine feelings of humility and uncertainty. The paintings were clearly more speculative in their process and more tentative in their appearance than the pure works of drawing upon which his early reputation rested. Later on, however, his hesitation arose from somewhat different circumstances. Beginning in the mid-1860s, and certainly by 1875, the act of painting had yielded to Menzel's fluent mastery about as completely as drawing had many years before. The dry complexity of Menzel's post-1875 works was pictorially antithetical to the looseness of his earlier paintings. If what he finally proposed as his major contribution to the art of painting was valid, and he certainly believed that it was, then that which occurred prior to absolute mastery was important only to him. The ultimate form of Menzel's hesitations with regard to his early paintings was very probably the most painful. During the last ten years of his life the much younger German Impressionists, in particular Max Liebermann, persisted in pointing to Menzel as a precursor in the kind of painting they now proposed. From his position as a venerable member of the Berlin artistic establishment, Menzel vehemently resisted being labeled a precursor for a kind of painting which he could never learn to tolerate. But, in the privacy of his studio, confronted with his early works, Menzel must have realized that Liebermann's citation of him was just. Perhaps, even more than this, he may very well have been driven to question, after many years of self-certainty, the relative qualitative achievements of his early and late works.

Like the best of his *Friedrich the Great* illustrations, Menzel's early paintings convey a sense of fortuitous discovery. This emerges both from the motifs which are presented and from the ways Menzel chooses, first to see, and then to paint, them. Descriptions of natural and artificial light and the way each acts to present color serve immediately to mark off the aspects of reality that Menzel's paintings are primarily intended to represent pictorially. In strictly positivistic terms these aspects only became accessible to Menzel once he began painting. As a draftsman he could only imply them with alternately soft or abrupt alterations of light and dark tones. Whether rendering one of the rooms of his family's Berlin apartment or a view of some bit of Berlin landscape, Menzel managed for over a decade to represent with passages of color-bearing paint the optical play of light in virtually every kind of "real" situation. He did so with disarming ease and artlessness. No picture prior to 1852 feels composed in the traditional sense. Instead views seem first discovered and then set down on canvas with only the barest hints of imposed surface organization and the slightest gestures toward pictorial space. The rather abrupt framing of many motifs in one or another picture parallels similar effects in early photography, as well as equally similar effects in Menzel's earlier illustrations.

Menzel's handling of oil paint in his early pictures is spontaneous and unmannered. Whether broadly brushed and patched or more delicately stippled, it responds more to relative contrasts of color and light than to any preestablished ideas of how a picture surface should ideally look. The result is a surface and a mode of covering it that seem invariably germane to the effects it discharges. That successive pictures tend to present different, and even opposed, surface qualities is largely irrelevant as long as Menzel can resolve each painting within the pictorial frame of reference he has established for it. Utility rather than fineness is the procedural rule in Menzel's early paintings; and this utility is often of a surprisingly beautiful, sensitive, and unpredictable sort.

There are many fundamental differences between Menzel's realist images and those of Courbet (or Manet) in France. One of the most important is that each of Menzel's pictures, seen individually, seems to suggest the possibility of a whole family of related images. These taken together might develop and consolidate into a definable pictorial bias through which certain aspects of reality could attain a primacy, enforced by something resembling style in the traditional sense of the term. This kind of image family is born and matured in the painting of Manet and Courbet, but it does not actually materialize in the work of Menzel. Instead, individualized realist images come rapidly one after the other. Each seems in the final analysis to be charged with confirming, or checking out, one or another pictorial possibility in order to establish that that possibility, along with many others, is available for future usage. Whatever qualities a particular painting achieves are stored, rather than developed directly, as Menzel proceeds to compile what becomes ultimately a technical compendium containing all of the records of his mastery of visual reality with paint.

In 1852 Menzel began to consult this compendium when he first attempted to translate his *Friedrich the Great* imagery into painted form in the *Flute Concert* (West Berlin, National Gallery). However, such consultations did not become an absolute rule in his work until much later. Menzel's trip to Paris in 1855 stimulated him to explore, in an incidental fashion, those unexpected bits of visual reality that appear so graphically to a traveler outside his homeland for the first time. While Paris provided him with new motifs, he did not actually begin to paint them until he returned to Berlin. Instead, he made sketches to use as reminders of what he had seen. The Paris paintings and those which follow over the next two decades demonstrate an increasing indirectness and complexity in Menzel's "realist" working methods. Gradually he introduced more and more preliminary steps (usually in the form of preparatory drawings) between the initial idea for a picture and its final painted form. The fact of a stimulating one-to-one reference between the painted image and its source in reality gradually lost its attraction for Menzel, until finally he began to concentrate his attention on the production of images which are unfortunately more informative sociologically than they are pictorially. Initially this disjuncture between reality and Menzel's images of it is not overly apparent. Many of his Parisian subjects, like the *Théâtre du Gymnase*, are still informed by much of the directness of his work from the late 1840s. By comparison, one of his crowd pictures from the early 1870s seems, in spite of its frenzy of light and color, more a self-induced regurgitation of visual reality than a straightforward response to it. Since Menzel could not, or chose not to, maintain firm connections between visual reality and the painting intended to represent it, it is hardly surprising that he did not generate any real following. His work was, in general, respected in Germany and in France, but it was seen more as a precursor (or perhaps a vague parallel) to later realist developments than as a source for them.

The kind of realist painting that happened in Munich in the decade 1865–75, dominated by the work of Wilhelm Leibl, was markedly different from the work of Menzel. The cosmopolitan character of the Munich art world, as compared to that of Berlin at the same time, virtually guaranteed that realism there would follow a more certain course: That it would, for a while at least, remain more securely within historically established traditions of painting and that it would be more responsive to related foreign influences, namely French. It was no historical accident that French realism, as represented by the paintings (particularly the figure paintings) of Courbet and Manet, made its deepest penetrations into Germany via Munich. The painters of no other German city were so clearly preattuned to the finely painted, old master aspects of French realism—those aspects which seemed both to emulate and to advance pre-nineteenth-century naturalist tendencies found in Dutch and Spanish painting. Further, no realist painters anywhere based their response to French developments so exclusively upon paintings of the human figure. While the tradition which Leibl and his associates established eventually became as international in its frame of reference and in its influences as that of the Nazarenes several generations before, its subject matter was for the most part restricted either to portraits or to reverie pictures—those undefinable half-portrait, half-genre subjects that place either single or assembled figures in physically inactive poses and present them as if they were daydreaming or engaged in some other form of contemplation. Portraiture had an established frequency in Germany and everywhere else, but reverie pictures happen as a result of such contemporary French precedents as Courbet's *After Dinner at Ornans* (1848, Lille, Musée des Beaux-Arts) and the more removed seventeenth-century Dutch prototypes of Jan Vermeer and Pieter de Hooch. The strong emphasis which Munich realism gave to portraiture (and to figure painting in general) both granted and actively supported a prevailing aspiration to seek out that painted poetry of touch which the Germans call *"Feinmalerie,"* when referring to painters like Rembrandt and Velasquez. While this aspiration may appear to contradict the notion of realism in the terms of Menzel, it does not in the terms of Leibl, or for that matter, of Courbet or Manet. Such a contradiction does, in fact, appear in the contemporary, eclectic, and fundamentally antirealist *Feinmalerie* of Lenbach.

Before examining directly the work of the Munich realists, it is helpful to look back, at least briefly, at some of the more important (and yet undiscussed) types of portraiture that were current in Germany after 1840 in order to gain a better idea of what sorts of stylistic departures the Munich painters actually proposed.

[24] Portraiture in Germany had long borne a distinctly Nazarene cast. At its best in the hands of an artist like MORITZ VON SCHWIND, the last and most influential second generation Nazarene in Munich, this kind of portraiture projected a tense, iconic formality which results more from a process of linear design than from direct observation, even though a portrait likeness is undeniably obtained. Compared to such late Nazarene portraits, almost anything which was softer and less strict in its design was bound to appear more responsive to actual appearances, whether it was or not. For example, Düsseldorf portraiture around [25, 26] the middle of the century (as exemplified by that of EMMANUEL LEUTZE) purports to be more attentive to actual description, but its methods are so dry pictorially and so essentially academic that the resulting portrait image is turgid and unfocused. Later Düsseldorf portraiture yields to contemporary French precedents, primarily those of Émile-Auguste Carolus-Duran, and ends up with images that are undeniably more sensitive than Leutze's, even though the pictorial means of achieving sensitivity are unabashedly secondhand.

[51] The only form of German portraiture which in any way anticipated the work of Leibl and his associates was that of the Saxon artistocrat and part-time painter, FERDINAND VON RAYSKI. In his portraits done between 1835 and 1865, Rayski developed an enormously powerful personal manner, based at first on the much earlier portraiture of Anton Graff and practiced upon descendants of many of the same still eminent families in and around Dresden that had previously commissioned Graff. A visit to Paris in 1834–35, undertaken after two brief periods of study at the Dresden Academy, served to update many elements of the style that Rayski had learned either from Graff or from the few examples of late eighteenth-century English portraiture that were available in Germany. In Paris, Rayski was impressed most by the work of Théodore Géricault who had died just ten years before Rayski's arrival.

At its best, Rayski's portraiture combines the paint handling finesse and the light scale of tones, characteristic of many of Graff's less formal works, with a bolder, more turbulently assertive presentation of the portrait image that derives generally from Géricault. In the paintings which result, Rayski manages to project both the truly visual presence of his sitters and his own pictorial self-assurance. All of this is conveyed by generally quite freely painted means. What distinguishes his portraiture most forcefully from the achievements of the Munich realists is the applied character of his special kind of painterliness as it appears in one or another of his portraits. Rayski seems to select the degree of looseness or density in his paint handling prior to the observation of his subject;

he rarely seems to discover real priorities as he works. Coexistence rather than integration characterizes the usual relationship between Rayski's actual perception of a sitter and the mode of paint handling he employs to represent it. One finally feels with Rayski's work that a kind of haughtiness and cynicism prevented one of the most formidable talents of the century from taking itself seriously. Rayski made no attempt to gain a public reputation and he quit painting altogether for the last fifteen years of his life, so there is at least some tangible basis for the assertion that he was a dilettante. As such he was frequently content with results which were in essence clever rather than sincere in a strictly artistic sense. One must, however, grant the few instances when this was not the case—when one or another of Rayski's portraits succeeds (whether fortuitously or because of some much stronger involvement in the process of painting it) in convincing the viewer of the combined rightness of its means and ends.

The work of the Munich realists proceeded without knowledge of whatever precedents existed in Rayski's portraiture. Instead it relied initially, as we have already noted, on those elements in seventeenth-century Dutch and Spanish portraiture (and figure painting in general) which seemed useful in pursuing more coherent and definite realist ends. It was increasingly aware of related developments in French art, and specifically so, as firsthand reports of what the painting of Courbet and others was like began to filter into Munich between 1865 and 1869. In 1869 the first great international art exhibition in Munich happened, and it included not only several of Courbet's most famous works, but also Manet's *Guitar Player* (New York, Metropolitan Museum of Art) and his *Philosopher with a Beret* (Art Institute of Chicago). As important as the paintings actually exhibited was the arrival of Courbet in Munich, in response to an invitation sent by a number of Munich painters. Courbet's arrival and his profuse praise of Leibl's portrait of *Frau Gedon* (Munich) served to finalize the ties between Munich realism and France. It also served to encourage LEIBL to visit Paris (something which many of his associates had already done) and to open up a French market for his work.

[67, 68]   Leibl's painting provides the best point of departure for understand-
[69, 70]   ing the basic character of Munich realism. It does so because the
[71]   qualities and the limitations which it presents pass (in greater or lesser degrees) into the art of every one of his associates—Wilhelm Trübner, Carl Schuch, Karl Hagemeister, Louis Eysen, and Hans Thoma, to mention only the most prominent. In general Leibl deals with the abstract problem of pictorial realism rather than with aspects of mood or with the psychology of individual figures. He does so by stressing the importance of precisely calculated color values. The most influential works from any point in his career use a bold, patchy kind of brushwork, somewhat in the old master tradition of Frans Hals and late Rembrandt, applied directly to the canvas without preliminary underdrawing and charged with articulating whatever sequential intervals of color value are necessary to represent the plasticity of the subject in consistent, optical terms. Leibl masters this kind of pictorial procedure in the late 1860s and it remains available to him until his death in 1900. The essential differences between early and late manifestations of this procedure reside in details of paint handling. The early works are broader, less flexible, and somewhat coarse in their brushwork.

They rely upon remnants of contour drawing to organize the strokes of the brush. This is not to say that drawing guides the brushwork, but rather that it remains available at any point in the making of a particular picture. Later works are less demonstrative with their brushwork and more confident in their ability to vary the handling of paint in whatever ways are necessary to carry an image to completion. Contour drawing is less available and less necessary, since the sensitive flow of paint itself seems capable of yielding whatever demarkations are necessary in presenting the image.

Most of Leibl's paintings conceived and brought to completion in this fashion necessarily occur in situations of weak natural illumination. A somewhat dark, interior setting (either actual or implied) usually provides the limited scale of color values which Leibl relies upon to support his particular way of evoking plasticity and image definition. It also represents the silence and provincial simplicity in which his images, and he himself, increasingly reside after the early 1870s. Leibl moved from Munich in 1873 and lived out his life in a succession of small villages in the Bavarian countryside.

The other side of Leibl's art, his so-called "hard style," seems to honor a completely different set of principles; and in many ways it does. The most likely explanation as to why Leibl began, around 1873, to cultivate a delicately etched linear realism in seeming opposition to his prevailing painterly mode exists in the fact that the latter had gradually forced him to abandon both the lighter side of his palette as well as independent effects of drawing. In order to repurchase what he had abandoned and to do so without interrupting the already secure painterly side of his art, Leibl forged an alternate set of pictorial conventions and set them to work on the same kinds of subjects which he had already rendered in another way.

It would be difficult to overemphasize the ambition to become a "complete" painter that resides in Leibl's cultivation of two styles. He was able to see that his initial pursuit of certain effects excluded others, and he regretted the loss. It is to his credit that he chose not to force his images to bear an incoherent combination of emphases; but he still wished, possibly as a result of Thoma's example, to cultivate all stylistic possibilities as long as they produced viable results. The paintings which Leibl produced in his "hard style" are not very numerous, but they are invariably impressive; first, for the refined Holbein-like delicacy of their details and, second, for their perfectly calculated design of whole images. Probably because Leibl came to his "hard style" from earlier, more painterly efforts, there remains an element of pictorial latitude in even the most totally drawn passages of these pictures. The drawing seems always to be permeated with light even when it does not itself convey strong color. It never completely flattens out, but instead tends to hover slightly in front of the picture surface, evoking a subtle plasticity that advances from the picture instead of residing within it.

Leibl's "hard style" does not continue directly into his late paintings (those after 1885), but its influence does serve to bring about some of the differences already noted between his early work (that from the late 1860s and early 1870s) and his late work in the 1890s. The greater freedom and mobility of Leibl's late paint handling, its ability to generate drawing and modeling from a single painterly act result, at least partly, from the discipline of his "hard style."

[78, 79]   The fact that neither Courbet nor Manet (nor any of Leibl's asso-
[80, 81]   ciates) felt the need to practice twin modes of realist style in order
for their work to develop, says nothing whatsoever about Leibl's achievement except that it evolved in a particular way. Other artists grappled, sometimes successfully, sometimes not, with similar problems (those of exclusive effects) in a less obviously dialectical manner. TRÜBNER and, to a lesser degree, HAGEMEISTER
schematized their brushwork into a system of similarly sized and generally regular patches in order to bring about a formal resolution between plasticity as
conveyed by sequences of color values and bright, natural light and color. Sup-
pressing both painterliness (in the sense of loose brushwork) and definite drawing
(in the sense of independent contours or accented details), both Trübner and
Hagemeister settled on a brushstroke which responded first to the light-reflecting,
plane surfaces within the image, but which also possessed a definite shape. It had
a passive but distinct ability to mark off limits and make edges, and it was by
definition a composite unit of painting and drawing. Both painters relied increasingly on the shape, scale, and general consistency of their brushstrokes to
unify pictorially whatever type of realist image (whether portrait, landscape, or
still life) they presented. Their solutions were more abstract and more reliant
upon a precise ideology of paint handling than Leibl's, and their results are more
predictable, if generally lower in quality. They were ultimately unable to resolve
their images any more straightforwardly and spontaneously than Leibl. Only the
French with their private brand of professional confidence, bred from generations of preeminent and uninterrupted artistic achievement, seemed able to
trust completely their intuitions and to react directly and in one move both to
what they saw and what they painted.

[85]   SCHUCH and Eysen pursued more circumscribed goals than those of
Leibl and Trübner. In the general context of Munich realism they were minor
figures. Schuch's characteristic still lifes often recall Leibl in the patchy, un-
drawn looseness of their paint handling and in the fineness of their rendering of
color values. Yet they seem always to stop short of making convincing points of
emphasis within the totality of their images. They look "set up" and "painted,"
but they feel finally anonymous and well made. What they project are characteristic effects rather than a real sensibility. This is as true of Schuch's work in
Munich as it is of his subsequent efforts in Paris from 1882 to 1894, the year of his
death. Schuch's Paris paintings appear more ambitious and modern than previous efforts, since they rely on French Impressionist compositional devices instead
of seventeenth-century Dutch ones, but their artistic substance remains elusive.
Admittedly Schuch intended that his paintings be optically pure and psychologically neutral, but he succeeded in proving that real artistic quality required more
arbitrary selfness than he was ever willing to expose.

[82, 83]   The works of EYSEN have many characteristics in common with
[84]   Schuch. They are equally impersonal and limited, either by an
inability or an unwillingness to make self-assertive decisions about the relative
visual importance of whatever effects they present. Eysen's paintings, which are
dominantly medium-sized landscapes or still lifes, depart from Schuch's in the
very different order of technical refinement which they feature. Eysen is soft,
vaporous, and multicolored where Schuch is comparatively firm in his handling
of paint and conservative in his color choices. Eysen's greatest charm, and his

61

greatest weakness, derives from the flexibility and the variousness of his pictorial effects. At times an undeniably attractive Corot-like richness of mood and atmosphere prevails in Eysen's work, providing it with a momentary sense of focus. But all too often Eysen is simply confused by the wealth of effects open to him and he is content to display them more or less randomly.

[72, 73]   Apart from the works of Leibl and Trübner, the most substantial,
[74, 75]   and the most varied accomplishments of Munich realism were those
[76, 77]   of HANS THOMA. In Thoma's paintings the gulf which appears to separate the mature blossom of German realism in Munich and the last form of German-Romanism as it appears in the art of Böcklin seems, at least momentarily, not to exist. For Thoma there seemed to be no irreconcilable oppositions between the intentions of Munich realism (with its French sources and parallels) and those of the young Böcklin. We have already mentioned the friendship which grew between Thoma and Böcklin during the former's residence in Munich from 1870 to 1874. What remains to be noted is the fact that Thoma was equally friendly with Leibl at the same time. Furthermore, he had, like Leibl, only recently returned from a visit to Paris (1868), duly impressed by the paintings of Manet and Courbet and perhaps those of the younger Impressionists as well. After leaving Munich, Thoma made a tour of Italy where he met both Marées and Fiedler. Throughout the 1870s he remained attuned to virtually every important manifestion of contemporary German and French painting, with the possible exception of that of Menzel. For a lesser artist, this active awareness of so much could have been fatal, but for Thoma it was not.

For all of his cosmopolitanism, Thoma retained a characteristically provincial ability, both to be impressed with what he saw and to maintain a basically commonsense awareness of his own capabilities. He was in certain respects like Courbet, particularly in his workmanlike attitude toward painting; throughout his life he remained basically an artist-craftsman. He never became a true intellectual. He pontificated a good deal both verbally and in writing, but he was not really inclined to examine what he did theoretically. He left that sort of thing to the likes of Marées or Trübner. Like van Gogh he was religious, both conventionally and privately. Further, he was sentimental in a very folkloric, German way about his family, his friends, and about certain aspects of nature.

Thoma was temperamentally unwilling to exclude anything from his painting on the basis of abstract principle. While attentive to (and prone to invoke) Goethe's dictum that a painter should make poetry with his touch rather than tell stories, Thoma never found it necessary to reject literary types of imagery. However, he always relied upon his own direct responses to nature to give actual form to whatever imagery he hoped to develop. His predisposition toward a kind of painting which featured combinations rather than exclusions goes a long way toward explaining his ability both to appreciate (and to emulate at times) such separate accomplishments as those of Leibl, Böcklin, and Marées. For as long as he kept sight of himself behind whatever "pure" or "impure" work he happened to be doing, he achieved aesthetic results of a very high order. Looking at his work, it is clear that basically realist intentions in the final analysis predominate, even when he includes much more than straightforward description of what he sees. Side by side with realist elements appears a definite tendency to develop resolutely two-dimensional and essentially decorative values; and this more than anything else lends a definably personal character to Thoma's painting. It also explains his desire to entertain simultaneously the painted aspects of Munich (and French) realism and the brightly colored, edgy linearity of Böcklin's paraphrastic old Germanism. Unlike Leibl, Thoma did not feel the need to hold such apparently contradictory pictorial tendencies in isolation and to paint in two styles. Instead he tried to express them in whatever combinations or sequences he could devise. As a result his essentially realist images are at once painterly and attentive to the rendition of plasticity through color values and also reliant on linearity, first, for overall two-dimensional organization and, second, as a pretense for brighter accents of pure colors.

Thoma's work developed in a strangely coherent fashion despite the fact that from 1860 to 1880 it explored a whole series of pictorial possibilities. At first it is a more loosely painted, and at the same time more brightly colored, variant of Düsseldorf realism recalling both Schirmer's landscapes and Leutze's portraits. Then, just prior to Thoma's visit to Paris in 1868 it became more reliant upon direct observation of its subjects under definite and definable circumstances of natural illumination. Thoma's portraiture and his anonymous figure subjects done around the time of his visit to Paris are enormously successful in their balance of psychological intimacy and decorative organization. The former quality is conveyed through a soft, self-assured handling of color values; the latter, through settings which spread a subtle but continuous linear network across the whole of the picture surface, punctuating it at one point or another with accents of pure color. In his many landscape views of the river valleys of the Rhine and the Main, done shortly after his move to Munich, Thoma relied increasingly on the act of confronting nature to assist him in refining either his perception of color values (and their painterly expression) or his more definitely colored decorative linearity. The particular views of landscape he chose finally to paint sponsor directly, through the simplicity or complexity of their aspect, the mode of pictorialization which Thoma will use to express them. Thoma's Rhine and Main landscapes are often compared to contemporary works by the French Impressionists. Such comparisons are appropriate, but what they underline is the far greater self-consciousness of Thoma's paintings. Thoma does not randomly explore the pictorial possibilities of landscapes. Instead he seizes upon a particular view for reasons determined in advance and having to do largely with the desire to explore a particular pictorial mode. He does not, as the French Impressionists very definitely did, engage in free and largely unpredictable visual dialogue with his landscape subjects. The results he achieves are finally less surprising if, at times, no less qualitatively secure.

Throughout the later 1870s and continuing on through Thoma's long life (he died in 1924), increasingly synthetic decorative values come to the fore in his work, even though visual reality continues in one way or another to hold them in check. Not surprisingly, Thoma undertook a considerable number of commissions for large-scale interior decorations during his many years of residence in Frankfurt (1876–99). Even though he continued to paint landscapes and figures, Böcklin-like religious and mythological subjects gain a certain currency in his work as well. His desire to achieve monumental images, organized by progressively more expansive complexes of linear design, gradually impels

63

Thoma toward the threshold of both a literal (represented) and pictorial (achieved) decorativeness that anticipates many aspects of the pan-European decorative movements of the 1890s—Art Nouveau in France and Belgium, and *Jugendstil* in Germany and Austria. Yet the parallel is never exact; the painterly realism that remains at the base of Thoma's work never completely gives in to a full-blown repeatable decorative formula. Instead, this realism serves to keep Thoma's decorativeness vital by constantly threatening it and forcing it to develop itself anew in each successive picture.

Munich realism in its various manifestations and the late German-Romanism of Böcklin and Marées together display the fecundity, the success, and the increasing focus that German painting achieved as it passed through the first two decades of Germany's existence as a national political entity from 1870 to 1890. However, the first truly new art of the Reich and that which, like the Reich itself, chose to center itself in Berlin, was German Impressionism. The fact that German Impressionism happened at least partly in Munich and operated on the basis of continuous references to French Impressionism in Paris is much less important than the fact that it became Germany's first truly national mode of artistic self-expression. Whether Germany accepted it as such is another story altogether.

German Impressionism, like its earlier counterpart in France, provoked scandal and public indignation for much of its history. It both caused and supported secessionist movements (directed against local academic exhibition practices), first in Munich (1893), then in Berlin (1899). By the turn of the century it was, from the standpoint of the German public, more notorious than praiseworthy. Yet in retrospect it is clear that German Impressionism succeeded more completely than any previous art movement in Germany in giving form to contemporary aspirations of artists from all parts of the country. The most important figures in the movement came from distant points in the Reich—Liebermann from Berlin, Slevogt and Uhde from Bavaria, Corinth from East Prussia. As a result of their shared dependence upon sources in France and in the realist tradition in Munich, all four painters found themselves working along generally similar lines by the mid-1890s. In the years thereafter they worked and exhibited in increasingly close concert. Uhde remained personally independent of the group once the other three painters had moved definitively to Berlin (Liebermann in 1884, Corinth in 1900, and Slevogt in 1901) leaving him behind in Munich, but his painting continued to share many elements in common with that of the others.

[86, 87] Looking at German Impressionism historically one must remember
[88, 89] that appearances of unity notwithstanding, it comprises the individ-
[90, 91] ual efforts of four artists from two distinct generations: LIEBER-
[92] MANN and Uhde born in 1847 and 1848 representing the first; and Corinth, born in 1858, and Slevogt, 1868, representing the second. Both Liebermann and Uhde made their initial acquaintance with French Impressionist painting around 1880. Both found in the Paris Salon of that year a hybrid Impressionist picture, Jules Bastien-Lepage's *Joan of Arc* (New York, Metropolitan Museum) which impressed them considerably. It did so because it represented the most successful attempt to date to combine the high-keyed palette of Impres-

sionism, developed with requisitely loose Impressionist brushwork, with a species of subject matter which, for all its apparent religiousness, conveyed through the figure of the impoverished peasant girl, social-realist, if not actually socialist, content. Prior to the appearance of Bastien-Lepage's picture, Liebermann had already shown a strong inclination toward the painterly presentation of social-realist subjects. This inclination was reinforced through his contact with contemporary realist painting in Holland. Bastien-Lepage's *Joan* gave him a sort of moral license to pursue a detailed exploration of French Impressionism as well. At first Liebermann looked at Impressionism simply as a source for technical and coloristic effects which he could use, as had Bastien-Lepage, to lend a greater visual immediacy to subjects that continued along social-realist lines. But the longer he looked, the more aware he became of the purely aesthetic values of Impressionism, and the more he came to emulate these to the exclusion of values residing directly in the subjects he portrayed. While never becoming quite as remote and neutral in his choice of subject matter as, for example, Monet, Liebermann worked steadily through the late 1880s and 1890s toward the most strictly aesthetic formulation which German Impressionism ever achieved.

[99, 100]   Along with Liebermann, and generally under his influence from 1880 to 1882, UHDE took a similar look at the external aspects of Impressionism, but his particular form of talent made it possible for him superficially to master most of the surface charm of Impressionism so quickly that he felt no pressure to look beyond it. Instead he spent the next fifteen years bound up in an artful, if inartistic, continuation of Bastien-Lepage's combination of Impressionism and popular religiousness. Not until the late 1890s, and not really until the first decade of the twentieth century, did Uhde stop to look at his work seriously and self-critically. When he did, he tried, as Liebermann had many years before, to get at the visual sources of what he was about. In a large group of paintings of his family, usually of his daughters, covering several years of work, Uhde explored basic Impressionist values of pure color, light, and paint handling. As he did so his work at least approached the purity of Liebermann's in the same period, even as it continued to rely upon precedents in Munich realism (especially in the work of Leibl) for many of the specific aspects of its intimate subjects.

While Liebermann and Uhde were forming their initial responses to French Impressionism, Corinth and Slevogt were enrolled as formal students at the Munich Academy. From such teachers as Wilhelm von Diez and Ludwig Löfftz, they absorbed a secondhand, academic realism which they proceeded to amplify by regular reference to whatever of Leibl's work they could see and through personal contact with Trübner. Following his stay in Munich, Corinth left for Paris in 1884 and enrolled in the atelier class of Adolphe-William Bouguereau and Robert Fleury at the Académie Julien where he worked for nearly two years. Slevogt enrolled in the Munich Academy a year later (1885), visiting Paris in 1889, but never actually working there as a student. Many of the characteristic aspects of Corinth's work begin to appear in his paintings from the latter half of the 1880s, while Slevogt's efforts remain tentative well into the 1890s.

[93, 94]   Corinth's early work (roughly 1885–89) is, for the most part, por-
[95, 96]   traiture; a refined comparatively light-toned painterly portraiture
[97, 98]   of his friends and members of his family that reflects precedents
in Leibl and Trübner. However, CORINTH had already begun to cultivate

a more rapid and spontaneous sketchiness and a more flexible, less predictable impasto than his Munich predecessors. As he does so the abrupt modeling qualities of his handling of light and the mysteriously flat, negative effects of his passages of shadow appear for the first time. Like contemporary paintings such as those from the late 1880s by the Norwegian Edvard Munch (which have not yet come to rely on the turgid, linear, coloristic, and psychological expressiveness of his better-known images from the 1890s), Corinth's feature a diluted indirect form of reference to Manet. While his work concentrates generally on the description of visual facts, there is an increasing predilection toward the mood-inducing development of light and dark tones which has its source in baroque (Dutch and Spanish) painting. This tends to moderate any truly direct and comprehensive response to Manet's art and that of the French Impressionists at least for a time. Further, it is something that remains in Corinth's art to varying degrees from beginning to end, providing the most dependable pictorial prop for the particular kind of optical-visceral expressiveness that becomes the most consistent autograph of his achievement as an artist. The human figure, especially the nude or seminude female, stands as the most consistent source and focus for this expressiveness.

The flamboyant and undisguised eroticism of Bouguereau's nudes was quite obviously attractive to Corinth, even though Bouguereau's manner of painting was waxy and unpainterly in the extreme. Returning to Germany, Corinth began in the early 1890s to explore successive ways of achieving a mutually reinforcing compromise between painterliness (in the form of a composite of Manet, Munich, seventeenth-century Amsterdam, and Madrid) and an almost tangible (essentially sexual) presence in his subjects. Depending upon the particular subject matter of a painting, Corinth's compromise may tend to evoke a comparatively delicate, at times even predominantly optical, presentation; or it may stress through its violence of paint handling the essentially materialistic "Teutonic frenzy," by which words Corinth admiringly described the surface appearance of many of Leibl's paintings. The form of compromise notwithstanding, Corinth assures by whatever means he chooses that the viewer will be forced unavoidably into a very direct manner of involvement with the completed picture. If his stress is optical and reminiscent of Liebermann, his subjects are seen like those of Runge nearly a century before—very close up. If his stress resides in paint handling per se, the subject is quite literally splayed across the surface, served on a platter, so to speak, regardless of its stated distance from the viewer.

Compared to Corinth's work from roughly 1890–1905, that of Liebermann from the same period seems far less physically urgent and, as already suggested, far purer (in the strictly visual manner of French Impressionism) in its intention. In the best and most interesting of his portraits Liebermann possesses a sufficient latitude of pictorial inflection to suggest very real and affecting comments upon the personalities of his sitters, but in the landscapes and urban scenes, which constitute an increasingly large part of his work, a rigid form of physical and psychological removal obtains. This removal is conveyed by a handling of paint which is, as we have already suggested, neutral—at times almost self-consciously ugly and inexpressive. It is as disciplined in its predominant regularity and lack of frenzy as that of Corinth is seemingly undisciplined and intentionally expressive. The ultimate goal, if not the appearance of Corinth's paintings, seems in many respects closer to that of the mature Munch than of Liebermann. They seek to express reality in terms of personal observations that are at once physical (visibly and tangibly) and psychological in origin. Since Munch cultivated more overt formal distortions to achieve his expression, his paintings appear to support different intentions from those of Corinth. However, apparent differences here are very deceptive. In the final analysis it is possible to propose that Corinth's work, featuring many superficial parallels with the increasingly "acceptable" art of Liebermann, prepared the most enlightened sector of the art public of Berlin for the more stylized expressiveness of Munich and that of the subsequent German painters who actually called themselves Expressionists. At the same time it remains resolutely true to itself and passes on much of its form and imagery to Max Beckmann and much of its sheer pictorial energy and flexibility to the late Hans Hofmann.

[101, 102]   MAX SLEVOGT's work, for all its undeniable qualities, is markedly
[103, 104]   less ambitious than that of either Liebermann or Corinth. Like Uhde, Slevogt very quickly developed an immense technical facility; and this, along with a clear eye for the achievements of other artists, guided his work in the absence of any preeminently personal artistic convictions. Slevogt's technical facility is most evident in his numerous pen drawings and illustrations; his tendency to create adaptations—often of major quality—rather than to be in any way distinctly original appears most frequently in his paintings. Initially (in the early 1890s) Slevogt is dependent upon Uhde and Corinth for artistic direction. His work re-creates and occasionally isolates effects from the most dramatic of their religious subjects. As it does so, his superior sense of theater and the more fluent lightness of his painted touch comes to the fore. In the most important of his works done prior to his move to Berlin in 1901, Slevogt walks a tightrope between the urgency of Corinth's physical and psychological directness and Uhde's often palling and inexpressive finesse. His paintings get their subjects across effectively, but with a minimum of stress on the viewer. Figures have sufficient presence to impress the viewer but not to hold his attention or to threaten him. Like those of Henri de Toulouse-Lautrec, Slevogt's figures have a kind of quickness that suggests more than it demonstrates.

Around 1900 Slevogt settled more or less conclusively upon a single exemplar —the art of Manet—around which to focus his mature work. Having moved temporarily to Frankfurt, he spent a considerable amount of time visiting the local zoo. In a group of paintings of familiar zoo animals, all rendered in a rapid, somewhat cursory manner, Slevogt started out to explore a wide range of stylistic effects, nearly all of which he borrowed from Manet. The images which result yield their source very readily. Slevogt makes no attempt to cover his derivativeness and, in fact, he has no reason to. Each painting first isolates and then resolves, usually in a quite convincing way, a characteristic Manet effect. In one instance Slevogt may sketch with paint around areas of thinly applied flat color; in another he may build up an impasto and caress it with Manet's kind of tonal and technical lushness. Slevogt's Frankfurt zoo pictures and his informal portraits made during the first decade of the twentieth century are for the most part extremely successful in reapplying in one or another successful paraphrase the most familiar conventions of Manet's painting. They honor Manet as completely and as sincerely as do the writings of the most important German critics

67

of the period. Unfortunately, Slevogt occasionally forces his emulation a bit too far, making it fussy and overly complicated. This tends to happen in his various actor portraits, which are based primarily on Manet's great portrait of *Jean-Baptiste Faure* (Essen, Folkwang Museum; with a full-scale sketch in the Hamburger Kunsthalle).

Taken together, the portrait painting of Slevogt and both the landscapes and portrait works of Liebermann demonstrate how remarkably able the Germans were in the period 1890–1910 to make both direct and productive use of contacts with modern, if not absolutely contemporary, French painting. Liebermann and Slevogt, like Leibl and Thoma before them, were able to do so because a national artistic momentum had begun to develop to parallel the increasingly focused nationalism of Germany as a whole in the period following the Franco-Prussian War. After 1870 France no longer appeared so different from Germany. The war served to show just how close, competitive, and (in many ways) interdependent the two countries had become. While remaining preeminent in most aspects of culture as a result of firm and long-standing tradition, France no longer possessed an exclusive ability to capitalize on her achievements. The Germans eyed her every move and on many occasions they developed a particular idea with greater thoroughness and over a more extended period of time than the French themselves would have believed possible. At the turn of the century Germany's political and cultural incorporation of France reached its peak of intensity and, in Berlin at least, both artistic and sociological Germanness of the sort that can be defined at almost every point in the nineteenth century seems to have vanished almost totally. In painting, only Corinth's work remained to suggest that it had not, that it was in fact only partly repressed, and that it would rise again.

ABBREVIATIONS

In the following discussions of paintings exhibited here, abbreviated references are used. In the list below these references are arranged alphabetically and correlated with the monographs, oeuvre catalogues, museum catalogues, etc. which they represent. All inventory numbers in the discussions below refer to the standard inventory system for the museum or collection lending a particular painting.

Allgeyer — Julius Allgeyer, *Anselm Feuerbach* (2 vols. Berlin and Leipzig, 1904).

Berckenhagen — Ekhart Berckenhagen, *Anton Graff: Leben und Werk* (Berlin, 1967).

Beringer — Josef August Beringer, *Trübner: eine Auswahl aus dem Lebenswerk des Meisters* (Stuttgart and Berlin, 1921).

Berlin — Berlin Nationalgalerie, *Verzeichnis der Vereinigten Kunstsammlungen Nationalgalerie (Preussischer Kulturbesitz) Galerie des 20. Jahrhunderts (Land Berlin)* (Berlin, 1968).

Börsch-Supan — Helmut Börsch-Supan, *Die Bildgestaltung bei Caspar David Friedrich* (Munich, 1960).

Cologne — Rolf Andree, *Katalog der Gemälde des 19. Jahrhunderts im Wallraf-Richartz Museum* (Cologne, 1964).

Corinth — Charlotte Berend-Corinth, *Die Gemälde von Lovis Corinth* (Munich, 1958).

Düsseldorf — Kunstmuseum, Düsseldorf, *Sammlungs-Katalogue* (Düsseldorf, 1959, 1962; *Katalogue der Düsseldorfer Malerschule* (forthcoming).

Essen — Museum Folkwang, Essen, *Gemälde—19. und 20. Jahrhundert* (Essen, 1963).

FR — Konrad Kaiser, *Der Frühe Realismus in Deutschland: Gemälde und Zeichnungen aus der Sammlung Georg Schäfer, Schweinfurt* (Nuremberg, 1967).

Hamburg — Eva Maria Krafft and Carl-Wolfgang Schüman, *Katalog der Meister des 19. Jahrhunderts in der Hamburger Kunsthalle* (Hamburg, 1969).

HS — Philipp Otto Runge, *Hinterlassene Schriften (herausgegeben von dessen ältestem Bruder)* (2 vols. Hamburg, 1841).

Imiela — Hans-Jürgen Imiela, *Max Slevogt* (Karlsruhe, 1968).

KR — Konrad Kaiser, *Klassizismus und Romantik in Deutschland: Gemälde und Zeichnungen aus der Sammlung Georg Schäfer, Schweinfurt* (Nuremberg, 1966).

Kuhn — Alfred Kuhn, *Peter Cornelius und die Geistigen Strömungen seiner Zeit* (Berlin, 1921).

Lutterotti — Otto R. von Lutterotti, *Joseph Anton Koch mit Werkverzeichnis und Briefen des Künstlers* (Berlin, 1940).

Meier-Graefe — Julius Meier-Graefe, *Hans von Marées* (2 vols. Munich and Leipzig, 1910).

Nathan	Peter Nathan, *Friedrich Wasmann: sein Leben und sein Werk* (Munich, 1954).
Pauli	Gustav Pauli, *Max Liebermann: des Meisters Gemälde*, Klassiker der Kunst (Stuttgart and Leipzig, 1911).
Prause	Marianne Prause, *Carl Gustav Carus als Maler* (diss. Cologne, 1963; republished Berlin, 1968).
Rave	Paul Ortwin Rave, *Karl Blechen: Leben Würdigungen, Werk* (Berlin, 1940).
Roennefahrt	Günther Roennefahrt, *Carl Spitzweg: Beschreibendes Verzeichnis seiner Gemälde, Ölstudien und Aquarelle* (Munich, 1960).
Rosenhagen	Hans Rosenhagen, *Uhde: des Meisters Gemälde*, Klassiker der Kurst (Stuttgart and Leipzig, 1908).
RR	Konrad Kaiser, *Romantik und Realismus in Österreich: Gemälde und Zeichnungen aus der Sammlung Georg Schäfer, Schweinfurt* (Vienna, 1968).
Scheffler	Karl Scheffler, *Menzel: der Mensch, das Werk* (2d ed. Munich, 1955).
Schmid	Heinrich Anton Schmid, *Arnold Böcklin: eine Auswahl der Hervorragendsten Werke des Künstlers* (4 vols. Munich, 1892–1901).
Stuttgart	Staatsgalerie, Stuttgart, *Katalog der Staatsgalerie Stuttgart: Neue Meister* (Stuttgart, 1968).
Thode	Henry Thode, *Thoma: des Meisters Gemälde*, Klassiker der Kunst (Stuttgart and Leipzig, 1909).
VE	Herbert von Einem, *Caspar David Friedrich* (3d ed. Berlin, 1950).
Waldmann	Emil Waldmann, *Wilhelm Leibl: eine Darstellung seiner Kunst, Gesamtverzeichnis seiner Gemälde* (Berlin, 1930).
Walter	Maräuschlein Walter, *Ferdinand von Rayski: sein Leben und sein Werk* (Bielefeld and Leipzig, 1943).
Weigmann	Otto Weigmann, *Schwind: des Meisters Werke*, Klassiker der Kunst (Stuttgart and Leipzig, 1906).
Wolf	Georg Jacob Wolf, *Leibl und sein Kreis* (Munich, 1923).
Zimmermann	Werner Zimmermann, *Der Maler Louis Eysen* (Frankfurt, 1963)

CATALOGUE

KARL BLECHEN
(1798 Cottbus–1840 Berlin)

Initial training as a banker in Berlin. 1822–23: Berlin Academy; studies with P. L. Lütke. 1823: summer, travels in Saxony; July, in Dresden, meets Dahl, Friedrich(?), Carus(?). 1824–27: recommended by Schinkel for work as set designer for Royal Theater in Berlin. 1828: travels on Baltic Coast and Rügen, then returns to Berlin; September 1828–September 1829: in Italy—Florence (November 1828 and September 1829), Rome (December 1828–May 1829, and July 1829), Naples (May–July 1829). 1831: professor of landscape painting at Berlin Academy. 1833: trip through Harz Mountains. 1835: short trip to Paris. After 1836: sick with disease of nervous system.

[1.] *View of Rooftops and Gardens* (ca. 1828)   PLATE 42
Stiftung Preussischer Kulturbesitz, Staatliche Museen, Nationalgalerie, Berlin

Oil on paper; 8″ x 10″; unsigned; *Berlin,* p. 28, Inv. no. NG 765; Rave, no. 1730

It is in Blechen's alla prima Italian sketches (cf. Rave, nos. 708, 818, etc.) that we first see him continuously employing this new manner of actually constructing on canvas, via changing sizes and shapes of brushwork and varying qualities of impasto, both a visual and a tactile equivalent of what he sees before him. Oiled pigment, with its possibilities for manipulation by brushes of differing sizes, shapes, and resistances, and the base color of the canvas or paper beneath are the only media he allows himself. The picture evolves from countless variations of surface texture, of color opacity or transparency, and of shapes within shape that result. The space that undeniably exists, punctuating the cottages and garden areas, seems to derive more from Blechen's general experience in structuring masses and voids as a stage designer than from any specific attention to established painterly or draftsmanly techniques for creating space.

Since Blechen did not often exhibit sketches such as this, preferring to rely on more elaborated, tightly structured pictures (usually containing bits of genre) like his romanticized park scenes and his large-scale views of fairly specified Italian landscape to carry his reputation, we are not able to date this sketch very precisely. He lived and worked in Berlin both before and after his Italian trip, producing for himself private views of her rooftops, her unseen back streets, and her work areas, while exhibiting views of her public parks, gardens, and castles. Whether this and sketches like it were done in the secrecy of his atelier before the Italian trip, laying a foundation for the type of relaxation and self-definition of style that evolves during that trip or whether they resulted from it is uncertain.

[2.] *A Bay near Naples* (ca. 1829)   PLATE 43
Städtische Kunsthalle, Mannheim (on loan from the Bundesrepublik Deutschland)

Oil on canvas; 11¼″ x 17″; unsigned; Inv. no. S-N 34; not in Rave

Rave (p. 301, no. 1022) illustrates a much smaller, looser version of this painting which was extended a good deal horizontally when enlarged. Blechen frequently made more than one version of his paintings, presumably because he found the idea and general conception of one or another sketch pleasing, but lacking in finesse, and so set out to tighten his composition, discipline his paint handling, and enlarge the size of the canvas in order to produce an ultimate finished picture for exhibition. (The century is not yet far enough advanced to value the properties of sketches almost more than those of finished pictures.)

In 1827 critical reviews first start comparing Blechen's work with Friedrich's and, from then on, frequently commend the "poetic life" or the "spirit" within his pictures. This view of part of the Bay of Naples at night, when the unearthly brightness of the moon dissolves and makes ghostly the jagged rock formations, is one of Blechen's most overtly Romantic pictures. We are reminded of the stillness and desolation in many of Friedrich's paintings and we sense the influence of Dahl and Carus in Blechen's manner of highlighting and in his interest in cloud patterns and the effects of natural light. (Many of his Neapolitan pictures seem to be primarily about light and what it does to things of substance.) But, unlike the painters in Dresden, Blechen is equally involved with the substance and malleability of his paint. *The Bay* ultimately relies as much for its effectiveness on the oiliness of its painted water and its scumbled ripples of waves as on its stark poetic imagery.

[3.] *The Interior of the Palm House on the Pfaueninsel* (1832)   PLATE 41
Stiftung Preussischer Kulturbesitz, Staatliche Museen, Nationalgalerie, Berlin

Oil on yellow paper mounted on canvas; 25⅝" x 22⅜"; unsigned; *Berlin*, p. 30, Inv. nos. A 1 617, NG 752; Rave, no. 1735. See Rave, pp. 436–43 for catalogue and illustrations of studies.

The Palm House, on the Peacocks' Island by the palace of Sans Souci at Potsdam, was designed by K. F. Schinkel to house the Foulchiron Collection of Palms acquired in 1830 for King Friedrich Wilhelm III by Alexander von Humboldt in Paris. In 1832 the king commissioned Blechen to paint two pendant views of the new building with its palms as a present for his daughter Charlotte, the Czarina of Russia. By 1834 these were finished and exhibited at the Berlin Academy. Apparently the king was so pleased by them that he then ordered another pair for his own castle at Charlottenburg (now in Potsdam). These are bigger, somewhat less loosely painted, and the large, red socle (today the only remaining trace of the building) and vase have been completely overgrown with foliage. The pendant to the painting shown here illustrates the whole central courtyard of the Palm House, with the odalisques reclining against the red socle (Hamburg). The series of paintings is in the same tradition as those of Gärtner and Hummel which celebrate the modern Prussian capital of Berlin with its pleasure places and impressive architectural monuments.

The Palm House, a very linear, highly articulated building containing a wealth of textures and colors in its painted decoration and in its greenery, provided Blechen with the type of subject matter he had sought time and again in nature without confronting him with difficult problems of perspective diminution and de-emphasis. With a stage designer's—even an architect's—precision, every member of the interior, with its own exact, but heterogenous, character of decoration, was incisively drawn, providing for the actual process of painting a skeleton no less complex and articulate than Schinkel had provided for the palms. Having chosen to work on yellow paper Blechen could count on a uniformly warm, hothouse tonality to pervade his picture. When he turned to the process of painting, it was with the same one-to-one relationship between the thing seen and the means used to render it that we have already observed in his *View of Rooftops and Gardens*. Every palm frond is made differently and each sits on the surface in the individualized separateness that it would have for the viewer walking through the collection and touching one or another plant. The odalisques provide the scene with a bit of synthetic, unconvincing orientalia.

[4.] *Rolling Mill near Neustadt-Eberswalde* (ca. 1834)   PLATE 44
Stiftung Preussischer Kulturbesitz, Staatliche Museen, Nationalgalerie, Berlin

Oil on panel; 10″ x 13⅛″; unsigned; *Berlin*, p. 31, Inv. no. NG 763; Rave, no. 1803

This is one of Blechen's late pictures, the end result of a series of eleven drawings (Rave, nos. 1804–13) showing various aspects of the new factory complex at Eberswalde. It has one specific preliminary drawing. Blechen also started a lithograph of the factory site (Rave, no. 492) and provided a pen drawing for the 1831 *Berliner Kalender* illustrating the park around the mineral springs at Neustadt-Eberswalde. This is the period in which Germany's belated industrialization resulted in many such new towns, built to house workers and factories alike.

Blechen's choice of this subject matter and his rather hesitant, distant treatment of the factory itself marks the beginning of a new direction in the type of naturalism that we have already observed in the *Palm House* and in Hummel's and Gärtner's views of Berlin. The subject is now specifically industry—modernness—at first gently noted and celebrated as a new visual aspect of the landscape (cf. Rethel's *Harkort Factory*, also 1834); later, in works by Menzel, revealed as an infernal, dehumanizing force, fascinating, all-consuming, and infinitely fearsome; and finally fled completely by Feuerbach, Marées, and Böcklin. Blechen's painting does not yet recognize the factory as an intrusion. Its stacks and arched windows not only echo the shapes of trees, bushes, and rocks, but apparently recalled to Blechen the late medieval architecture of Italy. The smoke, albeit black and noxious, blows away, leaving unsullied the quiet clear stream. The fishermen, still basically the same creatures who inhabit seventeenth- and eighteenth-century idyllic landscapes, remain undisturbed. Blechen's paint handling is relaxed and soft, almost Corot-like in its feathery dryness and pastoral effect.

73

ARNOLD BÖCKLIN
(1827 Basel–1901 San Domenico near Florence)

1841: studies drawing in Basel under Ludwig Kelterborn. 1845–47: at the Düsseldorf Academy under T. Hildebrandt and J. W. Schirmer. 1847: studies briefly in Brussels and Antwerp, then in Geneva under A. Calame. 1848: visits Paris. 1848–50: in Basel. 1850–57: first stay in Rome. 1853: marries a Roman woman, Angela Pascucci. 1856: meets Feuerbach briefly, much later contact in mid-1860s and late 1870s. 1857–58: back in Basel. 1858–60: in Munich. 1860: meets Graf Schack. 1860–62: teacher in Kunstschule Weimar. 1861: travels briefly to Genoa. 1862–66: second stay in Rome. 1866–71: in Basel, does frescoes for stairwell of Basel Museum. 1870: briefly in Paris. 1871–74: in Munich again, friendship with Thoma. 1874–85: generally in Florence. After 1875: much contact with Marées. 1885–92: in Hottingen near Zürich. 1889: given honorary degree from University of Zürich. After 1892: in Florence.

[5.] *The Artist with His Wife* (ca. 1863–64)   PLATE 56
Stiftung Preussischer Kulturbesitz, Staatliche Museen, Nationalgalerie, Berlin

Oil on canvas; 25¼″ x 20″; signed upper right "A. Böcklin Roma"; *Berlin*, p. 41, Inv. nos. A 11 589, NG 1517; Schmid, no. 143

This early portrait of Böcklin and his wife posed in an obviously synthesized (but generally naturalistic) bit of Roman landscape argues about as eloquently as any of the Böcklin's shown here the case for his pictorial sincerity and originality. The passages of landscape have an almost Blechen-like animation in their seemingly random development of both thin and impasted painterly effects and in their alternation of strong, localized colors with more tonal color which seems to respond to the muting effects of distance and atmosphere. In the painting of the figures of himself and his wife, Böcklin manages to describe details of costume and to focus firmly upon the portrait faces without abandoning a lightly stroked, small brush painterliness that fits very easily into his rendering of the landscape. However, Böcklin already demonstrates at least the first stages of a steadily increasing formal tendency to flatten out his pictorial space. This tendency becomes progressively more apparent in later phases of his work, inclining him to emulate aspects of style from fifteenth- and early sixteenth-century German and Netherlandish painting. The figures in this picture, as well as the more strongly colored bits of vegetation that stand to the right of them, have the feeling of being imposed against a generally calm and spatially quite lucid landscape vista. Böcklin makes no attempt to smooth out this sense of superimposition, either coloristically or by means of alterations in his setup of space. He is at this point in his work setting in opposition what seem to be mutually exclusive pictorial stresses —space conceived and developed tonally and comparatively strong, brightly colored, and surface-emphasizing shapes. In this picture the free and seemingly unforced employment of this opposition works, chiefly one feels as a result of its lack of precise formula.

[6.] *Blue Venus* (ca. 1869)   PLATE 57
Hessisches Landesmuseum, Darmstadt (on loan from the Bundesrepublik, Deutschland)

Oil on canvas; 54⅞″ x 31⅝″; unsigned; Schmid, no. 190

This painting, presenting the traditional subject of the birth of Venus, demonstrates the broad, formal characteristics of Böcklin's comparatively early and still naturalistically oriented "mythological style." It does so succinctly and with

74

considerable pictorial impact. While not the first, the *Blue Venus* is certainly one of the most successful and influential of Böcklin's long run of both mythological and allegorical figures of the female nude—his most favored device for simultaneously titillating and scoffing at his contemporary bourgeois audience.

Böcklin's success in presenting such ideated figures via a freewheeling composite of painterly naturalism and staunchly two-dimensional decorative linearity cast a spell of greater or lesser intensity and duration over two of his most talented colleagues, Thoma and Marées, as well as over a whole host of lesser artists. Böcklin's paintings (particularly those done shortly before and shortly after 1870) seemed to validate, through their unique and unpredictable formal conviction, the pursuit of a combination of naturalist and intellectual goals in painting. That they did so primarily because they were neither consistent in their dedication to expressing a truly personal confrontation with visible nature nor in any way very profound in their intellectual elaboration of images made little difference. Painters like Thoma and Marées wanted to believe in the viability of the pursuit Böcklin proposed and, given the undeniable vitality of images like the *Blue Venus* to go on, they could overlook much of Böcklin's subsequent pictorial insensitivity.[1]

[7.] *Self-Portrait with Death as the Fiddler* (1872)   PLATE 59
Stiftung Preussischer Kulturbesitz, Staatliche Museen, Nationalgalerie, Berlin

Oil on canvas; 30″ x 24⅜″; signed upper left "A. Böcklin pin. 1872"; *Berlin*, p. 41, Inv. nos. A 1 633, NG 772; Schmid, no. 218

Compared to Corinth's later and somewhat ambiguous juxtaposition of his own image with a studio skeleton, Böcklin's *Self-Portrait with Death as the Fiddler* illustrates a literal, but highly effective deus ex machina. The leering figure of death stands just behind the artist, scraping his one-stringed fiddle, while the artist pauses in the midst of his work to ponder his mortality. Even though the picture today seems overwrought in the explicitness of its illustrated content, it made a very powerful impression on Böcklin's contemporaries. Both Thoma (see Thode, p. 67) and Corinth were moved by Böcklin's picture and set out themselves to deal with its content in their own particular ways.

Perhaps the most obvious reason for the effectiveness of this particular self-portrait—at least in the eyes of Böcklin's contemporaries—had to do with the incredible presence and apparent reality of his figure of death, both as an image and as an idea. More than any other of Böcklin's mythical or allegorical images, death in this self-portrait adds a level of psychological conviction to the predictable ingenuity of its visualization. The dialogue between death and the artist occurs in a straightforward and acceptably real space. The picture as a whole is intimate in its focus, generally somber in its color, flexible and direct in its paint handling. There is little substantive variation expressed to distinguish the relative visual reality of the two figures, yet the self-portrait image is undeniably more palpable physically, primarily as a result of its dominant forward position in the picture. What seems finally to bind the two figures together so effectively is

75

1. For Thoma's variant of the *Blue Venus* see Thode, p. 115; and for a much later Corinth *Birth of Venus* à la Böcklin (combining aspects of the *Blue Venus* and subsequent Böcklin Venuses as well), see Corinth, no. 132.

the oddly parallel setup of death with his fiddle and Böcklin with his brush and palette. Because of the force of this parallel, death seems both to evoke mortality and, at the same time, to stand as one of the artist's attributes—or perhaps as his muse.

Böcklin did not reemploy the image of death in his later self-portraits, probably feeling—quite rightly—that this particular aspect of his self-image had already achieved its quintessential expression.

[8.] *Wedding Trip* (1875)   PLATE 58
Städtische Galerie, Frankfurt (on loan from the Bundesrepublik, Deutschland)

Tempera on wood; 28⅞″ x 21″; signed lower right "AB"; Schmid, no. 253

The *Wedding Trip* introduces the slightly murky Romanticism of Böcklin's artistic maturity. As it does so it harkens back, probably unconsciously, to many of the formal and psychological conventions of early romanticism—Friedrich's in particular—while at the same time reorchestrating them so that the form is pictorially richer (if no more compelling) and the content more circumscribed and definite (if finally less pressing). Two figures, both quite childlike in their appearance, are seated on a foreground rock from which they glance across a shallow abyss to the landscape vista beyond. The relationship between the figures and the distant landscape does not possess the terrifyingly abstract quality of alienation that appears in comparable Friedrichs, but it does evoke a fairly clear sense of the mysteries and uncertainties of human passage through as yet unknown times and places.

In this painting Böcklin's style continues the generally sensitive painterliness of the best of his earlier works, even though the shapes of the figures and the sections of landscape surrounding them have begun to assume the silhouetted and frequently apictorial stillness of Böcklin's later paintings. Both nature imagery and nature as something to be contended with visually combine to inform the image and to keep it securely within the realms of painting. For as long as this remains the case Böcklin's work is capable of achieving a formal significance in spite of the weight of whatever literary load its form is made to bear.

CARL GUSTAV CARUS
(1789 Leipzig–1869 Dresden)

1814: to Dresden, professorship in medicine at new academy after early work in chemistry, physics, natural sciences, and medicine followed by membership in faculties of medicine and of philosophy in Leipzig. 1816: exhibition of four *Sunday Paintings by an Amateur*. 1817: close friendship with Friedrich; general circle of friends includes Dahl, Thorwaldsen, A. von Humboldt, Tieck, Weber, and Goethe. 1827: becomes house doctor for Saxon King Anton. Various publications, 1831: *Nine Letters on Landscape Painting:* 1841: *C. D. Friedrich—the Landscape Painter;* 1843: *Goethe, zu dessen näheren Verzeichnis;* 1865–66: *Lebenserinnerungen und Denkwurdigkeiten;* and much criticism and natural philosophy (see Prause, p. 152, nos. 53–76). Various travels, 1819: Rügen (to retrace Friedrich's 1818 trip); 1820: Riesengebirge; 1821: Switzerland and Genoa; 1828: Italy—Florence, Rome, Naples, etc.; 1835: Rhineland and Paris; 1841: Florence (medical consultation for the duke of Tuscany); 1844: England and Scotland.

Kunstmuseum Düsseldorf

Oil on canvas (doubled); 11⅝″ x 8⅞″; signed lower left "Carus 1827"; *Düsseldorf*, no. 130; cat. no. 42 in 1827 Akademische Kunstausstellung, Dresden; bought there by Princess Johanna von Sachsen. Two drawings in Oslo concern similar subjects; one marked "2 July 1819" shows "the total interior of the boat"; another, "14 Aug. 1819," shows a view of boat between Greifswald and Rügen— both are apparently related to Friedrich's *On the Sailboat* (Leningrad). See Prause, p. 33 for a discussion of these drawings.

Although Carus employs in this picture many of Friedrich's most dependable props—a boat on the water, figures contemplating the landscape with their backs to the viewer, and a window opening from a closed space to the natural world outside—he arrives finally at an image which has more in common with the clarity and relaxed naturalism of Menzel's *Room with a Balcony* than with Friedrich's highly suggestive, personalized pictures of human and landscape moods. In much painting of the time, particularly in Dresden, the use of an open window in a picture had great currency; it suggested the disjuncture between man in his own space and the infinitude of nature; it existed as a visual pun between the actual portrayal of a window and the windowlike aspect of a picture; and it provided a reliable compositional unity based on interior shapes repeating the shape of the canvas. Carus is obviously aware of all these reasons for using a window. However his picture is not made from them, but from his intention to explore and then set down in paint exactly how and why light, color, even atmosphere, seem different inside and out. The interior of the boat glows with warm, reflected, even light whose slightly sandy or dusty texture obscures edges and confuses the viewer's perception of space. The brightness outside is too sharp to permit our eyes to see well indoors. Outside, light falls in almost arbitrary patches; it is crystalline, even cold, despite the intensity of the northern sun, and robs the figure of plasticity while defining the spatial extension of the bow of the boat. Shadows contain almost all the colors of the spectrum. The seated woman, half-obscured, half-lighted acts as a bridge between the two areas, making it clear that we are not considering two alien worlds, but the behavior of the same substances under differing circumstances. Carus's concerns, and ultimately his results, anticipate in many ways various paintings produced fifty years later by the Impressionists in France; for instance, Monet's views of the Gare St. Lazare or Manet's *Monet Working in his Boat at Argenteuil* (Munich).

77

"The view spread out before us is Dresden, with her lordly bridge and towers looming in the morning haze" (1827 catalogue. See Prause, p. 124, n. 190).

[10.] *Bacharach on the Rhine* (1836)　　　　　　　PLATE 34
Georg Schäfer Collection, Schweinfurt

Oil on canvas; 40⅝″ x 20⅜″; signed lower left "Carus 1836"; Inv. no. 449; *KR*, no. 12. Prause, p. 104, cites a lost drawing as the basis for the picture and mentions a replica (also lost) exhibited in Leipzig in 1839 (p. 142, n. 451). See also Carus's *Lebenserinnerungen . . . 2*, 209, 410.

In the 1836 Dresden Akademische Kunstaustellung catalogue this picture is no. 321, *Recollection of the Rhine, the Wernerikirche in Bacharach*. Carus spent quite a while in the Rhineland on his way to Paris in 1835 and his work from this period includes several memory pictures of sights he had seen there and in Paris. Hence, the visual facts of the painting are all accurate; the balcony peopled with vines instead of the counts and kings who walked there long ago was real, as were the ruined Gothic apse and the Romanesque tower of the Peterskirche in Bacharach by the river's edge. Unlike Friedrich, Carus did not feel the need to render into ruined form buildings that were still whole. But equally unlike his own earlier matter-of-fact acceptance of the physical and visual pleasures of boating in the open air, he here is captured by the romantic past of the Rhine Valley, with the result that his painting begins to approach the speculative, mood-inducing quality of Friedrich. As we can see from his careful description of separate leaf and tendril types and his attention to the way light reacts differently on the textures of the stone of the balcony, on the hill, and on the two churches, his naturalist inclinations are not completely set aside. But he was not compelled by simple visual facts to paint this view in the strange orange glow of neither day nor darkness, and he did not need to interpose a slight haze of dreaminess between the viewer and the scene before him. Perhaps most important of all, by choosing to place his picture in the arched Gothic format, he acknowledges as straightforwardly as possible that this is not a naturalist picture, but a Romantic one—a half-fairy tale, half-religious evocation of Germany's past.

[11.] *Balcony in the Moonlight* (ca. 1836–43)   PLATE 35
Georg Schäfer Collection, Schweinfurt

Oil on canvas; 40″ x 20⅞″; marked on back "Dr. K. G. Carus pinx. 1836"; Inv. no. 155; *KR*, no. 11

Despite the early nineteenth-century marking on the back of the canvas, the date of the painting is made uncertain by an 1843 review of Carus's book about Goethe in which it is suggested that Carus had recently started trying to give more poetic meaning to his works, citing as an example a recently exhibited "meaningful night piece, the subject of which he has borrowed from Shakespeare's Hamlet."[1] Of all Carus's extant works it is the one shown here which comes closest in spirit to the half-stormy, both matter-of-fact and dreamlike mood of Shakespeare's opening set. At the same time, in size, format (even to its roughly equal tripartite division into foreground, distance, and sky), and general handling of paint, it seems to be an intentional pendant to *Bacharach on the Rhine*. Even the openwork of the balconies in the two pictures is the same.

Consideration of Carus's marked preference for recognizable details that lend matter-of-factness or geographic accuracy to his landscapes provides us with no real solution to problems of date and subject. The church, with eight-sided turret and gable, is the Market Church in Halle which was still standing when Carus lived in Leipzig. There is no castle with a balcony overlooking this church, so the totality of the picture is definitively fantasy, or recollection. It seems as logical to suggest that Carus might employ such a solidly Romanesque structure seen by moonlight as a pendant for the delicately traced, late Gothic church in

1. From *Morgenblatt für gebildete Stände*, 1843, quoted in Prause, n. 455.

ruins seen at daybreak from a Rhine castle as it does to suggest that he would use the remembered church to lend credence to a setting for *Hamlet*.

We do know that *Bacharach* was exhibited alone in 1836, with no mention of a pendant. Perhaps the second picture was not yet finished. In 1841 Carus exhibited in Leipzig another primarily fantasy landscape in a Romanesque arch frame (*Frühlauten*, now in Essen). *Balcony in the Moonlight* shares with this painting a similar haze of distance, or dreaminess, between the immediate foreground and the rooftops beyond. A similar four-step, crenellated, gabled building appears in both pictures. Whether the *Balcony* was painted in 1836, four years before this second dream picture, or in 1843, three years after, cannot be definitively established, nor is it necessarily contradictory to suppose that a Hamlet picture could at the same time serve as a pendant for a Rhine picture at sunrise.

LOVIS CORINTH
(1858 Tapiau, East Prussia–1925 Berlin)

1876–80: student at Königsberg Academy, with a study trip to Weimar and Thüringen in 1878. 1880: moves to Munich; studies first with F. von Defregger, then at the Munich Academy under L. Löfftz. 1884: travels to Antwerp, then Paris, enrolls in Académie Julian under A. Bouguereau and Robert Fleury. 1885: briefly returns to Germany. 1886: back in Paris. 1887–1891: in Königsberg and Berlin. 1890: exhibits a pietà in Paris Salon, receives "honorable mention." 1891: moves to Munich again. 1898–99: spends winters in Berlin. 1900: moves definitely to Berlin. 1902: on executive committee of Berlin Secession. 1903: marries Charlotte Berend. 1906: trip to Florence. 1908: visits Holland. 1909: visits Paris. 1911: named chairman, Berlin Secession. 1912–13: visits to the Riviera. 1914: visits Rome and Switzerland. 1915: president of Berlin Secession. 1917: made honorary citizen of Tapiau. 1918: professor at Berlin Academy. 1924: in Königsberg for retrospective exhibition during Kant festival. 1925: honorary member of Munich Academy. Travels to Amsterdam to study Rembrandt and Hals for the last time. 1911–1912, seriously ill, weakened, and slightly paralyzed for remainder of his life.

[12.] *Portrait of the Artist's Father* (1888)   PLATE 94
Private collection

Oil on canvas; 46½″ x 39⅜″; signed middle right "Louis Corinth/Mai 1888"
Corinth, no. 56

This is one of four portraits of his father which Corinth painted between 1883 and 1888 (see Corinth, nos. II, 51, 56, and 57). Corinth's father, a tanner, died in 1889, less than a year after Corinth had painted him in his sickbed (Corinth, no. 57). One is reminded of Leibl's *Rosine Treuberg* by the broadly sketched, painterly setup of this portrait, even though Corinth is finally more reliant on both the pictorial energy and focus of his brushwork than Leibl. Like Leibl, Corinth terminated his work on the picture once he had fully realized the likeness of the sitter's face; but, unlike Leibl, he used the "unfinished sketchiness" of the remaining portions of the picture in a truly positive way. The sketchiness is left to evoke quickness and immediacy in the image as a whole. The degree (or quality) of sketchiness differs within the figure and outside of it in areas of background. The basic shapes of the figure, although thinly and cursorily painted, are relatively secure in their descriptiveness, without in any sense competing with the face in ultimate finish. The background is rapidly blocked in and painted in such a way as to project the figure through contrasts of tone; but, more importantly, to provide it with an outwardly radiating halo of vigorous brushstroke scribbles. Already in this early portrait Corinth is trying to develop a firm pictorial relationship between the cursive vigor of his brushwork (and the resulting surface appearance of his pictures) and the simultaneously physical and psychological excitement he feels in the presence of sitters or models. Unlike the painterliness of Liebermann (or even Trübner) Corinth's emphatic sketchiness is only half-optical in its intent. Its other half projects an earthy tactility which is enormously varied in the sensations it is capable of communicating to the viewer.

Corinth's recent work in Paris accounts for the rectangular framing of the figure and the general lightness of his palette—particularly its Manet-like combination of light earth tones and pure white. But the energy of his paint handling per se has its origins in Munich (in the work of Leibl especially), and it is already prototypically Corinth.

[13.] *Susanna in the Bath* (1890)   PLATE 95
Museum Folkwang, Essen

Oil on canvas; 63⅝″ x 44⅜″; signed middle right "Lovis Corinth KBG 1890"; *Essen,* no. 218, Inv. no. 349; Corinth, no. 74.

Two virtually identical versions of this picture are listed in Corinth, p. 62, but the current whereabouts of the version listed as the first is unknown. One of the versions (which one is unclear) was shown in the Paris Salon of 1891; this fact goes a long way toward explaining many of the painting's most prominant aspects. The standard French academic design of the picture—its use of a geometrically framing background—and the similarly academic evenness of the modeling of Susanna's flesh in smoothed passages of light and dark tones indicate that Corinth is bowing very courteously to the formal standards of a Salon jury. At this point in his career he is actively searching for prospective patrons and in the *Susanna* he pulls all of the predictable French stops. The subject itself quite obviously reflects Bouguereau's titillating nudes, which were enormously popular in France (and elsewhere) at the time. And, of course, Corinth had only recently left the Académie Julian, where he had worked under Bouguereau, so his knowledge of the older man's painting was definitely comprehensive and firsthand.

While one can easily catalogue the academic Bouguereauesqueness of Corinth's *Susanna,* the image does not really feel forced, either in its subject matter or in its manner of painting. Corinth shared a good deal more with Bouguereau than just ambition. A rather steamy, almost voyeuristic eroticism was basic to the sensibilities of both artists; and its traditions in earlier nineteenth-century academic art in France (beginning with David and Ingres) had a good deal to do with the popularity which that art enjoyed with the mock puritan French middle class. The almost wax-figure presence of academically modeled nudes had, throughout the century, conveyed an almost corpselike fleshiness that opportunistic painters and the general public alike found erotically appealing and legitimized by academic rule.

For his *Susanna* Corinth simply accepted all this, while energizing his image pictorially with a brilliant, painterly treatment of drapery, a few carefully selected accents of bright local color, and a distinctly Rembrandtesque heaviness of atmosphere and shadow. In his development of the subject, the physical closeness of Susanna and her invader is sexually pressing even by prevailing French standards.

[14.] *Self-Portrait with Image of Death* (1896)   PLATE 93
Städtische Galerie (Im Lenbach Haus), Munich

Oil on canvas; 27⅛″ x 35⅛″; signed upper right "Lovis Corinth 38 J. a. 1896"; Inv. no. G 2075; Corinth, no. 135

The two prevailing, interconnected (and nearly obsessive) themes apparent in Corinth's paintings of the 1890s are the immediate (usually the erotic) pleasures of the flesh and the threat of death (or castration) which is an inevitable hand-maiden of these pleasures. His numerous paintings of succulently displayed studio nudes and his bacchanalian scenes carry out the first of these themes; his paintings of Samson, and Salome with the head of John the Baptist objectify the second.

Seemingly in contrast to all of this, Corinth presents in his great *Self-Portrait* of 1896 what appears to be a disarmingly straight image of himself (in all of his self-indulgent and alcoholic corpulence), the interior of his studio, and, through the studio window, the world outside. By correlating himself with definite and apparently characteristic bits of the strictly visual reality in which (and with which) he lived, he tries to set his personal obsessions momentarily to rest. As if to emphasize the dispassionate optical factualness of the image, he develops it in a painterly manner, generally reminiscent of Liebermann, even though passages of modeling with definite shadow exist in the foreground and passages of city-scape, less clearly toned and less rigidly painted than one finds in comparable Liebermanns, fill the painting's background.

Yet, for all of the apparent visual objectivity of the portrait, it is hardly as neutral in its subject matter as, for example, a comparable Liebermann self-portrait. Instead, the juxtaposition of the self-portrait figure and the studio skeleton directly recalls the "vanitas" and "mortality" image of death the fiddler in Böcklin's famous self-portrait of 1872. The skeleton may be just a studio prop, but it is death as well, and it waits just behind the no longer young (thirty-eight-year-old and already physically dissipated) painter. In the same way the intersecting mullions of the studio window are factually just mullions, but they create a jaillike separation between Corinth—an artist in isolation—and an outside world, which experiences none of the terror and force of his obsessions and which instead will gratuitously inherit, as a matter of course, the works of his tormented genius. While appearing to provide a purely visual self-image this self-portrait, in fact, expresses Corinth's inability to escape his feelings and to live like Liebermann through his eyes alone.

81

Oil on canvas; 44″ x 22″; signed below on border "suae XXXII Lovis Corinth Pinxit Anno 1897"; *Hamburg,* no. 1640; Corinth, no. 141

Eckmann, a minor *Jugendstil* painter, was one of Corinth's closest friends in Munich. For his portrait of Eckmann, Corinth assembled a pastiche of elements reflecting sources in English art of the so-called "aesthetic" sort. Whistler and late pre-Raphaelite conventions are simultaneously evoked and the image assumes a distinctly Wildeian air. Eckmann's figure is painted as though it were without substance. Except for the head, shoulders, and hands the figure is physically undefined, seeming almost to levitate from the vaporously painted lower portions of the smock. The indefiniteness of these portions is made very emphatic by the flat band bearing the picture's inscription which runs directly beneath them.

Corinth's reasons for painting Eckmann in this particular way had a good deal to do with Eckmann as an artist and his own stance in the art world of Munich in the 1890s. Eckmann and artists like him exemplified the substantial influence which Whistler as a painter, a personality, and a representative of English aestheticism in general exerted in Munich after 1888—the year Whistler first showed in an international exhibition there. Whistler's influence was something which Corinth himself probably had difficulty understanding and accepting; but, as a friend of someone like Eckmann, he could hardly ignore its currency. In the Eckmann portrait, Corinth set about making his own painterly comment upon it, and the comment contains a considerable element of good humor. Adopting the somber tones of Whistler's palette, the thinness of his impasto, and the cramped portrait setup characteristic of Whistler's late works, Corinth produces a distinctly self-conscious paraphrase of Whistler's style and molds Eckmann's figure to fit it. However, he does not stop there. His finishing touches "correct" Whistler by firming up contours in the lower arms and hands, by focusing on details of drawing and modeling in the face, and by increasing the apparent velocity of the brushwork in general. The result is clearly Whistlerian, but more hectic, and finally more vital.

82

Oil on canvas; 30″ x 48″; signed lower right "Lovis Corinth"; Inv. no. 187; Corinth, no. 179. (The painting reuses a previously painted canvas.)

This is one of four studio nudes painted by Corinth in 1899 (see Corinth, nos. 176–79). Two of the others (nos. 176 and 177) are posed rather conventionally; the third (no. 178) shows a model in bed, half-asleep, and partly covered. The Bremen picture, in contrast to all of these, conveys the overwhelming desire on Corinth's part to generate with paint and with the seductive display of female flesh an ur-pictorialization of sexual ecstasy, or at least of the anticipation or remembrance thereof.

Compared to other great nineteenth-century nudes—Ingres's *Bather of Valpinçon* (Paris, Louvre), Manet's *Olympia* (Paris, Louvre), Courbet's *Woman with a Parrot* (New York, Metropolitan Museum—and clearly the most direct source for Corinth's picture), or Gauguin's innumerable Tahitians—Corinth's is unbelievably literal in both the form and content of its presentation. The raucous, painterly swirl of the bedclothes, the pulsing masses of loosely painted flesh, and the flamelike frenzy of the hair are all drawn up to the picture surface and virtually heaved at the viewer. Pictorial coherence is severely threatened by the heated comprehensiveness of Corinth's erotic display; but it is finally secured, largely as a result of the forceful design of the figure and her bed into a continuous (if sagging under the weight of flesh) path across the center of the picture and the reinforcements given to this path by the lateral breadth of Corinth's brushwork. In the eight years which have passed between the painting of the *Susanna* and this nude, Corinth has abandoned all the props of the typically academic tableau vivant. He now states and elaborates his content in unabashedly straightforward terms; he makes this content relevant as painting through the simple urgency and the conviction of his brushstroke-oriented and paint-positive mode of pictorial construction.

[17.] *The Family of the Painter Fritz Rumpf* (1901) PLATE 98
Stiftung Preussischer Kulturbesitz, Staatliche Museen, Nationalgalerie, Berlin

Oil on canvas; 45⅛″ x 56″; signed left middle "Familie Rumpf, Dezember 1901 Lovis Corinth pinx"; *Berlin,* p. 50, Inv. nos. A 11 596, NG 1525; Corinth, no. 219

Of the paintings by Corinth shown here, the *Rumpf Family* is clearly the masterpiece. In fact it is one of the most totally successful and moving images Corinth ever achieved. His close friendship with the painter Fritz Rumpf (see Corinth, no. 218 for a portrait of Rumpf alone) and with the members of his large family during the first years of his residence in Berlin stimulated Corinth to produce, in terms very much his own, a group portrait worthy of standing beside those of the two masters of seventeenth-century Holland whom he most venerated, Hals and Rembrandt. In spite of his increasingly close association with Liebermann and Slevogt in Berlin, and with the evidently French (generally Impressionist and predominantly optical) bias of their art, Corinth clearly demonstrates in this picture that the basic tenor of his own best work reflects the influence of Holland, filtered at times through the simultaneous pictorial intensity and painterly excitement of Leibl. This is not to say that Corinth was unaffected by certain technical aspects of Liebermann's and Slevogt's modern Frenchness; but, rather, that the combined psychological and optical values that informed his most successful paintings required a relatively traditional reliance on the mood-inducing aspects of shadow, as well as on a more modern description of painted light. Even the latter has an obvious admixture of tradition in Corinth's work as a result of Hals's continuing influence.

The *Rumpf Family* uses the almost uncomfortably closeup viewpoint that appears in so many of Corinth's works. The viewer feels forcibly pressed into the physical and psychological intimacy of the family group. Figures are arranged so as to occupy virtually every section of the canvas. Their deployment, both spatially and across the picture surface, is incredibly compact and, at the same time, warmly informal. The various portrait faces are seen alternately in full face, in three-quarter profile, or in full profile as Corinth seeks a balance between spectator engagement and figural engagement (or individual disengagement) within the painted group. Silhouettes (expressed in profiles) are also used to firm up the basic axes of the picture's overall design in two and three dimensions and to provide a foil for the flickering, but pictorially secure, brilliance of Corinth's modeling with assertive lights and withdrawing, almost negative shadows. The prevailing tonal warmth of the coloration draws disparately shaped and positioned figures together, while seeming to welcome the viewer's presence. Breaks in the tonality (e.g. the foreground parrot and the background window) serve to suspend all of the figures in a zone of comparatively constant tonality. The essential humanity which the image projects finally defies precise description; but every bit of it is ultimately derived from the pictorial integrity of Corinth's vision, the complexity of its sources notwithstanding.

PETER VON CORNELIUS
(1783 Düsseldorf–1867 Berlin)

Early studies with his father (a staff member of the Düsseldorf Gallery) who painted in a late baroque manner. 1803, 1804, 1805: submitted entries to Weimarer Kunstfreunde competitions. 1809–11: in Frankfurt. 1809: begins work on Goethe's *Faust* illustrations. 1811: autumn, to Heidelberg, then Rome via Lugano, Milan, Piacenza, Parma, Modena, Bologna, Florence, Siena; October, arrives in Rome; lives in same house as Thorwaldsen. 1813: summer in Orvieto; December, in Florence. 1815–17: work on the Casa Bartholdy frescoes. 1817: spring, commission for the Casino Massimo frescoes; October, arrival in Rome of Ludwig, crown prince of Bavaria. 1819: September, leaves Rome for Munich. 1821–24: directorship of Academy in Düsseldorf; works there in the winter; in Munich during the summer. 1824: directorship of Munich Academy. 1841: called to Berlin by Frederick Wilhelm IV. 1859: cartoon of *Four Horsemen of the Apocalypse* exhibited in Berlin. Residence in Rome 1830–31, 1833–35, 1843–44, 1845–46, 1853–61.

[18.] *The Five Wise and the Five Foolish Virgins* (ca. 1813–19)   PLATE 20
Kunstmuseum, Düsseldorf

Oil on canvas; 45½″ x 61″; unsigned; *Düsseldorf, no.* 4062. Begun in Orvieto, summer 1813; left unfinished in Rome in 1819, in Koch's studio. Bought by Thorwaldsen and taken to Copenhagen, then returned to Rome by 1848. Bought for the Düsseldorf Gallery by the Galerieverein at the Second Universal Exhibition of German and Historic Art in Cologne, 1861.

In October 1814 Cornelius wrote to the art publisher Riemer that he had a

'rich composition' near completion. 'It concerns the parable of the Five Wise and the Five Foolish Virgins. The moment is as the bridegroom appears (he is here Christ Himself, with saints from the Old [figure with book] and New [St. Peter with key] Testaments, surrounded by a glory of Angels); the wise virgins are welcomed in his splendour, the foolish are shut out. It would take too long to explain to you all the motifs; I say only that I have worked a year on this picture with supreme love and effort. I can also simply say that it is the most mature and the best art that I have produced so far.' (Düsseldorf, no. 4062)

Cornelius's major period of work on *The Wise and Foolish Virgins* was during 1813, a year in which he was in Rome, Orvieto, and Florence exploring various different approaches to fresco painting in order best to fulfill his own dream of revitalizing fresco as an art form relevant for nineteenth-century Germany. It was through his work on the large oil of *The Wise and Foolish Virgins* (a surrogate fresco) that he evolved the precise type of composition and figure style that suited his own conception of how a fresco should work.

An early drawing for *The Wise and Foolish Virgins* places Christ and St. Peter at the top of four steps, with the five foolish virgins sitting in despair on or below the steps to the left, while the five wise virgins rhythmically ascend the steps on the right. The resulting loosely pyramidal ring of figures enclosing empty space is obviously modeled on the center group of the *School of Athens* (Kuhn, p. 115). Given Cornelius's residence in Rome and his strong connections with Overbeck, whose dominant stylistic reliance was on the art of the young Raphael, we are not surprised by Cornelius's initial impulse toward Raphael's major early frescoes. The transformation between the early drawing and the final composition echoes the changes between David's first drawings for *The Oath of the Horatii* (Paris, Louvre) and its completed form. In both cases the painters decided that the immediacy of impact and the friezelike monumentality they desired were not produced by figures placed in a perspective arrangement around a core of space.

Cornelius's discovery of styles more relevant to his own principles took place both in Orvieto and Florence. In the cathedral at Orvieto he realized that Signorelli's taut, sharply incised, massive forms, organized across the plane of the wall, communicated an immediacy and a type of single-minded unity with their setting lacking in the generalized, spatial, and classically balanced *School of Athens*. But the character of Signorelli's forms was not pleasing to one who had learned by copying eighteenth-century pictures and for whom Titian, Raphael, and Correggio were as gods. In Florence Masaccio's frescoes in the Brancacci Chapel presented fully formed, dignified figures in yet another form of planimetric organization that emphasized their monumentality by compressing their space. *The Wise and Foolish Virgins* shares much with *The Tribute Money*, both in specific figure types and in general compositional effects. Like Masaccio, Cornelius makes his figures cramped and large, allowing them to purchase space only with devices that simultaneously assert surface decoration, such as their rounded rhythms and the patterned intervals of emptiness around their feet.

85

What remained for Cornelius when he returned to Rome was a reassertion both of the baroque amplitude of forms he had cultivated in his youth and of the possibilities for drama inherent in tautly outlined, obtrusively near figures. These tendencies are part of the late works of Raphael, along with freely flowing decorative articulations of drapery and rhythmic forms. We are reminded of Raphael's tapestries in the Vatican and those others of his late works that exhibit a close kinship with Mannerism, which seems also to have profited Cornelius in the interplay he sought between sculptural plasticity and substanceless monumentality. The cool acidity of colors in *The Wise and Foolish Virgins* both reflects Mannerist inclinations and anticipates the technique of fresco, in which all hues are bonded together by the absorbency of the white plaster surface.

In summary, Cornelius's mature work, and his best, was demonstrably that of fresco, although both its high quality and its pictorial forms are foreshadowed by *The Wise and Foolish Virgins*. His late baroque beginnings, given character and individuality by a study of Dürer and then infused with the late Raphael's power, resulted in the monumentality of his forms. His practice in classical line drawing permitted him to describe and control surface contours, shadow patterns, and rhythms for a maximum effectiveness. And, finally, the neoclassicizing spirit which informed his drawings for Goethe's *Kunstfreunde* made him confident in his final abandonment of theatrical space. We have only to look at his 1805 drawing of *Hercules in the Underworld* (Berlin, Kuhn, p. 12) to realize that in 1814–15, in his *Wise and Foolish Virgins* and his Casa Bartholdy frescoes, Cornelius's creative methods had not been altered, they had simply come into their own.

JOHANN CHRISTIAN CLAUSEN DAHL
(1788 Bergen, Norway–1857 Dresden)

1811–18: studies at Copenhagen Academy with C. A. Lorentzen and, after 1816, C. W. Eckersberg. 1818: autumn, to Dresden via Berlin; shares house with Friedrich. 1820: membership in Dresden Academy. Autumn 1820–February 1821: travels in Italy (Rome and much time in Naples). 1824: trip to Riesengebirge; becomes professor at Dresden Academy. 1827: membership in Copenhagen Academy; 1832, Stockholm Academy; 1835, Berlin Academy. 1847: trip to Paris. 1826, 1834, 1839, 1844, 1850: trips to Norway.

[19.] *Cloud Study* (1834)   PLATE 36
Stiftung Preussischer Kulturbesitz, Staatliche Museen, Nationalgalerie, Berlin

Oil on paper; 10″ x 11⅛″; signed lower left "Dahl d. 17 May 1834"; *Berlin,* p. 53, Inv. nos. A 11 92, NG 1383

This is one of a large number of cloud studies executed by Dahl throughout his lifetime. Roughly contemporary with similar concerns in the works of John Constable and R. P. Bonington, they permit us an insight beyond the dominantly rather synthetic Romanticism of Dahl's full-scale pictures to his primarily naturalistic powers of observation and his stenographic quickness and sureness of paint handling when privileged to work in an un-self-conscious manner. It is through consideration of pictures such as these, where composition comprises no more than the particular segment of sky and horizon observed by the painter at his moment of painting, and the quality and textures of paint handling and all variations of light and color values are determined by particularities of the weather passing before him, that we are made to realize exactly how essential the role of the sketch was in predicting the types and extent of the realism that began to surface after 1845 in Germany.

[20.] *The Copenhagen Harbor by Moonlight* (1837)   PLATE 37
Georg Schäfer Collection, Schweinfurt

Oil on canvas; 21⅝″ x 28½″; signed lower left "Dahl 1837"; Inv. no. 34261857. According to Dr. Konrad Kaiser there are: an unsigned replica in Dresden (inv. no. 3609); and preliminary studies in Oslo: for the storage sheds on the left, dated 1834; for the standing figure and steamship, dated 1826.

This painting makes obvious reference to a general group of harbor-by-moon-light pictures by Friedrich, perhaps most specifically to his *Evening on a Baltic Beach* (VE, no. 103, dated 1831). The figure seems to look yearningly out to sea and boats drift in the harbor, while a full moon is troubled by clouds. But, while Carus in his best pictures recasts Friedrich-like images to evoke the joys and pleasures of living a healthy life in nature, Dahl seems to rely more on the presence of these images to construct a basically illustrative genrelike scene—neither emotionally immediate nor purely naturalistic. The compact figure, standing solidly on spread legs, seems too confident, too perfectly contoured to touch us; while the steamship and the warehouses, both recent mechanical intrusions into man's age-old relationship with the sea, are apparently intended to impress us with the modernity of Copenhagen's harbor. The thrusting anchors, whose steely sharpness is exaggerated by the hard lines of light at their edges, carve out foreground space in a distinctly obtrusive way. The whole, when assembled, reminds us of a stage set, in which the comparatively naturalistic and self-reliant observation and recording of cloud patterns which still obtain seems rather out of place and not really part of the same picture.

LOUIS EYSEN
(1843 Manchester, England–1899 Munich)

Born of German parents in England. Family returns to Frankfurt shortly after his birth. 1860: enrolls at Städelsches Kunstinstitut (Frankfurt) under K. F. Hausmann. 1863–65: studied wood engraving with Alexander Stix. 1866: traveled to Berlin and Munich. 1867: meets Victor Muller (recently returned from Paris) and is introduced to Leibl. 1869: to Paris, meets Otto Scholderer. Enters the studio of L. Bonnat and meets Courbet. 1870: back to Frankfurt, but remains in regular touch with Leibl circle and especially Thoma. 1873–78: lives in Kronberg (Taunus mountains). After 1879: in Meran (Tirol) where Wasmann had spent much of his life.

[21.] *Still Life with Apples and Quinces* (ca. 1869–70)   PLATE 82
Städtische Galerie, Frankfurt

Oil on canvas; 9⅞″ x 13⅜″; unsigned; Inv. no. SG 497; Zimmermann, no. 2

This still life is one of Eysen's earliest known works. It may have been painted in Paris; but, whether or not this was the case, it already demonstrates the basically skillful, assimilative, and ingratiatingly attractive essence of his mature art. The style in which Eysen casts his three pieces of fruit is distinctly French in the prevailing lightness and delicacy of its brushwork and general coloration. It recalls in its appearance certain still life details in Manet's *Luncheon in the Studio* of 1868 (Munich) and Renoir's *Odalisque* of 1870 (National Gallery, Washington, D.C.), as well as the pure still life works of Fantin-Latour. The picture unfortunately lacks a definite personality of its own. Eysen prefers to play down the independent importance of both color intervals and brushwork in favor of an uncomplicated (and unpressing), jewellike preciousness that later becomes a trademark of his work. In a purely technical sense Eysen was one of the most talented artists of his generation in Germany; but, as one can see even in this early effort, he was not inclined to push his talent to the point of marking out truly original pictorial qualities.

[22.] *Flower Still Life with Delft Vase and Brass Ware* (ca. 1882)   PLATE 84
Staatliche Kunsthalle, Karlsruhe

Oil on canvas; 22⅝″ x 17¼″; signed upper right "Eysen"; Inv. no. 955; Zimmermann, no. 83

This still life is essentially a more skillful and learned variant of the previous picture. It embraces the old-master qualities of seventeenth-century Dutch still lifes (particularly those of Willem Kalf), while remaining cognizant of Manet, Renoir, Fantin-Latour, and, perhaps most important, Thoma (see Thoma's *Bouquet of Wildflowers* of 1872 in Berlin). As it stands, the picture is unbelievably rich—opulent in its illusionism and in its varied coloration. Elsewhere in the nineteenth century only the still lifes of Delacroix present a comparable richness of effects. Once again, however, the kind of pictorial stresses and selections that might have made Eysen's image both totally successful and truly original are lacking. The treatment of polished surfaces tends to overwhelm (and nearly obviate) the color; the color competes similarly with the polished surfaces, and the whole becomes somehow less than the sum of its many, technically brilliant parts.

[23.] *White House on a Hill* (ca. 1887)   PLATE 83
Städtische Galerie, Frankfurt

Oil on canvas; 13¼″ x 21⅜″; signed lower left (on a stone) "Eysen"; Inv. no. SG 616; Zimmermann, no. 107

In landscape subjects the combined influences of Corot, Daubigny, and Thoma supported many of Eysen's most successful achievements. The varied, almost diffuse, greenness of the *White House on a Hill* recalls Daubigny (see Daubigny's *View of the Hermitage, Pontoise* from 1866 in Bremen), as does the space-compressing angle of Eysen's viewpoint. The slight softening of intervals between color values and the resulting slightly vaporous atmosphere recalls Corot. Thoma's influence is more pronounced in other of Eysen's landscapes where the motif calls for a more extended palette.

As in the previous still life, that quality of the picture which is distinctly Eysen's resides in the delicate interweaving of brushstroke textures and colors which are closely related tonally. The image which results is fragile, but undeniably pleasant.

ANSELM FEUERBACH
(1829 Speyer–1880 Venice)

1845–48: student at Düsseldorf Academy under W. von Schadow, C. Sohn, and J. W. Schirmer. 1848–50: student at Munich Academy under K. Schorn. Friendship with and much influenced by K. Rahl. 1850–51: studies in Antwerp under G. Wappers. 1851: moves to Paris. 1852–54: student of T. Couture in Paris. 1855: travels to Venice. 1856: to Rome via Florence. 1856–72: generally in Rome. 1861–67: liaison with Nanna Risi. 1862: meets Graf Schack and agrees to his financial support in exchange for paintings. Meets Böcklin, Fiedler, and later Marées and Hildebrand. 1873–76: professor at Vienna Academy. Paints ceiling panels for assembly hall of Vienna Academy. 1876–80: mostly in Venice with visits to Rome.

[24.] *Youthful Self-Portrait* (ca. 1852–54)   PLATE 52
Staatliche Kunsthalle, Karlsruhe

Oil on canvas; 16⅞″ x 13⅛″; unsigned, signature removed by early framing; Inv. no. 946; Allgeyer, no. 93

The dating of this self-portrait is not exactly certain. Based on the recollections of the painting's first owner, Professor Heinrich Carl Shaible, it was a product of 1851–52—the period before Feuerbach's work with Couture.[1] This date is confirmed by Allgeyer and most later writers. However, in the forceful directness of Feuerbach's painterly draftsmanship and in the vigorous frontality of the portrait pose, there is a kind of pictorial self-confidence that is not really apparent in Feuerbach's painting prior to his work with Couture, so one suspects that this portrait may well be closer to 1854 than to 1851.

Seen in the great run of nineteenth-century self-portraits, this early one by Feuerbach is unabashedly Romantic. Feuerbach provides a self-image which, in its combination of fixedness and informal, painterly flourish, successfully evokes the turbulence and the concentration of archetypally frenzied genius. Judging from his early letters, this painted self-image properly reflects the manner in which Feuerbach generally conceived of himself, his artistic powers, and his destiny; hence, the picture's undeniable conviction, despite some indecisively resolved problems of modeling in certain areas of the portrait head.

[25.] *Nanna* (1861)   PLATE 53
Wallraf-Richartz Museum, Cologne

Oil on canvas; 29⅜″ x 22⅛″; signed lower left AFeuerbach"; *Cologne*, p. 41, Inv. no. 2372; Allgeyer, no. 384

After several years of work in Rome, Feuerbach discovered Nanna Risi while out for an afternoon walk on the Via Tritone early in 1860. She appeared with a child in her arms, standing under an open window. In her heavy, statuesque beauty and with her overpowering shock of black hair she seemed to Feuerbach's eyes to be the objectification of all the great women of classical art. Her impact on Feuerbach, both as a painter and as a man, was enormous, and it lasted for nearly seven years. To begin with, Nanna was just a model—first for a *Madonna* (Dresden) and then for a whole series of basically subjectless costume pictures which were devised for the sole purpose of displaying the various formal perfections of her heavy-featured and nearly overwhelming physical image. In the process of displaying this image, designing and caressing it pictorially, Feuerbach tried to work out the steadily mounting moral tension that Nanna's presence as his mistress, as well as his model, generated. He did so by converting this moral tension into a series of formal tensions that made possible the attainment of a level of artistic quality that his earlier work had promised

89

1. *Anselm Feuerbach* (Staatliche Kunsthalle, Karlsruhe), p. 12.

but never really achieved. Around the almost pathologically loved and feared figure of Nanna all of the eclectic pieces of Raphael, Titian, Rubens, van Dyck, and Couture, which had for years informed Feuerbach's eyes and guided his hands, suddenly achieved a focus.

The Cologne *Nanna* is one of the smaller of Feuerbach's images of his model, muse, and mistress. Unlike the larger, more formally posed images in Stuttgart, Munich, and Magdeburg, this one is seen quite close up, so that the lucid sculptural progression of the forms of Nanna's formidable figure confront the viewer (and the artist) very directly. In the pictorial contrasts which Feuerbach develops between the rocklike firmness of the silhouette of Nanna's head and the almost waxen softness of his modeling of the flesh of her face and that which appears between the dignified, if rhythmically unpredictable, contours of her cloak and the intensely nervous cross-hatched painterly treatment of modeling with color values within the cloak, one finds the source of a pictorial and psychological energy which is both urgent and undeniable. The image finally evokes the opposite of that somber, decorous, and aristocratic calm which it pretends to display with such tonal refinement. The detail which represents the psychological discomfort of the image most directly is the prominantly displayed Roman snake bracelet that clings almost like a leech to the wrist of Nanna's hugely scaled left hand. It seems to focus an almost strangling sequence of serpentine rhythms from the drawn folds and the brushwork of the cloak and direct them toward Nanna's neck.

Nanna posed for several other painters, both before and after her liaison with Feuerbach. In 1859 she sat for Frederic Leighton, in 1869 for Ferdinand Keller, and in 1874 for Nathaneal Schmitt.

[26.] *Paolo and Francesca da Rimini* (1864)   PLATE 55
Städtische Kunsthalle, Mannheim

Oil on canvas; 30⅜″ x 23⅛″; signed lower right "A. Feuerbach"; Inv. no. 84; Allgeyer, no. 417

The themes of Dante's *Paolo and Francesca* and Shakespeare's *Romeo and Juliet* fascinated Feuerbach for obvious reasons during the years of his illicit liaison with Nanna. The Mannheim picture is either a preliminary version or a projected variant of a painting by the same title (Allgeyer, no. 415) which Feuerbach gave to Graf Schack in 1864 in partial exchange for his regular financial support. Unlike the Schack painting, this one features relatively small-scale figures in an extensive landscape setting. In the Schack version the figures are large and occupy nearly all the available area of the painting in the same way as they do in most other of Feuerbach's works.

As a sketch, and as one featuring landscape, the Mannheim picture provides an interesting sidelight to Feuerbach's work—one which is not seen directly in any other of his works shown here. Couture's influence is displayed very clearly in the flat and relatively unmodulated blocking in of the landscape in abrupt patches of light and dark. This same basic technical procedure obtains in the figures, although the scale of individual brushstrokes is reduced considerably. Feuerbach's paint quality has the rather dry, acidic temper of Couture's, and the very fact of making a free, oil sketch which at least begins from nature

90

definitely reflects Couture's precedents and teachings. One is reminded of comparably Couture-like oil sketches by Manet from the mid- and late 1850s. There is, however, no missing Feuerbach's own personality in this picture. The steep, vertical setup of the painting is one to which he returns many times. The very nervous busyness of the brushwork, which renders the highlights of the landscape and, with darker tones, lays out the silhouettes of the trees, is comparable in its expressive effect to that already noted in the *Nanna*. Even within the apparent poetic calm of this sketch Feuerbach's carefully restrained (but only partly concealed) feelings seem to scream for pictorial recognition.

[27.] *Portrait of the Artist's Stepmother* (1867)   PLATE 54
Kurpfälzisches Museum, Heidelberg

Oil on canvas; 42⅜″ x 33″; signed lower right "A. Feuerbach p. 67"; Inv. no. G 155; Allgeyer, 406

Feuerbach's stepmother (the former Henriette Heydenreich) treated him, usually by letter, with a combination of sympathetic indulgence and ambitious maternal encouragement. Judging from Feuerbach's response to his stepmother's letters and to her presence during his various return visits to Germany, neither the sympathy nor the encouragement concealed very effectively a significant degree of sourness that derived from her feelings of both financial and emotional neglect. Widowed early in her marriage, she refocused her world around her stepson and his career; but one was too distant and the other too erratic to give her any genuine and lasting satisfaction. Feuerbach worshipped her, partly, one feels, out of guilt and partly out of real affection; but, as with Nanna—the other female object of his adulation—affection, a certain coefficient of terror and a longing for a simpler, more direct emotional relationship went hand in hand. Granting the generally similar and comparably problematic emotional bonds that held Feuerbach to Nanna and to his stepmother, it is not surprising to find a disconcertingly direct connection between his successive paintings of the two of them.

The Heidelberg *Portrait of the Artist's Stepmother* derives many of its aspects of pose and many of its sensuous stresses and suppressions from earlier images of Nanna. While the *Stepmother* is much more staid and angular in her pictured demeanor, Feuerbach's inflated treatment of her ringlets of hair and of her hands expresses an undeniable physical (and partly sexual) discomfort, which seeks objectification almost against his will.

91

[28.] *Iphigenia* (1871)   PLATE II
Staatsgalerie, Stuttgart

Oil on canvas; 77″ x 56″; signed lower left "A. Feuerbach 71"; *Stuttgart,* p. 63, Inv. no. 770; Allgeyer, no. 535

Feuerbach first conceived of the idea for an Iphigenia in 1858. In a letter to his stepmother in June 1858 he described a composition with a large figure of Iphigenia sitting at the gate of the temple of Diana with two children playing at her feet. Iphigenia's glance was to be directed across the sea toward Greece, the homeland to which she could not return. Feuerbach hoped that the image could achieve an aesthetic abstractness of sentiment that would make it like "silent music."

Not until several years later, after the advent of Nanna, was Feuerbach inspired to develop his idea for an *Iphigenia*. In a painting finished in 1862 (Allgeyer, no. 393, now in Darmstadt and first owned by Fiedler) he used the idea of *Iphigenia* as a vehicle for a seated full-view figure of Nanna. He described the beginning steps of this *Iphigenia* in a letter of May 22, 1861. He was most pleased by the fortuitous simplicity of the image, which restricted itself essentially to a single monumental figure (Nanna's), and he believed that he had managed, as he had intended, to express a sentiment without "sentimentality." His enthusiasm for the picture was summarized thus: "never has a picture spoken so directly from my soul."

In the winter of 1871–72 Feuerbach planned a second *Iphigenia;* this one featuring Nanna's successor as his model and mistress, the less inspiring (but somewhat less emotionally troubling) Lucia Brunacci. In February 1872 he reported to his stepmother that this painting was going well—that it was "a painting before which one could sit for hours—broad, clear and soulful." It is this second version of *Iphigenia* which is shown here.

Between the first and second *Iphigenia* there is the passing of a decade of Feuerbach's life as a mature artist and there is a general cooling off of the emotional tone of his work in the last part of that decade, after Nanna's abrupt departure. These two factors—one historical and one psychological—are keys to the differences between two equally impressive, but essentially distinct (despite the shared subject), pictures. The languishing sensuousness of the almost Pontormo-like figure of Nanna in the first *Iphigenia* is completely altered in the second, where a more classically rectilinear severity of pose locks the figure tightly to the bench on which she sits and to the wall on which she leans. A somber, slightly icy coloration (stressing whites, blues, greens, and grays) is constant in both pictures; but the linear intricacy of the first version gives way to a stately, marvelously formal, and beautifully formed painterliness in the second, where the aesthetic sensuousness of the painting as a whole dominates the specifically erotic sensuousness of the figure itself in the first version. The first version depends upon Feuerbach's ability to render his personal passion for Nanna into some poetically generalized aesthetic form; the second depends upon his ability to move from a position of greater aesthetic self-certainty to an individual embodiment of that certainty. In both instances he succeeds and, in doing so, he manages to express the two-part character that Iphigenia assumed for Goethe in his re-creation of the myth, which Feuerbach read in 1860. For Goethe, Iphigenia was both an intensely real woman and an impersonal tool of mythical fate. She was as seductive in one guise as she was a poetically abstract, sublime, and finally classical female archetype in the other.

CASPAR DAVID FRIEDRICH
(1774 Greifswald–1840 Dresden)

First art teacher is Johan Friedrich Quistorp, friend of Kosegarten. 1787: brother, Christopher, dies, falling through ice. 1794: enrolled in Copenhagen Academy. 1798: to Dresden, works with landscapist Zingg then with Klengels and Siedelmann in perspective drawing. 1801–02: in Greifswald; travels on Rügen; meets Runge. 1802: summer, returns to Dresden; acquaintance with Tieck, Novalis, other "early romantics." 1805: wins second prize in Weimarer Kunstfreunde; meets Goethe. 1808: January, article in *Journal des Luxus und der Moden* states that "Friedrich has recently been painting successfully in oil"; November, finishes *Tetschner Altar* (Dresden). 1810: exhibits *Monk on the Edge of the Sea* (first mentioned *Journal des Luxus und der Moden,* February 1809) and *Abbey amidst Oak Trees* (bought by Prussian crown prince) at Berlin Academy exhibition; later made member of Berlin Academy. 1816: membership in Dresden Academy. 1818: marries Caroline Bommer; shares house with Dahl. 1824: made ordinary professor at Dresden Academy (he never received a chair); first appearance of Carus's *Nine Letters on Landscape Painting.* 1835: arm paralyzed by a stroke, convalescence aided by Russian royal family's purchase of pictures. 1837: able to work briefly, then succumbs again. Various walking tours and trips: Greifswald, 1801, 1802, 1806, 1809, 1818, 1820; Rügen, 1801, 1802, 1806, 1818; Northern Bohemia, 1807–08; Riesengebirge, 1810 with Kersting; 1811, Harz Mountains.

[29.] *Woman in the Morning Light* (ca. 1809)   PLATE 6
Museum Folkwang, Essen

Oil on canvas; 8¾″ x 12″; unsigned; *Essen,* p. 20, Inv. no. G 45; VE, no. 36. Some landscape elements appear in Rügen sketchbook from 1806 (Börsch-Supan, p. 20).

In this, one of Friedrich's earliest paintings (Börsch-Supan, 1809), we may observe many of the compositional devices Friedrich evolved to support his first attempts at oil painting. As in the *Monk on the Edge of the Sea* (VE, no. 27), space is extended horizontally in three layers of approximate foreground, distance, and sky. Whatever pictorial depth we might infer from Friedrich's coloristic changes between layers is contradicted, or at least confused, by the vertical figure of the woman who seems to stand in the immediate foreground and yet appears at the same time to become part of the (barely visible) geometric system of light rays fanning out from behind the most distant of the mountains. Friedrich has relied on a system of axial symmetry devolving from the vertical center (almost the actual center point) of his canvas to organize his composition.

Given the clearly emblematic, as opposed to pictorial, significance of the woman silhouetted darkly against a light sky (we find the same symbolic indication of sunrise in the *Tetschener Altar* [VE, no. 26]) we are reminded not of Friedrich's later, purer landscapes, but of Runge's ambitions for his *Four Times of Day.* Friedrich clearly knew at least the engravings for these; we may imagine that his *Woman in the Morning Light* was conceived in sympathy with, if not as an actual counterpart to, Runge's *Morning.* (Runge had begun his final campaign to render his *Morning* into painted form in 1807–08, shortly before Friedrich's painting.) Hence the superimposition of the orant figure, hands spread open to receive the sunrise, over a straightforward, albeit somewhat cursorily described, landscape which may also owe its increased foreground specificity to Runge's example. Like Runge, Friedrich found it necessary to evolve a basically unyielding geometric armature to support the emblematic intent of his picture; unlike Runge, he realized that the types of pictorial contradictions and disjunctures which emerged could be used, more effectively than the emblems themselves, to make pictures that were immediate and deeply expressive.

[30.] *Riverbank in Fog* (ca. 1816–20)   PLATE 9
Wallraf-Richartz Museum, Cologne

Oil on canvas; 8¾″ x 13⅜″; unsigned; *Cologne,* p. 42, Inv. no. 2667; no VE number

Because Friedrich constitutionally believed that pictures should need neither signatures nor dates ("each picture is more or less a characterization of him who made it; so that it sings out in every respect his inner worth"[1]), it is small, generally undocumented pictures like this that pose problems of chronology. However, in Friedrich's career the years between 1816 and 1820 represent a period of searching, of rethinking and extending his vocabulary of motifs and pictorial solutions; it was at this time that he turned most frequently to description of small, almost totally insignificant bits of nature to help him in his development. Neither strong symmetry nor overt oppositions between pictorial space and the picture surface are evident here, nor is his later inclination to search out natural events which lend themselves to psychological (or mood-inducing) interpretation. Compared with the thinly painted, stenographic approximations of grasses and leaves in *Woman in the Morning Light,* the flowers and bushes along the riverbank are described actualities of nature, varied and more richly hued. Space and atmospheric light are tangible. It is paintings like this, and like his masterly conveyance of nature's more unassuming moods in the *Four Times of Day,* ca. 1820 (Hannover, VE, nos. 75–78), that make it possible for his mature style to employ elements of naturalism in the service of almost hyperreal psychological expressiveness.

[31.] *The Lone Tree* (1823)   PLATE 7
Stiftung Preussischer Kulturbesitz, Staatliche Museen, Nationalgalerie, Berlin.

Oil on canvas; 22″ x 28⅜″; *Berlin,* p. 66, Inv. no. NG 77; VE no. VII. Background tree is from a Riesengebirge study, July 6, 1810 (Chemnitz); tree on left is from the sepia *Hun's Grave by the Sea,* 1806 (Weimar, VE, no. 16); and lone tree is from a study, May 23, 1806 (Hamburg).

94

In 1828 J. A. Bonte's catalogue of the Sammlung Wagener (Consul in Dresden) described this and the following picture *(Moonrise on the Sea),* both painted in 1823, as pendants representing morning and evening. Subsequent discussion has questioned whether the *Lone Tree* is not perhaps a Harz Mountain landscape, at evening.

Like its human counterpart *(Woman in the Morning Light),* the tree stands alone in the center of the painting, facing the sun rising behind clouds. Unlike the woman, it is an actual part of nature, described and elaborated within its own surroundings, which Friedrich has invested with the task of embodying man's (or at any rate his own) feelings before and within nature. The painting rep-

1. Carus, *Friedrich der Landschaftsmaler,* p. 18.

resents Friedrich's closest rapprochement between his basically pantheistic Christianity and his pure, nature imagery. Like the cross in the *Tetschener Altar* (Dresden) the tree rises above the mountains, silhouetted against the first stormy light of day. Flanked by two lesser trees, and supporting the small figure of the shepherd leaning against it, it seems to serve as a key to unlock within every man his ability to feel, through images which are part of universal experience, the stirrings of his most basic Christian beliefs.

[32.] *Moonrise on the Sea* (1823)   PLATE 8
Stiftung Preussischer Kulturbesitz, Staatliche Museen, Nationalgalerie, Berlin

Oil on canvas; 22″ x 28⅜″; unsigned; *Berlin*, p. 66, Inv. no. NG 78; VE no. 91. 1821 version is seen from a higher viewpoint with two men standing on a rock in the middle ground and two women seated on rock in foreground; all rocks are smaller in scale (Leningrad). There is also a figure study, tusche on tracing paper (East Berlin).

This painting is part of a general group of Friedrich's works in which he seems to explore man's time-bound, always somewhat poignant and uncertain, humanity by placing him beside the infinite and unconquerable ocean. His figures share the heavy solidity of the rocks; yet, silhouetted tersely against the brightness of the moon, they seem to yearn for the lightness of the ships. But, like most of Friedrich's ships, these are neither coming to shore nor setting out to sea; they are still and silent, caught in some half-way calm between the heaviness of earth and the freedom of the winds. The figures watch them as though they were seeing the plight of their own half-clay, half-eternal souls. Yet because of their tense, jagged, imperious contours, it is the human beings who seem ultimately the dominant, most alive creatures in this world of half-lights, mists, and ghostly presences.

[33.] *Man and Woman Contemplating the Moon* (ca. 1820–24)   PLATE 10
Stiftung Preussischer Kulturbesitz, Staatliche Museen, Nationalgalerie, Berlin

Oil on canvas; 13⅝″ x 17⅜″; unsigned; *Berlin*, p. 67, Inv. nos. A 11 887, NG H 6; not in VE. An 1819 version shows two men and brings the large rock and several branches closer to the foreground in front of the tree (Dresden, VE, V); a study for the woman is in reed pen and tusche on tracing paper (Berlin).

Since there are two known versions of this picture and since there were apparently several commissions for further replicas left outstanding, we can assume that this was one of Friedrich's most appreciated pictures. From our historical viewpoint the painting seems somewhat overwrought, slightly secondhand in its impact. Very little in it is being expressed for the first time. The composition reminds us of the vortical, chaotic rhythms and centripetal forces that dominate many of Friedrich's mountain grave or landslide pictures; but here the rhythms have been tamed to such a degree that the painting seems slightly wide or too big for itself. Frequently, too, Friedrich has employed contrasts between intense, warm light in the distance and a somber, dark foreground in order to confound our sense of spatiality—seemingly to turn a picture inside out and leave us feeling discomforted by the result. However, in this instance, the moon, almost pulsing through the window formed by the trees, is more pyrotechnical than affecting. Finally, in the disposition of the tree, half-torn from the earth and counter-balanced by the heavy rock, is a lingering reminiscence of Jacob van Ruysdael's *Jewish Cemetery* (Dresden), a picture that no doubt haunted Friedrich in his wanderings through the Royal Collections in Dresden.

In the final analysis, this painting of a *Man and Woman Contemplating the Moon* seems to us to be more illustrative than sincere. Hence we are, perhaps, close to the mark in assuming that Friedrich was working less from his own experience than from that of others, specifically the final meeting between Franz Sternbald and Dürer in the moonlight in a shadowed wood, described by Tieck in his *Franz Sternbalds Wanderungen*. In this second version of the picture, Friedrich has replaced one of the two men with a woman, presumably to lessen the speculative content of the image and to insure that the feelings evoked by such an archetypally "Romantic" moment be more universal and more accessible to recall by a larger number of viewers.

[34.] *Neubrandenburg Burning at Sunset* (ca. 1834)   PLATE 11
Hamburger Kunsthalle

Oil on canvas; 28⅞" x 40½"; unsigned, and unfinished; *Hamburg,* no. 1050; VE, no. 92

The fact that this painting was left unfinished (perhaps as a result of Friedrich's stroke in 1835) allows us to observe firsthand Friedrich's picture-making process, which changed very little throughout his lifetime. The existence of a sketch for one tower (the New Tower, second from right) from 1809 (Oslo) and a landscape drawing of the stones, foreground fields, and background city, dated October 1824 (Dresden), remind us that Friedrich did not work from nature directly, but permitted a picture to form in his mind before setting it on canvas— often with the help of such preliminary sketches. Reliance on simple geometric intervals (parallels, perpendicular intersections, radial diagonals) gave him a certain amount of assurance with which to face his blank canvas. Drawing, in this case both the fairly broad ink sketching in the foreground and the tight finesse of the engraver's line with which he rendered the city, provided an armature for his thin, transparent layers of paint.

This painting shares the openness and comparative lack of intensity of most of his very late works. Like many early paintings of ruined churches and graves, it depicts not the actual ravages of time or of fire but imagined destruction, nature reclaiming, or at least moving back into and penetrating, what man has made. But neither the vital forces of nature nor the jagged hardness of man's building confront us now; they are removed, distant, closer to dream than to actuality. The delicacy of Friedrich's drawing is still evident, and his almost childlike awe before phenomena of nature and in the individual lives of things is apparent, but the concentrated focus which brought these together and conveyed their almost unbearable reality has passed.

EDUARD GÄRTNER
(1801 Berlin–1877 Berlin)

1806: moves to Kassel with his mother. 1811–12: studies with F. W. Müller in Kassel. 1813: returns to Berlin. 1814–21: apprenticeship as porcelain painter in Berlin. 1821–22: works as assistant to theatrical scene painter, C. Gropius. 1822: first showing of work at Berlin Academy exhibition. 1825: travels to Paris and works with F. E. Bertin. 1827: back in Berlin working on architectural subjects. 1833: member of Berlin Academy. 1834–35: does six-part panorama of Berlin for Winter Palace of Russian Czar. 1837–39: in Russia to do three-part panorama of Kremlin. 1870: exhibits for last time at Berlin Academy.

[35.] *The New Guardhouse* (1833)   PLATE 39
Stiftung Preussischer Kulturbesitz, Staatliche Museen, Nationalgalerie, Berlin

Oil on canvas; 18⅞″ x 30⅞″; signed lower right "E. Gärtner 1833"; *Berlin,* p. 71, Inv. nos. A 1 917, NG 910

Compared to his older Berlin colleague, Hummel, Gärtner is a rather neutral artistic personality. His skill as a painter of architectural panoramas was considerable and his painted records of Berlin are enormously compelling from a documentary standpoint, even though they inevitably lack, or purposely play down, the kinds of surprising objects or incidents that so enchanted Hummel. What seems, above all, to interest Gärtner is the clarity and amplitude of Berlin's great urban spaces and the architectural framework that described these spaces with such precision. In Gärtner's hands the stern, blocky bulk of Schinkel's neoclassic guardhouse (1816–18) and the late eighteenth-century aspect into which it is fit become urbanly and visually one. For Gärtner, all architecture is a series of variations on the theme of panoramic urban design, a definer of space which is then available to him to paint.

In this particular painting his use of the foreground monument with its wrought iron fence and the tree at the right edge of the picture provide a spatially congested foil against which the remainder of his obliquely viewed perspective blossoms in an apparently limitless vista. His technique is generally linear and rather fussy, but the tonal simplicity of his color keeps the image as a whole from being uncomfortably severe. Everything is clearly defined, articulate in its placement, and almost frighteningly at ease in its nearly military anonymity and impersonality.

JOHAN JACOB GENSLER
(1808 Hamburg–1845 Hamburg)

Early studies with Gert Hardorff d. Ä in Hamburg. 1824–26: studies with Tischbein in Eutin. 1828: to Munich, via Dresden and Nuremberg. 1828–30: Munich Academy; also contact with Kobell, J. A. Klein, and H. Bürkel; probably, Wasmann. 1830: Vienna Academy; trip through Tirol. 1831: returns to permanent residence and work in Hamburg, as genre and landscape painter. 1841: trip through Holland. 1845: Wasmann is among mourners at his funeral.

[36.] *Beach near Blankenese* (1842)   PLATE 33
Hamburger Kunsthalle

Oil on paper; 13¾″ x 19¾″; signed bottom middle "J.G. (under) Blknse, Octbr. 8, 1842"; *Hamburg,* no. 1319

Jacob Gensler was the second of three painter brothers and the most varied and talented in his art. The oldest, Günther, primarily made portraits in a manner not unlike Wasmann's slightly primitive, rigidly posed style; while the youngest, Martin, contented himself with Isabey-like views of picturesque old alleys, buildings, and dark, close Romanesque interiors and Gothic halls. Jacob's work includes portraits, relaxed and unconventional in style (in some cases almost anticipating Leibl), genre scenes, and landscapes, of which the one shown here is typical and one of the best.

Beach near Blankenese reflects the growing nineteenth-century concern with uncomposed, seemingly almost empty, pictures which are made only of light (as expressed in color or tone values), the quality of the artist's paint handling per se, and his visual sensitivity to the world around him. We are reminded both of the open, light-conscious transparency of R. P. Bonington's work and that of the English watercolorists around him near the beginning of the century and of the relaxed painterly work of Boudin later on. As he frequently did, Gensler has here chosen a wide, horizontal format in which land and things of actual substance are distant from the viewer, leaving the foreground free for his soft, broadly brushed passages of water, sometimes transparent and textured by the sand underneath, at other times light-reflecting and greasily impasted. The clouds, made of scumbled, wispy brushstrokes, seemingly directed by confused beachside wind patterns, echo the light-dark variations of sea and shore.

CHRISTIAN FRIEDRICH GILLE
(1805 Ballenstadt, Harz–1899 Wahnsdorf near Dresden)

1825: enters Dresden Academy to study landscape engraving; works with G. A. Frenzel. 1827: begins oil painting under Dahl. 1830–33: works as engraver of pictures for the Sächsische Kunstverein. Continues to work as painter and lithographer in Dresden.

[37.] *The Brühlsche Terrace in Dresden* (1862) PLATE 38
Niedersächsiches Landesmuseum (Landesgalerie), Hannover

Oil on canvas; 13⅜″ x 21⅛″; signed bottom middle "C. Gille 62"; Inv. no. PNM 449

According to Prause (p. 57) Gille's small-scale landscape studies are reminiscent of contemporary French Barbizon painting in their impasted, tonal color handling and sense of intimacy with landscape.

In this larger, more formal picture little unconventionality and freedom of handling are evident. Instead an attempt has been made to present, through bravura effects of light and depiction of the differing, but related, transient shapes and textures of clouds and steam a tour de force of vivid description of contemporary Dresden and her inhabitants. Although Gille has clearly learned much from Dahl, both in his acuity of observing momentary effects of weather and his loving accuracy in rendering them, and despite the fact that his figures are edged with light in the manner of both Dahl and Carus, we cannot help but know from this picture that an epoch in Dresden painting has definitively passed. Friedrich, then somewhat differently, Carus and Dahl, valued both the countryside and the city of Dresden for the varying moods they sensed in them and for the natural and pictorial beauty which they could find. Gille, on the other hand, finds it necessary to imbue Dresden and her Elbe River with all the bustle and steam of modern industry. His painting does not individualize the city nor his own feelings for her; instead, in the best tradition of contemporary illustration, it proves to the viewer that Dresden is as modern as any other city of the 1860s.

The Brühlsche Terrace overlooks the Elbe from a point near the Zwinger.

ANTON GRAFF
(1736 Winterthur, Switzerland–1813 Dresden)

1753–56: student of drawing and painting in Winterthur under J. H. Schellenberg. 1757: Augsburg. 1758: Ansbach, assistant to Leonhard Schneider. 1759–65: Augsburg, working independently. Associated with J. F. Bause (Halle) and Salomon Gessner (Zürich). 1766: member Dresden Academy. 1778: meets Goethe in Berlin, also meets Daniel Chodowiecki. 1783: honorary member Berlin Academy. 1788: professor Dresden Academy; thereafter Dresden. 1801: Runge arrives in Dresden, meets Graff. 1812: honorary member Munich and Vienna academies.

[38]. *Portrait of Johann Adolf Freiherr von Thielmann in Saxon
Husar Uniform with the Order of St. Heinrich* (ca. 1797)   PLATE 2
Germanisches Nationalmuseum, Nuremberg

Oil on canvas; 80″ x 45⅔″; unsigned; Inv. no. GM 1532; Berckenhagen, no. 1371. Formerly in the collection of Günther Freiherr von Thielmann, originally in the collection of Siegfried Freiherr von Thielmann.

Thielmann was generally considered to be the most talented Saxon officer of his generation. During the Napoleonic period he held an erratic sequence of commands. He began in the service of Prince Louis Ferdinand of Prussia. Then in 1806 and 1807 he served the king of Saxony, acting as a mediator in the armistice between Napoleon and Saxony. From 1808 to 1810 he aided the French, abandoning them to command Saxon forces after 1810. In 1815 he returned to service in the Prussian army.

For his portrait of Thielmann, Graff has drawn heavily upon slightly earlier sources in England. The basic formula of the portrait recalls Gainsborough, Reynolds, Lawrence, and Romney in the formal presentation of the figure against a rich landscape background and in the painterly elaboration of details of costume. However, Graff's dramatic use of shadow and his sensitive, personalizing adjustments of Thielmann's pose make the image both human and slightly vulnerable in the manner of Géricault's single-figure military subjects which appear about fifteen years later. Berckenhagen lists two drawings of Thielmann by Graff. The first (Berckenhagen, no. 1370) is a study of hand and leg details for this portrait; the second is a later bust portrait (Berckenhagen, no. 1372) from about 1810.

99

[39.] *Portrait of the Printmaker Bause* (ca. 1807–08)   PLATE 3
Bremen Kunsthalle

Oil on canvas; 28⅔″ x 22¾″; unsigned; Inv. nos. 670, B 61

This is one of seven known portraits in oil of Johann Friedrich Bause—the earliest from 1759, the last from about 1808. There are also at least five portrait drawings. Berckenhagen has catalogued all of these as numbers 51–62.

Bause (1738–1814) was for many years one of Graff's closest friends. He worked for most of his life as an engraver of portraits, living alternately in Halle, Weimar, and Berlin. In 1786 he was made an honorary member of the Berlin Academy and in 1805 named a professor there. Graff's Bremen portrait is the second of a group of three closely related variants from 1807 to 1808. The first is in Halle (Staatliche Galerie Moritzburg); the third is in the University Library, Leipzig (see Berckenhagen, nos. 60, 62). A lithograph of the portrait was published in 1838 by Friedrich Pecht as the frontispiece to a catalogue of Bause's engravings.

Graff's portrait is developed along quite clearly eighteenth-century French lines. One is reminded of the bust portraits of Nattier, Peronneau, and Duplessis —many of which Graff would have known through copies and engravings. What distinguishes Graff's work from its French prototypes is a more robust and slightly flatter drawing with paint and a more coarsely modulated handling of bright flesh tones. These qualities make the portrait image sit less decorously and emerge with greater physical directness than comparable French works. Runge's respect for Graff's painting can be understood, at least partly, on the basis of the coloristic freshness, the forceful formal and psychological presence of portraits such as this.

KARL HAGEMEISTER
(1848 Werder–1933 Werder)

1871: studies in Weimar with Friedrich Preller. 1873: meets Schuch. 1874: meets Trübner in Brussels. 1876: in company of Trübner and Schuch, visits Italy briefly. After 1876: lives and works in Ferch on the Schwielowsee. Visited in summers by Schuch. After 1890: in Werder. 1913: published a biography of Schuch. Mid-1880s: interested in Manet and French Impressionism, together with Schuch.

[40.] *White Poppies* (1881)   PLATE 81
Niedersächsisches Landesmuseum (Städtische Galerie), Hannover

Oil on canvas; 31⅝″ x 46¾″; signed lower right "K. Hagemeister 1881"; Inv. no. 1912/158

Hagemeister's work carves out a middle path between Schuch (and his obsession with color values) and Trübner (and the primacy of systematized brushstrokes, forceful shapes, and brilliant, frequently almost ungraded, local color). The *White Poppies* make probably greater pictorial sense of this middle path than any other of Hagemeister's paintings. The tension between strongly shaped areas of whites and greens in the foreground and the slightly lowered values of the background produces a truly glorious optical clatter. The flowers almost leap from the surface of the canvas, remaining part of a coherent total image as a result of the edgy, but consistent, breadth of Hagemeister's brushwork. One is reminded of Blechen (even Runge) in the brashly demonstrative weight of Hagemeister's painted surface and of Manet in the lush display of large areas of pure white and high-value green.

100

Hagemeister was not always successful in achieving the surprising force of optical impact which this picture possesses. His work tends, rather, to be flashy and indecisive, since he rarely found subjects as fortuitous in their support of his composite style as the *White Poppies.*

PHILIPP FRIEDRICH VON HETSCH
(1758 Stuttgart–1838 Stuttgart)

1771–75: enrolled in the local (Stuttgart) military academy. Meets F. von Schiller and the sculptor, J. H. Dannecker. Studies with N. Guibal and assists him with decorative projects. 1775–80: studies painting at Karlsacademy in Stuttgart. 1780–82: travels to Karlsruhe and then on to Paris to study with J. M. Vien; meets David. 1782–85: in Stuttgart with regular visits to Paris. 1785–87: works in Rome; maintains contact with David. 1787: made honorary member of Academy in Bologna. 1787–94: professor at Karlschule in Stuttgart. Koch and Schick among his students. 1795–96: in Rome. 1797: appointed director of the Ludwigsberger Schloss and royal painting gallery in Stuttgart. 1801: named member of Berlin Academy. 1802–03: to Rome again, visits Schick. After 1803: generally in Stuttgart.

[41.] *Allegory of Washington* (1793)   PLATE 1
Georg Schäfer Collection, Schweinfurt

Oil on canvas; 43⅝″ x 35⅛″; signed lower left "Hetsch 1793, Stoutgard"; Inv. no. 2902

Hetsch's artistic and political sympathies were distinctly French and he passed them directly to his two most talented students, Koch and Schick. His friendship with David and his frequent visits to France in the years prior to the French Revolution served to instill republican ideals which were in no way undercut by the "reign of terror" that followed. In his *Allegory of Washington* he pays tribute to the American Revolution which he rightly saw as a basic stimulus to revolutionary republican sentiment in Europe. By signing the picture with his hometown rendered in its French spelling, he implied a connection between the American, French, and a "potential" German revolution very explicitly.

The painting itself is neoclassic in the generic, rather than the truly heroic, sense of the word. Its poetic quiet recalls Vien rather than David, even though its decor is quite up-to-date. The two female muses, posed in the act of conceiving the allegory, are appropriately Greco-Roman in dress and neoclassic in the complex linearity of their poses. The composition as a whole is generally frieze-like, even though the half-drawn curtain does open up a background space that contains a sculpture group of "victory crowning virtue." This opening makes the picture space more complicated and less lucid than David's, for example, but the rhythmic interweaving of foreground figures keeps the spatial complexity from becoming very pronounced. Similarly, the clearly zoned, schematic hardness of the painting's coloration helps to secure the predominance of surface arrangement over pictorial space.

The painting is, finally, learned and cosmopolitan—exactly the sort of thing that Goethe later hoped might provide a basis for nineteenth-century German art. But, partly for aesthetic and partly for political reasons, this evidently

French kind of neoclassicism became an anathema to the Germans, even to those trained in it, after Napoleon moved to occupy one part of Germany after another. The apparent morality and republican virtue which the style seemed initially to objectify vanished, like many of the liberal ideals of the French Revolution itself, under the heavy, if deceptively benevolent, hand of the emperor.

JOHANN ERDMANN HUMMEL
(1769 Kassel–1852 Berlin)

1782: begins to study architecture at Kassel Academy. 1786: becomes assistant to Kassel Hofmaler, Böttner. 1790: enters painting class at Kassel Academy. 1792–99: in Rome where influenced temporarily by Carstens and Flaxman. 1799: returns to Kassel. 1800: moves to Berlin. 1803: does theatrical costume designs for Royal Theater in Berlin and works as an illustrator. 1808: meets Goethe in Weimar and encouraged to develop his interests in optics and perspective. 1809: hired to teach same at Berlin Academy. 1811: member of Berlin Academy. After 1812: many paintings of architectural subjects. 1824–44: publishes several teaching manuals on perspective and geometric construction.

[42.] *The Granite Dish in the Pleasure Garden, Berlin* (ca. 1832)   PLATE 40
Stiftung Preussischer Kulturbesitz, Staatliche Museen, Nationalgalerie, Berlin

Oil on canvas; 26⅜" x 35⅝"; unsigned; *Berlin,* p. 101, Inv. nos. A 1 843, NG 934

Hummel's combination of a learned professionalism in the working out of illusionistic problems of optics and perspective and the almost childlike naïveté of the bits of incidental reality that move through his pictures produces images that are positively delightful in their quirkish disjunctivity. The most fortuitous subject matter Hummel ever found to support his particular kind of pictorial magic was the great granite bowl, manufactured in Berlin and set up in a public park in 1831. In four paintings Hummel followed the monument from its manufacture through its installation. In a view of the bowl in the limited confines of the factory where it was made (cf. Berlin, Nationalgalerie inv. no. A 1 844, NG 933) Hummel first achieved the powerful illusionistic play between an architectural perspective space and a perspective projection of the bowl within that space. This continues into the picture shown here. In the earlier picture he also introduced the elegantly curved mirror reflections that re-create pictorially the highly polished surface of the bowl. But what was done simply in the earlier picture is redone with an almost unbelievable degree of optical complication, as Hummel moves outdoors into the park where the monument was set up and looks up at it from a sort of average spectator's distance. From his chosen viewpoint a whole complex of primary (direct) and secondary (inverted) reflections in the front lip and underside of the bowl appear. With consistently firm drawing and with systematically graded colors Hummel renders these reflections and then proceeds to the figures and the architectural elements that surround the bowl and provide the detailed basis for what its surface actually reflects.

In the image as a whole there is no question as to what primary visual fact dominates the picture—it is the bowl. Everything seems arranged for the pictorial benefit of the bowl. The variously moving and gesturing figures come almost as an afterthought to remove some of the optical fixedness and severity of the pictured setup and to provide some comforting genre relief, both in fact and in reflection. Yet, in the airless depth of Hummel's perspective, many figures become so small (and at times so ambiguous) in their relative scale that the specificity of their action seems absolutely surreal. The resulting confrontation between this surreal specificity of the figures and the inflated, hyperoptical presence of the bowl generates, almost by accident, qualities of art, rather than simply of fact.

WILHELM VON KOBELL
(1766 Mannheim–1853 Munich)

Early training from his father Ferdinand Kobell and at Mannheim Academy under Agidus Verhelst, an engraver, and Franz Anton von Leydensdorf, a painter; schooling includes copying old masters in Mannheim and Düsseldorf galleries. 1784: wins prize at Mannheim Academy. 1791: made member of Berlin Academy. 1792: November, summoned to Munich as court painter to Elector Karl Theodor. 1793: August, begins permanent residence in Munich. 1796: beginning of Napoleonic occupation. 1797: spring, marriage to Anna Maria Theresa von Krempelhuber; September, aquatint sold to private collector in London. 1803: publication of military scenes in *Rheinische Zeitung*. 1806–07: commissioned by King Max-Joseph of Bavaria to make cycle of battle pictures as present to Marshall Alexandre Berthier, minister of war for Napoleon. 1808: June, made member of art committee of Bavarian Academy of Pictorial Arts; made member of Vienna Academy. 1809: commissioned by Crown Prince Ludwig of Bavaria to paint twelve large battle pictures for a Victory Room (banquet hall) in Munich Residenz; June to October, in Vienna. Winter 1809–April 1810: in Paris. 1814: October, becomes professor of landscape painting at Munich Academy. 1815: finishes battle pictures. 1817: knighted by Bavarian royal family, henceforth Wilhelm von Kobell. 1824: Cornelius becomes director of Munich Academy. 1826: Kobell released from Academy, as Cornelius sees no need for professorship in landscape painting.

[43.] *Horses in the Isar near Munich* (1815)　　　　　　　　PLATE 12
Georg Schäfer Collection, Schweinfurt

Oil on canvas; 8⅞″ x 12⅜″; signed lower left "Wil:Kobell 1815"; Inv. no. 2051; *FR*, no. 142. Later variant (1819) in Munich.

Although the breadth and depth of this Isar landscape recall the discomfortingly full panoramic effects of Kobell's great battle pictures, everything here has been scaled down and softened in keeping with its small size and basically quiescent subject, depicted in the heavy atmosphere that seems to precede a summer thunderstorm. The delicacy of Kobell's drawing and the simultaneously individualized, but incredibly distant and fragile, shapes of the Munich skyline remind us more of the serenity and emptiness of his small-scale etched views of Munich and environs (published in 1818) than of the bustle and edgy clatter of the big battle scenes.

Despite the somewhat dioramic two-dimensionality of the flatly lighted horses and the back lit silhouette of the woman, the landscape itself derives from an

103

atmospheric totality which seems actually to contain light in a way which, although lacking any positive paintedness, recalls the soft shadowing and weblike continuity of Monet's works from the mid-1880s. This softness of paint handling is a debt which Kobell still owes to the combined influences of his seventeenth-century Dutch sources and the eighteenth-century French traditions of his family.

In general, the pictorial integration of the figures into the landscape results largely from the fact that this is one of the first times that Kobell has painted figures like these and that he has had to rely on the totality of what he sees in order to render them. Hence, contours are somewhat unpredictable and the resulting negative shapes are sometimes unsure and arhythmic. The organization of the figures and the intersections between them are not exactly geometric. In this painting, unlike many of Kobell's later works, we are not made to feel that all the possible visual questions arising from the group of figures were answered prior to the act of painting.

[44.] *Landscape with Hunters near Schorndorf* (1823)   PLATE 13
Museum Folkwang, Essen

Oil on canvas; 17⅝″ x 25⅛″; signed lower right "WKobell 1823"; *Essen*, p. 33, Inv. no. 307

This picture presents us with a fine example of Kobell's mature manner of painting. He has shifted to a slightly low viewpoint; the sky fills almost two-thirds of the canvas and what seems to be foreground is comparatively wide and recedes abruptly—to end suddenly at the beginning of distance. The figures, sandwiched by shadows into a sort of implied middle ground, seem sharply folded out toward us; perched on a steep incline and silhouetted crisply against the sky, they are thinned and extended into long, elegant shapes. No longer does it seem as though we are looking at the scene through a gauzy curtain, instead edges and transitions between highlights and shadows are stereometrically clear. Light is not contained within the picture, it is directed boldly from a source outside, resulting in almost Piero della Francesa-like subdivisions of already geometric shapes and patterning the ground with long shadows. Pebbles stipple the ground with reflected light, but in a passive, somewhat diagrammatic way—the fact of light remains without any surface-enlivening effects.

In his mature work it seems as though Kobell returned for inspiration to his battle pictures, focusing closely on one or another figure group in order to make whole pictures out of what had been the necessarily diorama-based organization of many small units into a coherent, historically accurate whole. Nothing in the late pictures is left to visual happenstance: Intervals and intersections are calculated with mathematical precision; groups and the figures within them are simplified or slightly distorted to fit into the basically elongated, geometric shapes of rectangles, ovals, triangles, or diamonds; and every figural recession is either stopped and turned back parallel to the picture plane or contradicted by a corresponding projection before illusionistic space can possibly threaten the coherence of Kobell's presented entity. In this landscape the secondary diagonal leading from the dog to the horse to the smaller background figures fulfills its double intention with the utmost qualitative success. The fact of distance is stated with absolute certainty, while a coherent unit of organization upon the picture surface is defined and maintained.

In Kobell's best late pictures we are haunted by the clarity of his images and by the loneliness of a world in which exaggerated gesture and angular motion have the communicative impact of pistol shots in a crystalline silence.

JOSEPH ANTON KOCH
(1768 Obergibeln bei Elbigenalp, Tirol–1839 Rome)

1782–83: primary training in Dillingen and Wittislingen under the guidance of Bishop J. N. Freiherr von Ungelter. 1784: works in Augsburg with the sculptor Ignaz Ingerl and the painter I. I. Metterleiter. 1785-91: in Stuttgart as student in Hohe Karlschule where he meets Hetsch and Schick. 1791–94: in Switzerland —first Basel, then Bern, Biel, Neuchâtel, and Bernese Alps. 1794: travels to Italy—Milan, Bologna, Florence, Rome, and Naples. 1795: in Rome, sees exhibition of Carsten's work. 1795–1812: regularly in Rome. 1812–15: in Vienna where he meets Ferdinand Olivier and Friedrich Schlegel. 1815: returns to Rome as permanent residence. 1825–28: works with Nazarenes on frescoes for Casino Massimo.

[45.] *Mountain Landscape* (1796)   PLATE 15

Oil on canvas; 44″ x 64½″; signed lower left "peint par Koch/1796"; *Cologne, no.* 2601; Lutterotti, G. no. 3

This is one of the largest and earliest of Koch's landscapes. It is related to a watercolor of 1792–93 done in Switzerland (Lutterotti, Z. no. 652) which is now in Vienna. While clearly demonstrating Koch's respect for seventeenth-century French-Italianate landscape—a respect which had developed during his years in Stuttgart—this painting suggests as well Koch's personal romance with mountains. Born in the Tirol, Koch returned to the mountains of Switzerland for the three years prior to his removal to Italy. The *Mountain Landscape* was painted shortly after his arrival in Rome and the memory of the Alps in general, and particularly of the highlands around Bern, was still fresh in his mind. Before surrendering to the imagery of definitely French-Italianate landscape, Koch paused to give monumental form to his experience of the turbulent irregularities of the nature he knew best—a kind of nature which appealed increasingly to later generations of more overtly Romantic artists.

The experience of mountains and the way Koch expresses it pictorially in this painting has a distinct influence on his subsequent work. The space-compressing aspects of mountain scenery with its confusion of near and distant vistas and its bold rhythms of faulted landscape and falling water impels Koch to stress variety, rather than stereometric clarity and precise focus in his composition. He forges a coherence from his various elements by developing formal relationships in a strictly two-dimensional fashion. This kind of coherence, conveyed both tonally and through continuous contours, persists throughout Koch's life as a painter, giving a distinctly personal accent to perpetual borrowings from Nicholas Poussin, Gaspar Poussin, and Claude Lorraine.

105

[46.] *Waterfall by Subiaco* (1813)   PLATE 14
Stiftung Preussischer Kulturbesitz, Staatliche Museen, Nationalgalerie, Berlin

Oil on canvas; 23¼″ x 27¼″; signed lower left "G. Koch fece 1813"; *Berlin,* p. III, Inv. nos. A 1 407, NG 554; Lutterotti, G. no. 25

This painting is the second painted version of a subject first treated in drawings from 1805 to 1806 (Lutterotti, Z. nos. 896, 991, Vienna and Berlin respectively) and in a painting of 1811 in Leipzig (Lutterotti, G. no. 18). According to Lutterotti the painting was ordered from Koch by his dealer and friend, Robert von Langer, in 1812 as a present for Langer's father. Koch himself described the picture and its relationship to the earlier (Leipzig) one in a letter of October 20, 1812, to Langer: "It is (a view) of the area around Subiaco with a waterfall, the same one that appears in Herr von Asbeck's picture (Leipzig) but seen from the other side. The view is completely in the taste of Gaspar Poussin but more vibrantly colored" (Lutterotti, p. 206).

Compared to the previous *Mountain Landscape* this picture conveys more directly Koch's regard for the pictorial values of seventeenth-century French-Italianate landscape. Various landscape elements—mountains, trees, water, and sky—are clearly defined and comparatively isolated from one another in their disposition within the total composition. The constructed illusion of space is more consistent, even though Koch still tends to resolve the important elements of his composition in two dimensions, permitting the image to grow upward across the surface. Like his French-Italianate predecessors, Koch suggests in his foreground "staffage" figures a traditional narrative subject; here a *Flight into Egypt.*

[47.] *Grotta Ferrata* (ca. 1834)   PLATE 16
Niedersächsisches Landesmuseum (Landesgalerie), Hannover

Oil on canvas; 30¾″ x 41⅝″; signed lower left "J. K."; Inv. no. PNM 492; Lutterotti, G. no. 85

There are three closely related versions of this subject, all from around 1834. The first (Lutterotti, G. no. 84) is in the museum in Stettin; this Hannover painting is the second; the third (much reduced in size) is also in Hannover (Lutterotti, G. no. 86). Related drawings for the subject are in Darmstadt (Lutterotti, Z. no. 152), in Weimar (Lutterotti, Z. no. 650), and in Vienna (Lutterotti, Z. no. 686). Except for minor details of vegetation and topography (and for changes in the relative scale of figures to setting in the third version), all three of Koch's pictures seem virtually identical. The question of sequence in the group is not very problematic, since the Stettin version alone possesses whatever complications of detail there are and these all disappear from the two Hannover pictures.

Grotta Ferrata represents one aspect of Koch's late style—that aspect which continues to refine French-Italianate elements and gradually surrenders the more vigorously personal characteristics of Koch's earlier modes of landscape expression. Gone almost completely is the surface excitement of the *Mountain Landscape* and the *Waterfall.* Koch's viewpoint is lowered and his horizon drops correspondingly, so that pictorial space expands at the expense of two-dimensional cogency. Bright, slightly brittle, Nazarene color appears both in figures and in the landscape, echoing the lucid hardness of the landscape prospect in general. In his friezelike arrangement of the figures around the well and in the swirling rhythms of the tree shapes above them, one can feel Koch trying to hold on to at least some of the planimetric energy of his earlier landscapes.

[48.] *Macbeth and the Witches* (ca. 1834)   PLATE 17
Von der Heydt-Museum, Wuppertal

Oil on mahogany; 14⅝″ x 21¾″; signed lower right "J. K."; Inv. no. G 78; Lutterotti, G. no. 87

This picture also appears in three closely related versions. The first from 1829 (Lutterotti, G. no. 73) is in Basel. The Wuppertal picture adopts the same basic images, adding some smaller figures in the right middle ground and the group of witches flying across the sky in the center of the picture. These additions also appear in a much larger Innsbruck version (Lutterotti, G. no. 88). Lutterotti suggests (p. 224) that the Wuppertal picture is a preliminary study for the one in Innsbruck, but his explanation is not totally convincing. It could just as well have been a second, smaller version. Whatever the case, a preparatory water-color of the flying witches is in Cologne (Lutterotti, Z. no. 432) and a completed (and squared for transfer) preparatory drawing (Lutterotti, Z. no. 606) is in Rome.

The Macbeth pictures appear shortly after Koch's completion of his Dante frescoes at the Casino Massimo. Together with the frescoes, *Macbeth* demonstrates the essential characteristics of Koch's work as a painter of dramatic narratives. Like Carstens (and Runge) before him, Koch generates narrative excitement through the wild nervousness of his drawing and through jarring contrasts of scale and shape. The visual (illustrated) equivalents for drama are, as a result, quite literal and, from a pictorial point of view, not very convincing. Compared to the contemporary illustrations of Goethe and Shakespeare by Delacroix, Koch's seem enormously overcomplicated, primarily as a result of the leathery stiffness of his sense of form and his rather schematic development of color and tone. In landscape Koch's style was the successful outgrowth of the combined experiences of nature and art. In narratives like the *Macbeth*, this style was forced to support ambitions of a visually far less direct sort and it was not totally adequate to the task.

WILHELM LEIBL
(1844 Cologne–1900 Würzburg)

1861–64: student of H. Becker in Cologne. 1864: moves to Munich. 1866–68: student of A. von Ramberg. 1869: student of K. von Piloty. Exhibits *Frau Gedon* (Munich) in International Exhibition in Munich. Meets and is much praised by Courbet. 1869–70: in Paris. 1870: in Munich again, meets Thoma and later Schuch and Trübner. 1870–73: informal group of painters forms around Leibl, includes Hagemeister and the above. 1873: moves from Munich to the country, first to Grasslfing. 1875–77: in Unterschondorf. 1878–82: in Berbling. After 1882: in Bad Aibling and Kutterling. 1898: travels to Holland.

[49.] *The Painter Eduard Fischer* (1875)   PLATE 67
Wallraf-Richartz Museum, Cologne

Oil on canvas (doubled); 17⅝" x 26⅝"; signed lower right "W. Leibl. / 1875"; *Cologne,* no. 2011; Waldmann, no. 145

Fischer, a landscape painter from Berlin, was one of a large and somewhat random group of artists working outside Munich with greater or lesser degrees of personal contact with Leibl in the last three decades of the nineteenth century. This portrait is one of the most successful early examples of Leibl's so-called "hard style," which developed in the years following his removal from Munich and which culminated in the great *Three Women in Church* (Hamburg) of 1878–82. In contrast to Leibl's work prior to 1873 and after 1885, where loose, painterly brushwork applied directly to the canvas (usually without preparatory drawings) renders figural plasticity and definition through the careful calculation of color values, Leibl's "hard style" recalls the elegantly sensitive linear effects and the crisp flesh tones of sixteenth-century German portraiture in the general tradition of Hans Holbein the Younger.

In paintings like the portrait of Fischer it is clear that Leibl's "hard style" is truly felt and not simply adopted. The drawing is enormously searching, unpredictable, and capable of giving a remarkable sense of immediacy to the image. The light and delicate brushstrokes that Leibl uses to specify relative textures and tones effectively pull the figure outward from its silhouetted flatness, causing it to hover vibrantly at a point just in front of the picture surface.

[50.] *Countess Rosine Treuberg* (1878)   PLATE 69
Hamburger Kunsthalle

Oil on canvas; 41⅝" x 32⅞"; signed lower left "Leibl 1878"; *Hamburg,* no. 1535; Waldmann, no. 161

The subject was the wife of one of Leibl's most important patrons and friends, Count Ferdinand Fischler von Treuberg, Herrn auf Holzen. The commission for this portrait derived from Leibl's visit to Holzen in 1877, at which time he painted a slightly smaller and less ambitious portrait of the Countess (Vienna, see Waldmann, no. 162) and began the Hamburg picture, which he hoped to develop fully in the painstaking technical terms of his current "hard style." The painting was never finished, but it stands, even in its unfinished state, as a lucid demonstration of how Leibl painted at the time and as an at least partly successful picture. Leibl's desire to handle comparatively light tones, delicately modulated in their values, developed simultaneously with his "hard style" and seems directly, if not totally, responsible for it. The Treuberg portrait demonstrates a variety and delicacy of coloration which Leibl was never able to achieve (and, in fact, never really pursued) in the more painterly style of his earlier and later years.

Leibl's work on the Treuberg portrait, and the mechanics of his "hard style" in general, proceeded systematically from the loose blocking in of the image with broadly brushed passages of thinned oil paint. Basic shapes, their disposition, and general coloration were established in this fashion. This initial procedure was basically similar to that which Leibl had followed previously in his more painterly works. However, instead of continuing to work up the image with units of increasingly focused brushwork, Leibl now proceeded to seek out the precise linear definition of one area after another. He did not begin with drawing, but he, so to speak, changed over to it in the middle of his work on a picture. Linearity was an extension rather than a new foundation of his manner of pictorializing images. Unlike traditional "linear" artists such as Holbein, he never reproduced draftsmanly values in paint; but as a painter he tried to achieve with linearity an ultimate degree of painterly refinement.

In the Treuberg portrait, Leibl attempted linear resolution of only the head and upper bodice. His most difficult task was to maintain simultaneously rhythmic and descriptive coherence in the move from generalized to more specific contours. In a simple, frontal image, such as the Vienna portrait of the Countess, the task was dealt with quickly and effectively. But, in the Hamburg portrait, the situation was complicated largely as a result of the off-center, three-quarter, profile pose. The somewhat compressed and unresolved contour of the left side of the subject's face seems, for example, to fight the overall shape of the figure in order to respond to the curves of the black neckband. Working out difficulties of this sort took Leibl an incredibly long time—in the case of the *Three Women in Church,* nearly four years.

[51.] *The Wife of the Bürgermeister of Kutterling* (1892)   PLATE 68
Georg Schäfer Collection, Schweinfurt

Oil on canvas; 26″ x 19¾″; signed lower right "W. Leibl 92"; Inv. no. 79146125; Waldmann, no. 206

This portrait is a splendid example of Leibl's painterly style—his so-called "direct painting." More than any other of Leibl's pictures shown here, *The Wife of the Burgermeister of Kutterling* conveys the particular qualities for which Munich painting was internationally famous in the 1880s and 1890s. The image is, quite literally, made of paint. The facts of brushwork and pigment are preeminent, even though the sitter's likeness is rendered very convincingly. Color values, as conveyed through the variously scaled and shaped marks of Leibl's brush, carry the major burden of describing the sitter's appearance in pictorial terms, which are at once plastic and forcefully two-dimensional in character. The rich painterliness of Leibl's picture recalls, in certain respects, the seventeenth-century portraiture of Hals, Rembrandt, and Velasquez; but his bonding of the image to the continuous and spatially undifferentiated membrane of the canvas surface is unique.

Unlike his painterly works of the late 1860s and early 1870s, those of the 1890s benefit indirectly from the linear impulses of Leibl's "hard style." Brush-strokes are less carefully arranged in the 1890s, their shapes and relative densities less predictable, and their ability to inflect both edges and flat surfaces more secure.

[52.] *The Description of the Hunt* (1893)   PLATE 70
Wallraf-Richartz Museum, Cologne

Oil on canvas; 29⅜″ x 34⅝″; signed lower left "W. Leibl 93"; *Cologne,* no. 1168; Waldmann, no. 212

Leibl became interested in this type of subject in the late 1860s. The term "reverie picture" has been coined to describe generally the semianecdote, semi-portrait, semi-figure painting for the sake of figure painting nature of such

109

subjects. The most important recent precedents for these subjects were Courbet's *After Dinner at Ornans* (Lille) and Manet's *Luncheon in the Studio* (Munich). These pictures, and Leibl's after them, assemble figures around or beside a table and make "conversation" (actual, potential, or concluded) the emblematic anecdote that binds figures together. Leibl's first important essay on this subject, the *Group Seated around a Table* in Cologne (1872–73), became the prototype for many others that followed, particularly in the 1890s. In that picture, and in the *Description of the Hunt,* conversation is portrayed very definitely. Figures either speak or listen. In the later picture there are fewer figures. Their shapes are more complicated and each possesses an individualized and truly monument- al presence. Seen against their somber, turgidly angular settings, the figures of the hunter and the old woman come alive through the rude, inelegant clumsi- ness of their respective poses, while the murky consistency of Leibl's color and the pictorially unifying character of his instinctively flexible (but fluent and continuous) brushwork draws the various parts of the image together.

Both figures in the picture have been identified (Cologne, p. 71). The man is Joseph Holzmaier; the old woman was named Tumin. There is a drawing of the latter in Munich and an earlier oil sketch, reproduced in Waldmann (no. 211).

[53.] *Kitchen in Kutterling* (1898)   PLATE 71
Wallraf-Richartz Museum, Cologne

Oil on canvas; 33⅝" x 25¾"; signed lower left "W. Leibl 98"; *Cologne,* no. 1165; Waldmann no. 248

This painting is a variant of a picture with the same title in Stuttgart; it is related to two partially preparatory drawings (one in Munich and another in a German private collection). Like the *Description of the Hunt,* the *Kitchen in Kutterling* is a "reverie picture"; but, unlike the *Description,* it does not use literal conversation to relate two figures anecdotally. Instead, both figures are lost in their own daydreams, possibly about each other, possibly not. Both seem to be engaged in a simple manual activity, but neither seems able to concentrate.

In the Stuttgart picture the two figures are grouped more compactly and a more direct psychological connection is implied. However, for this variant, Leibl has spread the figures apart, both laterally and spatially, and emphasized their isolation by the two separate windows on the wall behind them. This second solution required the intermediate steps of the two drawings mentioned above; but the painting is finally as direct and resolute pictorially as any of Leibl's late works. Compared to the *Description,* this painting gives greater emphasis to the plasticity of individual figures and to the spatial coherence of the setting they mutually inhabit. Seen together, the two pictures demonstrate the manner in which Leibl used the articulation or nonarticulation of pictorial space to underline the form of psychological connection that exists between figures. This, along with the unity or separateness of Leibl's conception of in- dividual figures (and their location within the total pictured setting), suggests the latitude of narrative expression which Leibl permits himself, while relying finally upon a purely optical resolution of the whole of his images.

The sitters' identities are known. They are Therese Haltmaier and Nicholaus Ebersberger (Cologne, p. 73).

EMANUEL GOTTLIEB LEUTZE
(1816 Swäbisch Gmünd–1868 Washington D.C.)

As a child emigrates to America with his parents. 1839–40: studies in Philadelphia under John A. Smith. 1841–42: back in Germany; studies in Düsseldorf under C. F. Lessing. 1842–45: travels to Munich and then to Italy. 1845: returns to Düsseldorf and paints subjects from English and American history (cf. *Washington Crossing the Delaware*, 1850 in Bremen). 1848: takes part in the founding of "Malkasten." 1856: one of the administrators of the Deutsche Kunstgenossenschaft. 1859: called to Washington to do paintings for the assembly rooms of the Capitol building.

[54.] *Frau Oberst Lottner* (ca. 1845)   PLATE 25
Staatsgalerie, Stuttgart

Oil on canvas; 22″ x 18⅞″; unsigned; *Stuttgart*, pp. 109–10, Inv. no. 1489

The two portraits by Leutze shown here both represent members of the family of his in-laws, the Lottner's. *Frau Oberst Lottner* was his mother-in-law; Ferdinand *(Herr Lottner)* was his brother-in-law. This is the only known portrait of his mother-in-law, but Leutze did two other (both earlier) bust portraits of Ferdinand. One is in a private collection in Munich, the other (a miniature) is in a private collection in Basel.

The *Frau Oberst Lottner* is a very characteristic example of a kind of German portraiture in the middle of the nineteenth century that was rather indiscriminately international in its appearance and generally untouched by prevailing Nazarene conventions. One is reminded of many similar works by Rayski and by that most eminent painter of European royalty, F. X. Winterhalter, who was born in Germany and trained there, although he made his reputation in France and England. Like Rayski and Winterhalter (particularly in their early works), Leutze fixes his image very sternly and stresses its matter-of-factness, rather than attempting to probe its particular psychology. Yet, he does not draw it with any evident firmness or consistency, preferring instead to map out basic details of costume and physiognomy in a cursory fashion—thereafter distributing highlights and accents of color in a way which seems quite loose and painterly, but which is, in fact, distinctly mannered. As in the case of so many of Winterhalter's portraits, one senses in this particular Leutze a form of nearly automatic and unfeeling flattery with paint. Whatever visual presence the sitter may have had is surpressed rather than objectified in her painted appearance.

The tendency of so much later Düsseldorf painting to rely on a painterly superficiality that mimics, rather than really contends with, visual reality is directly anticipated by Leutze in this portrait, even though he, fortunately, lacks at this time the technical skill to be totally arrogant and insensitive pictorially.

[55.] *Herr Lottner* (1852)   PLATE 26
Kunstmuseum, Düsseldorf

Oil on canvas; 52⅜″ x 40″; signed lower left "E. Leutze 1852"; Inv. no. 4268

The *Herr Lottner* is in almost every respect a more ambitious and successful

111

portrait than the *Frau Oberst Lottner*. The distinctly rubbery formlessness of the latter has largely given way to a more interesting and forcefully designed setup of the figure and a more carefully observed and clearly focused expression of the sequences of light and tone through which it is elaborated pictorially. Leutze's handling of color values is impressive in its precision and extremely effective in projecting the essential plasticity of the figure without compromising the overall strength of its posed shape. The bright flesh tones of the face and the accent of red-orange in the lining of the hat (lower left) state the extremes of tone, while the warm browns and grays of the subject's wool mantle carefully respect both the modeling of the figure and the linear echoes, within the folds of the mantle, of the overall shape and axis of the figure as a unit.

The portraiture of Titian, Tintoretto, and Van Dyck, which Leutze had studied in Italy, has a considerable influence on his conception of the *Herr Lottner*. The three-quarter length pose and the relatively small scale of the head in relation to the figure's upper body are effects drawn directly from sixteenth- and seventeenth-century Venice and reapplied here with genuine success. The image which results is both extremely dignified and humane in its bearing. The somewhat turgid, mechanical, and academic aspect of Leutze's paint handling does not exactly extend the purely visual qualities of the image; but it does not, in the final analysis, obviate them.

MAX LIEBERMANN
(1847 Berlin–1935 Berlin)

1866: enters Berlin University and studies painting informally; visits Karl Steffeck. 1868–73: studies at the Weimar Kunstschule under two Belgian history painters, Ferdinand Pauwels and Charles Verlat. 1871: briefly in Düsseldorf, visits M. L. von Munkácsy. 1873–78: in Paris. 1874: spends summer in Barbizon Forest. 1871, 1872, 1875: visits to Holland. 1876: exhibits *Workers in a Turnip Field* in Paris Salon. Spends entire summer in Holland. 1878: visits Venice, then Berlin. 1878: moves to Munich, meets Leibl. 1881: exhibits *Twelve-Year-Old Jesus in the Temple* (Hamburg), painting causes considerable public debate. 1880: onward, regular visits to Holland, regular visits to Paris and many works exhibited there. 1884: moves to Berlin. 1892: a member of a group of painters called the "XI"—a pre-Secessionist alliance. 1897: an exclusive showing of his work at the Berlin Academy and named professor there. 1898: founding of the Berlin Secession, first exhibition in 1899. 1899–1912: president of the Berlin Secession. 1912: honorary doctor's degree from Berlin University. 1917: exhibition honoring Liebermann's seventieth birthday. 1920–32: president of the Berlin Academy. 1927: retrospective exhibition at Berlin Academy. After 1933: forbidden to paint or exhibit.

[56.] *The Bleaching Ground* (1882)   PLATE 86
Wallraf-Richartz Museum, Cologne

Oil on canvas; 43⅝″ x 69¼″; signed lower right "M. Liebermann 82"; *Cologne,* no. 2939; Pauli, p. 60

Pauli lists four studies for this picture—three of details of landscape and of various figures and a final watercolor mock-up for the finished painting (Pauli,

p. 244). *The Bleaching Ground* is the earliest of Liebermann's works shown here. It represents the particular form of his initial accommodation of late Barbizon (cf. Jules Breton) social realist subjects and a diluted, essentially academic, form of Impressionism, based generally (like Uhde's work at this time) on the contemporary paintings of French artists such as Bastien-Lepage, but containing a strong admixture of effects from contemporary realist painting in Holland.

The Bleaching Ground is one of the most successful of Liebermann's works in this vein and its presents several qualities which are developed further in his later work. The painting also presents an interesting sidelight to contemporary developments in France where, between 1882 and 1885, the young neo-Impressionists, Seurat in particular, had begun, in a way not unrelated to Liebermann's, to stress firmness and regularity in the drawing of figures (frequently emulating Millet) and greater breadth and clarity in the construction of pictorial space than one finds in the art of Manet or in French Impressionism of the 1870s. Liebermann's manner of designing space is a good deal more perspectival (in the sense of traditional linear perspective) and more literally vacant in the effects it produces than Seurat's and his drawing less systematic in its construction of hierarchical units of rhythm; but a similar impulse toward a greater pictorial definiteness than Impressionism featured is evident.

Coloristically *The Bleaching Ground* is bright in its patterned greens, blacks, and whites; and, by Impressionist standards, optically unsubtle. Yet, the hardness of the color, combined with the general inelegance of pictured shapes and the cultivated emptiness of the pictorial space makes the painting unpredictable and alive. The half-perspectival, half-surface pattern aspect of Liebermann's deployment of the sheets draped across the grass anticipates the play between sunspots (or shadows) and perspective axes in many of his later works.

[57.] *Bürgermeister Petersen* (1891)   PLATE 90
Hamburger Kunsthalle

Oil on canvas; 82⅜″ x 47⅝″; signed lower right "M. Liebermañ"; *Hamburg*, no. 1696; Pauli, p. 90

In the *Bürgermeister Petersen* Liebermann's enormous talent as a portrait painter appears for the first time in an image of major dimensions. The commission for the portrait was an important one, coming as it did before Liebermann's reputation was truly established. Petersen had been a distinguished figure in Hamburg city government for many years. He had served in the local Senat since 1855, and he was bürgermeister in 1876 and 1892. His portrait was commissioned from Liebermann for the "Collection of Pictures from Hamburg" which had been founded in 1889. Prior to beginning the final version of the portrait, Liebermann made several studies of his subject's face, figure, and finally of the composition as a whole (these are detailed in *Hamburg*, p. 184). Yet, for all of the importance of the commission and the numerous preparations, the painting finally presents one of the most humane, pictorially fresh, and concise portrait images of the century. Of other nineteenth-century artists only Ingres, and only then in a few instances, was able to make portraiture as pictorially and psychologically viable as Liebermann did in this picture.

113

Echoes of Hals and Velasquez undeniably abound in Liebermann's picture; but they neither condemn it, nor do they guarantee its unique qualities any more than do the echoes of Raphael and David in Ingres's portraits. It is finally Liebermann's own balance of painterly sensitivity to contours and to color values and the perfection of his integration of the portrait likeness into the whole of the painted image that makes the picture work. The qualities of the *Petersen* are largely self-evident, but they seem even more pronounced when compared to Slevogt's *William Henry O'swald* of 1905 (also Hamburg) which is based directly on the *Petersen*, but which unfortunately loses itself in technical display. Liebermann did some repainting on the *Petersen* in 1903 and Slevogt probably scrutinized the picture closely at that time—but not closely enough.

[58.] *Papageienallee, Amsterdam* (1902)   PLATE 87
Bremen Kunsthalle

Oil on canvas; 35⅛″ x 29″; signed lower right "M. Liebermann"; Inv. no. 690; Pauli, p. 139

In Liebermann's work from the late 1890s and during the first decade of the present century the purely optical values of Manet's art and of French Impressionism in general make a belated, but direct, impact. In contrast to the earlier *Bleaching Ground,* the *Papageienallee* (a promenade in the Amsterdam Zoo) relies on the general regularity of brushstrokes, the distribution of bright colors, and the handling of color values to maintain visual interest. The informativeness of the subject matter is markedly reduced. Clarity in the layout of pictorial space and in the drawing of individual figures remains, at least up to a point, as a carry-over from paintings like the *Bleaching Ground;* but this now stands in a kind of calculated opposition to the essentially two-dimensional and continuous aspect of Liebermann's paint handling per se. One of the most prominent characteristics of Liebermann's later style is precisely this sort of calculated pictorial opposition between apparent space and seemingly definite figures and a picture surface, the flatness of which is emphatically endorsed by the literal weight and evenness of the paint it bears.

[59.] *Terrace in the Restaurant Jacob, Nienstedten* (ca. 1902)   PLATE 88
Hamburger Kunsthalle

Oil on canvas; 28″ x 40″; signed lower left "M. Liebermann"; *Hamburg*, no. 1597; Pauli, p. 142

114

The dialogue of pictorial oppositions between Liebermann's diagram of pictorial space and the unequivocal surface emphasis contained in his distribution of brushstrokes and of accents of bright colors continues directly from the *Papageienallee* into this picture. But here it is, if possible, even more marked. The overall design of the painting is enormously space-emphasizing. Liebermann's viewpoint is quiet low in level and the terrace recedes in an emphatically perspectival fashion via the row of trees running from the right of center toward the upper lefthand corner of the picture. In order seemingly to intensify this recession Liebermann arranges the empty chair and the table edge in the right foreground to provide a geometric shape that repeats (in a proportional reduction) the shape of his picture as a whole. The remainder of the image appears as though it should move both rapidly and articulately back into the pictured depth of the terrace; but it does not. Once again the patchy regularity of Liebermann's paint handling and the edgy brightness of his accents of pure color draw the image forward to the surface and a truly exciting pictorial ambiguity results.

Compared to similar two- and three-dimensional equivocations in the paintings of some of the French Impressionists—Monet or Pissarro, for example—Liebermann's are carefully weighed and calculated in every particular; often, one feels, overly so. Paintings such as the *Terrace* present, in French terms, a somewhat academic and too studied appearance. What can be said in Liebermann's defense is that his work may be in certain respects academic, but that it is the most vital and compelling form of academicism that ever happened.

The painting was commissioned from Liebermann by the Hamburger Kunsthalle in 1902.

[60.] *Portrait of Freiherrn Alfred von Berger* (1905)   PLATE 92
Hamburger Kunsthalle

Oil on canvas; 44⅞″ x 34¾″; signed upper right "M. Liebermann 1905"; *Hamburg,* no. 1591; Pauli, p. 161

Berger was a distinguished theatrical impresario in Hamburg and Vienna. He was by education an aesthetician (he had qualified as a lecturer at the University of Vienna). His career in the theater began when he was named artistic secretary of the Burgtheater in Vienna (1887–1900). From 1900 to 1910 he was director of the Deutsches Schauspielhaus in Hamburg and from 1910 to 1912 he was director of the Burgtheater in Vienna. Liebermann's portrait exists in two versions—this one from Hamburg and a second in Dresden. There is one preparatory drawing (Hamburg).

For the Berger portrait Liebermann chose an informal, rather conversational pose, recalling that which Ingres had developed in his great portrait of the journalist, Bertin, in 1832 (Paris, Louvre). The closeup immediacy which the pose conveys seems calculated to produce a very active, almost aggressive image. The comparative hardness of Liebermann's color and the stiff, slightly angular breadth of his paint handling acts, like the swelling turbulence of Ingres's linear rhythms in the *Bertin,* to generate pictorially a sense of mobility and life in the prevailing heaviness of the sitter's shape, while a kind of almost animal vitality is expressed in Liebermann's undeniably phallic positioning of the burning cigar butt.

[61.] *Self-Portrait* (1908)   PLATE 91
Saarland Museum, Saarbrücken

Oil on canvas; 38⅞″ x 30⅜″; signed upper right "M. Liebermann 08"; Inv. no. NI 2209; Pauli, not listed

Liebermann painted a large number of self-portraits, particularly during the last three decades of his life. This is one, possibly the best, of four from 1908 (see Pauli, pp. 211–13). The self-portraits appear to serve as a kind of proving ground for poses and effects which Liebermann later develops in his commissioned portraits. They test out various figure positions and directions; they experiment with the relative scale of the figure in relation to the background against which it is set and with the relative definiteness of that background. Yet, despite the experimental aspect of the self-portraits, they are almost invariably successful pictures—in many instances much more so than some of Liebermann's commissioned portraits. Liebermann's visual familiarity with his own appearance and with the various articles that surrounded him in his studio was obviously greater than that which obtained with second person sitters. This fact seems to have put Liebermann truly at ease artistically and the fine (sometimes overly fine) calculation of effects that appears in his commissioned work is thankfully absent from the self-portraits.

In the simple, frontal pose of the figure, slightly off-center to the left, with the rectangular shapes of two other paintings leaning against a background wall abutting it to the right, the Saarbrücken self-portrait achieves a fortuitous directness of design that recalls the figure paintings of Corot. Like Corot, Liebermann stresses the interrelations of patchy brushstrokes and close color values in the image as a whole and he finally achieves an almost unbelievable delicacy of optical refinement in his handling of white, gray, and yellow-brown tones. This emerges in spite of the evident weight of the paint surface itself. Like the *Petersen* portrait, this self-portrait suggests the generally more dependable quality of Liebermann's predominantly tonal works. When painting with pure and contrasting colors he tends to be optically demonstrative rather than truly sensuous.

Compared to the self-portraits by Corinth and Böcklin shown here, Liebermann's avoids any outright dramatization of his self-image as an artist. He makes himself a quietly passive object of perception, rather than the subject of a self-emulative disquisition.

[62.] *Beach at Scheveningen* (ca. 1908)   PLATE 89
Von der Heydt-Museum, Wuppertal

Oil on canvas; 26⅛″ x 31⅞″; signed lower left "M. Liebermann"; Inv. no. G 1123; Pauli, p. 198

The tonal security and the apparent optical effortlessness of the self-portraits from 1908 emerge equally in a group of landscapes of the beach at Scheveningen done at about the same time. Pauli lists a total of nine of these (pp. 194–202). In the best of the Scheveningen pictures the tonal continuum of sand, sea, and sky predominate, while the contrasting shapes and tones of figures and sun huts punctuate the image, without challenging its overall simplicity of tone and design. Liebermann's brushwork is both sensitive and extremely flexible in these pictures, easily stretching to encompass the undifferentiated textures of the sand and the more definite appearance of one or another figure, without ever losing its sense of pictorial neutrality and consistency.

The essential "purity" of Liebermann's mature art, its fundamental indifference to anything that is not apprehensible and expressible visually emerges in full force in these landscapes. In the final analysis the quality of paint or, to put it more directly, paintedness, predominates. Liebermann seems in his best work actually to see via paint, rather than to make illusionistic replications with it. The shape, weight, and load of his brushstrokes is far less conditioned by what is being described (in particular) than it is by a method of optical construction which uses paint as its basic material to realize pure vision in general.

HANS VON MARÉES
(1837 Elberfeld–1887 Rome)

1847: family moves to Koblenz. 1853: enters primary class at Berlin Academy. 1854–55: studies with K. Steffeck in Berlin. 1855–57: military service. 1857–64: in Munich. 1864: meets Graf Schack and is dispatched along with Lenbach to Italy. 1864–69: in Rome. 1864: meets Feuerbach and accompanies him on visits to Siena, Perugia, and Orvieto during the following year. 1866: meets K. Fiedler. 1867: meets A. von Hildebrand. 1868: breaks relations with Schack. 1869: visits Spain, France, Belgium, and Holland with Fiedler. 1870: recalled for military duty in Germany. 1870–72: in Berlin with Hildebrand. 1872–73: in Dresden. 1873: to Naples with Hildebrand to do frescoes for German Zoological Station there. 1874–75: works with Hildebrand in Florence (living at the Cloister of San Francesco). 1875: breaks relations with Hildebrand. Travels to Naples, then to Rome. Periodic contact with Feuerbach and Böcklin during this final stay in Rome.

[63.] *Foraging Soldiers* (1862)   PLATE 61
Von der Heydt-Museum, Wuppertal

Oil on canvas; 21⅛″ x 29⅝″; signed lower left "Hans von Marées 1862"; Inv. no. G. 190; Meier-Graefe, no. 74

The arcadian theme of humanity at ease with nature in a mythic, endless summer that informs so many of Marées's late paintings (cf. his series of polyptychs in Munich) first appears, in rather more specific contexts, in his work from the early 1860s. Paintings like the *Foraging Soldiers* (the finished version of a composition which was developed first in an oil sketch [Meier-Graefe, no. 73] in Vienna) present the theme in the guise of a military subject, which still depends slightly upon the horse paintings of Marées's teacher in Berlin, Karl Steffeck, but perhaps more importantly, upon the currently popular works of Spitzweg in Munich. These paintings further indicate the extent of Marées's involvement with seventeenth-century Dutch landscape genre—an involvement which also developed during his years in Munich.

The technical brilliance of the *Foraging Soldiers,* as expressed in the handling of light and in the security of Marées's painterly draftsmanship, demonstrates just how well he had mastered the naturalist mannerisms of both Spitzweg and a whole host of minor Dutch masters in the years prior to his departure for Rome. In the warmth and unpredictability of his half-shadows and in the flexibility of his handling of color values generally, there is at least the suggested beginning of that intensely serious and self-critical quest to understand the perceptual mechanics of pictorial vision which marks Marées's mature work. But, there is also the suggestion of a definite potential to be overtaken by his own fluency—a potential which Marées himself recognized and which he avoided only by erecting for himself the most formidable formal and technical standards imaginable.

117

[64.] *Self-Portrait with Hildebrand and Grant* (1873)   PLATE 60
Von der Heydt-Museum, Wuppertal

Oil on canvas; 32″ x 32⅜″; unsigned; Inv. no. G. 153; Meier-Graefe, no. 218

As a result of his concentrated study (both alone and in Fiedler's company) of the preeminent painterly traditions of old-master painting—those of sixteenth-century Venice and seventeenth-century Spain and Holland—in the years immediately preceding the Franco-Prussian War, Marées's work just after 1870 began to search in a cautious and rigorously self-critical way for a kind of essential painterliness of its own. What Marées hoped to discover was not so much a style or a formula as a confidence in his own knowledge of how to proceed from the perceptual particulars of nature to both the optical and structural universals of great art.

In 1873, with Fiedler's assistance, Marées obtained permission to do fresco decorations for the new German Zoological Station in Naples. Working there, together with Hildebrand, he had his first real opportunity to test on a large scale the aesthetic validity of what he had so far managed to discover about the possibility of generating monumental art from a combination of clear, architectural design and the pictorially flexible expression of his perceptions of visible nature. For the theme of his decorations he chose to develop, half as allegory and half as paraphrased visual reality, a complex image of human life at the edge of the sea. Using the arcing landscape of the Bay of Naples to unify three of his four walls, he distributed figures of fishermen, peasants, an old hermit, and a group of urban visitors to the seaside to provide a catalogue of the various forms of actual and spiritual intercourse between man and the sea.

The Wuppertal "portrait" of the artist with Hildebrand and their friend, Charles Grant, is in fact a full-scale oil study for a section of the east wall of the Naples frescoes—a section showing these figures and two others grouped around a table in the shade of a pergola. In what is, then, a small detail from a single section of his whole decorative scheme, one can see very clearly how Marées proceeds to state and adjust his microcosmic units of form so that each will echo through its architectonic clarity of shape and rhythm the essentially structural character of his total design. The outlines of his figures are broadened and slightly geometricized, with the result that the forms, both individually and together, are statically secure. The informal forward movement of the center figure of Marées himself is the only break in the almost terrifyingly formal calm of the group. Against this stability and calm Marées models his figures in a comparatively loose, painterly fashion, so that sequences of light and tone have the appearance of deriving from and reexpressing pictorially an instant of real vision. In the tension between the seeming permanence of his architecture of shape and the optical incidentality of his modeling lies the unique quality of Marées's Naples frescoes and of his mature work in general.

118

[65.] *Orange Picker* (1873)   PLATE 62
Stiftung Preussischer Kulturbesitz, Staatliche Museen, Nationalgalerie, Berlin

Oil on canvas; 79⅛″ x 39⅛″; unsigned; *Berlin*, p. 136, Inv. nos. A 1 1024, NG 1222; Meier-Graefe, no. 210. Formerly in the collection of Adolf von Hildebrand.

Like the above "portrait" this picture is a full-scale oil study for a section of the Naples frescoes. The figure of the *Orange Picker* dominates the righthand panel of the south wall. This wall, unlike the other three, presents its figures in the context of a Mediterranean landscape, rather than at the edge of the sea.

In the left panel two women in stylish urban dress sit conversing on a bench in front of a well-groomed stretch of forest. In the right panel a young boy lies nude in the foreground. Behind him an old man turns over the soil with a shovel, while the figure of the *Orange Picker* occupies the right half of the panel. Here, more than anywhere else in the Naples frescoes, the mythic, golden age imagery of Marées's late works emerges, with its impersonal, nude figures formally choreographed in an ideally ordered and productive landscape.

In the Berlin study of the *Orange Picker* the incredible power and concentration of Marées's manner of eliciting pictorial form is apparent. The precisely controlled interplay between flexible, but decisive, contours and a kind of painterly modeling, which seems capable of inflecting whatever degree of relative plasticity, tactility, or flatness Marées desires in one or another area of his figure, is conveyed by the consistently broad and apparently generalizing strokes of his brush. These kinds of contours and brushstrokes continue directly into the frescoes, recalling finally, in their emphatic boldness, the formal and technical certainties of Roman fresco painting in nearby Pompeii.

[66.] *Boys Bathing* (ca. 1874)   PLATE 63
Von der Heydt-Museum, Wuppertal

Oil on canvas; 32″ x 40″; unsigned; Inv. no. G 373; Meier-Graefe, no. 290

The *Boys Bathing* comes, according to Meier-Graefe, from the period in Marées's career just after the Naples frescoes. Hence, the obvious parallels of form and imagery between it and the frescoes in general. Compared to the *Orange Picker,* this picture represents a less completely resolved state of a Marées image—an image which was, in fact, never directly extended beyond the point of this study.

In its sketchy, rather provisional state the *Boys Bathing* presents us with a valuable opportunity literally to see inside the process of Marées's picture making. His simultaneous quest for ideal, equilibrated, individual forms, for a rhythmic unification of these forms in the context of a painted group, and for an appropriately flexible optical means of generating both general and incidental plasticity in his modeling, appears here almost in diagram. Paralleling, as has been noted many times, the tentative and probing formal character of Cezanne's numerous bather subjects, Marées's unfinished images declare very clearly the tense, invariably problematic, yet highly expressive combination of two distinct modes of pictorial vision—one a painter's and one a sculptor's. Marées, in a letter to Fiedler of June 3, 1877, recognized what he felt to be almost a fated necessity to maintain and elaborate this combination. "It seems to have been predestined that I would always be influenced to some extent by sculpture." In the *Boys Bathing* it is at many points almost impossible to sort out sculptural and painterly priorities in one or another of Marées's drawn or painted accents. The most unresolved parts of the image are those where Marées's next move would have required a definite decision of whether to design absolute plasticity or to evoke it optically. In the most resolved sections the decisions have been made in such a way that both pictorial options seem to have been maintained and brought into balance.

ADOLF VON MENZEL
(1815 Breslau–1905 Berlin)

1828: Menzel's father, Carl Erdmann Menzel, establishes lithographic print-ing business. 1830: family moves to Berlin and Menzel studies briefly at the Berlin Academy. 1832: father dies, Menzel takes over printing business. 1833–36: Menzel's first lithographic projects. 1840–42: pen designs for Kugler's *Friedrich the Great*. 1855: first visit to Paris (fourteen days). 1867: second visit to Paris (four weeks). 1868: third visit to Paris (also four weeks). 1873: visits Vienna. Trips to Verona: 1880, 1881, 1883. 1885: named "Chancellor" in the Order "pour le mérite." Honorary doctor's degree Berlin University. Honorary citizen of the city of Breslau. 1895: named to the "True Secret Council" of Prussia. Honorary citizen of Berlin. Named "Knight of the Order of the Black Eagle."

[67.] *The Room with a Balcony* (1845)   PLATE 46
Stiftung Preussischer Kulturbesitz, Staatliche Museen, Nationalgalerie, Berlin

Oil on paper; 23¼″ x 18¾″; signed "A. M. 45"; *Berlin,* p. 140, Inv. nos. A 1 744, NG 845; Scheffler, frontispiece. From the artist's collection.

This is one, and perhaps the best, of a group of paintings of the interior of Menzel's family apartment in Berlin done sometime between 1845 and 1850 (see also, *The Living Room with the Artist's Sister* in Munich and *The Artist's Sister Asleep* in Hamburg). Anticipating similar subjects by Whistler and Degas by over a decade, Menzel is incredibly successful in seeking out self-composing points of view and in discovering the most forceful pictorial abbreviations for expressing them.

In *The Room with a Balcony* Menzel's attention to color values of weak greens, browns, and reds and his fortuitous use of architectural axes and details of interior furnishings bring about an image which is at once intimately in-formal and visually concise. He opposes his angled view into the corner of the room with surface-emphasizing reflections in the mirror and broad patches of paint on the floor and rear wall. His paint handling is highly flexible, searching, and genuinely intuitive, moving easily between passages of detailed description and passages of sheer paintedness. The abrupt cutoff of the image at all sides of the picture recalls similar effects in photography, but here the result is perfectly calculated to express the random emptiness of a private place, minus those for whom it is private.

120

[68.] *View of a Factory Fire* (ca. 1854)   PLATE 47
Private collection, Germany

Oil on cardboard; 8¾″ x 13¼″; unsigned; Scheffler (1922 ed.), p. 59

This is a sort of outdoor equivalent to *The Room with a Balcony*. Like most of Menzel's landscapes (and cityscapes) from the late 1840s and early 1850s it is enormously concerned with the painitng of light effects. Here, in the image of a factory fire at night, the light effects really constitute the subject of the picture. Foreground buildings, trees, and terrain are reduced to diaphanous silhouettes, while Menzel scumbles together orange, black, and gray paint to render the ghostlike image of the burning factory, aglow with heat and spewing smoke and flames of every description. Once again an almost unbelievable rightness of pictorial emphasis is achieved as Menzel sets up his picture in the simplest, most straightforward way and then makes his paint represent as accurately as it can what appears. Nothing seems forced or dramatized in a very conscious way, even though the picture finally harbors a kind of urban-realist equivalent to the constructed and essentially Romantic nature spectacles of Friedrich.

Compared to night pictures by Whistler from the 1870s and later, Menzel's has the feeling of genuine visual discovery, rather than appearing to support preestablished decorative intentions.

[69.] *Théâtre du Gymnase in Paris* (1856)   PLATE 49
Stiftung Preussischer Kulturbesitz, Staatliche Museen, Nationalgalerie, Berlin

Oil on canvas; 18⅜″ x 24¾″; signed lower left "Menzel 1856"; *Berlin,* p. 144, Inv. nos. A 1 981, NG 984; Scheffler, facing p. 24. From the artist's collection.

For this painting Menzel relied on drawings from the sketchbook he took to Paris in 1855 (East Berlin). The result is something of a tour de force of light effects from earlier paintings, like *The Room with a Balcony* and the *Factory Fire.* By the time of the *Théâtre du Gymnase* Menzel had come to the point of being able to regenerate certain effects without actually experiencing them as he painted. This picture seems very real, more completely and documentarily so than comparable subjects from the same date by Daumier or later by Degas. Every aspect of the spectacle of the theater is given a place in Menzel's picture. The viewpoint is calculated to place the orchestra, the boxes, and the stage in equal off-center view. Space is developed (more diagrammatically than illusionistically) through abrupt shifts in the source of light. Because of the bold division of the image into areas of contrasting shape and tone, much of the pictorial conciseness of earlier pictures is maintained, but within each zone the kind of literally descriptive busyness of Menzel's later style begins to emerge. Yet considerable vitality of a truly visual sort exists as well, particularly in Menzel's brilliant development of silhouettes jutting upward from the orchestra into other areas of the picture and in the consistent and effective warmth of the color.

[70.] *King Wilhelm I's Farewell to the Army on July 31, 1870* (1871)   PLATE 48
Stiftung Preussischer Kulturbesitz, Staatliche Museen, Nationalgalerie, Berlin

Oil on canvas; 25¼″ x 31¼″; signed lower right "Ad. Menzel Berlin 1871"; *Berlin,* p. 146, Inv. nos. A 1 323, NG 490; not reproduced in Scheffler

This is the general type of painting that established Menzel's reputation during his lifetime. Compared to the three earlier paintings shown here, it is pictorially diffuse, hard in its effects, and overly concerned with visual documentation at the expense of art. The wealth of bright color and the undeniable energy of Menzel's drawing makes the image impressive, but the descriptive complications are finally so extreme and so small in scale that genuine expressiveness is dissipated into an exercise in craft. One of Menzel's Impressionist contemporaries in France might have found material for half a dozen paintings in a spectacle such as this; but Menzel, acting the role of a "modern history painter," assembles everything into one, carefully documenting numerous particular people through portraits (based on preparatory drawings) in a complicated urban setting at a definite time on the eve of war with France. Individual aspects of the picture seen alone possess qualities which, unfortunately, vanish in combat with the image as a whole. By the time of this painting Menzel has lost the ability to be guided by what he sees. Instead he manufactures an elaborate product from visual raw materials which are important because of what they are, rather than how they appear.

[71.] *The Wall of the Studio* (1872)   PLATE 50
Hamburger Kunsthalle

Oil on canvas; 44⅜" x 31¾"; signed lower right "Menzel Octob 72"; *Hamburg,* Inv. no. 1266; Scheffler, facing p. 192

This is one of two paintings of the wall of Menzel's studio. The first (Berlin) is from 1852. Strangely, the cold, ghostlike fragments of his plaster casts of human anatomy seem to have gripped Menzel more directly than almost any other subject in the last thirty years of his life. In his representation these fragments emerge with a degree of visual presence that is almost terrifying in its impact. The image as a whole seems at once obsessive, almost necrophiliac, despite the apparently random, if not clinically inhuman arrangement of the casts. Groups of plaster heads act out the same kind of silent (but viscerally apprehensible) intercourse in death that appeared earlier in the century in paintings of corpse fragments by Géricault. In the center of the picture the splayed breasts of a truncated female torso hang threateningly above the vicious steel points of two large drawing compasses and a hugely scaled cast of a human hand. The psychoanalytic implications of this tripartite central image, which is surrounded by male heads and a male torso in half shadow, are numerous and complicated—especially so, when one considers the fact of Menzel's puritanical bachelorhood and the recurrent image of his sister in his work from the 1840s and early 1850s.

At this point in his career Menzel found within the walls of his studio the only available outlet for the intimate human passions and fears that had become increasingly concealed beneath the overbearing descriptive mechanics of his mature art. This outlet was made of plaster rather than flesh; but in the long run this was less important than the fact that it was at least there and that it had in one picture, at least, brought the young Menzel back to life.

FERDINAND OLIVIER
(1785 Dessau–1841 Munich)

Early studies with Carl Wilhelm Kolbe. 1802–03: studies with Unger, a woodcut maker in Berlin. 1804–06: Dresden, with young brother Friedrich; friendship with Romantic circle. 1807–09: in Paris with brother Friedrich. 1810: travels in Harz Mountains. 1811–30: Vienna; friendship with Koch and other Nazarenes and Romantics. 1815 and 1817: visits Salzburg. 1816: made member of Brotherhood of St. Luke. 1830: moves to Munich. 1833: becomes professor of art history at Munich Academy.

[72.] *Jesus and His Apostles* (ca. 1840)   PLATE 22
Georg Schäfer Collection, Schweinfurt

Oil on paper; 9⅞″ x 11⅞″; unsigned; Inv. no. 3919; *KR,* no. 105; *RR,* no. 105

Jesus and His Apostles, like many of Olivier's late paintings, seems to be primarily a restatement—much more confident and, therefore, less challenging to the viewer—of most of the premises behind his early work. His friendship with Koch and knowledge of his precedents are evident, both in the careful, successively diminished layers of fore-, middle, and background in the center of the picture, held in check and tied to the surface by framing elements along the edge, and in the somewhat pantomimic separateness of the figures. Like his early drawings, but much less starkly and effectively, the landscape is less naturalistically rendered than constructed of basically similar formal units; these punctuate the rhythmic, distant hills as the figures do the foreground. Olivier's reliance on primarily tonal handling of color (a substitution for the rich variations of gray that work so well in his drawings) serves to integrate these figures into the painting by doing away with the need to draw edges. As well, his granular, slightly fuzzy paint handling (recalling both Koch's early works and his own early training in graphic media) makes them part of a uniform surface texture. Nonetheless, the two foreground groups still seem bodiless, almost transparent—more dreamed into the landscape than observed there.

The content of the imagery derives from Matthew 12:1–8.

FRIEDRICH JOHANN OVERBECK
(1789 Lübeck–1869 Rome)

1806: January, in Hamburg to visit Runge; April, in Vienna; May, enrolls in Vienna Academy under Director Heinrich Füger. 1809: July 10, founding of Brotherhood of St. Luke by Overbeck, Pforr, K. Hottinger, J. Sutter, L. Vogel, J. Wintergerst. 1810: June 20, departure for Rome with Pforr, Hottinger, Vogel; September, residence at Cloister San Isidoro as cloister brothers, or Nazarenes, until autumn 1812. 1812: July, death of Franz Pforr. 1813: April 13, conversion to Catholicism. May 1816–July 1817: frescoes at Casa Bartholdy. 1817–29: frescoes at Casino Massimo. 1831: July–November, travels in Germany (Munich, Heidelberg, Frankfurt, Cologne, Zurich). 1855: second trip to Germany.

[73.] *Italia and Germania* (ca. 1811–69)   PLATE 19
Georg Schäfer Collection, Schweinfurt

Oil on canvas; 8¾″ x 10¼″; unsigned; Inv. no. 3455; *KR,* no. 114, *RR,* no. 111

Because this particular oil sketch is not specifically documented within the history of Overbeck's final version of *Italia and Germania* (Munich), we shall briefly summarize the evolution of the theme and its various embodiments before suggesting a probable position for this sketch within the spectrum.

The painting which Overbeck ultimately designated *Germania and Italia* when he wrote of it to his patron, F. Wenner, on January 31, 1829, was germinated from a drawing made by Pforr some twenty years earlier. That drawing, called *Friendship* (the name Overbeck gave Wenner as an alternative to *Germania and Italia*), showed two seated women, or brides, embracing. One version of this markedly Düreresque drawing, which contained a wealth of traditional symbols of faithfulness and friendship, was emblematically inscribed P(forr), O(verbeck),

P(assavant). From 1808 to Pforr's death in 1812 this rather loose theme became more and more personalized. It was lavishly embellished and came to stand as an emblem for Overbeck's and Pforr's deep mutual interdependence as men and artists. Overbeck conceived the desire that each man should make for the other a painting which would embody the essential beauty and singularity of each one's artistic ideal. Pforr, in a typically idiosyncratic, Nazarene way, personalized these ideals both by his drawing and in his allegorical manuscript, *The Little Book of Sulamit and Maria,* still in Overbeck's possession when he died. Sulamit (the beloved in *The Song of Solomon*)—traditionally a symbol for the Old Testament—was the personification of what Italy and her art meant to Overbeck, fully formed, chaste but passionate—the beauty and clarity of Raphael's art. Maria belonged to the North, with its Germanic heritage of folk wandering, of Gothic Christianity, of legend—the forces which informed Pforr's art. Each woman was to be symbolically the bride of the painter who embraced her ideals; together the two brides celebrated the union of the two dominant forces of Nazarene art.

In the diptych Pforr completed for Overbeck he contrasted Maria, combing her hair alone in a small cell containing many of the household articles used by fifteenth-century Northern painters to symbolize the Virgin Annunciate, with Sulamit, seated in the sunlight in a verdant garden, offering a pomegranate to the child on her lap, while birds and a lamb look on. Waiting at the entrance to the garden is a male figure whose features resemble those of Overbeck. The background is a classical landscape. The polarities between North and South are evident, as are the transforming, or delivering, qualities which the South and Italy were seen to have on the Northerner.

With the exception of the Schäfer oil sketch we have left no traces of exactly what Overbeck's pendant to Pforr's diptych was to look like, although its existence is clearly documented in various diary entries[1] and letters by Overbeck. On October 3, 1811, his diary says that "later I spent a beautiful hour with Pforr in my cell, before the cartoon for Sulamit and Maria." On February 17, 1812, he states that he has "traced the cartoon of Sulamit and Maria and has begun to work it up." After Pforr's death in July of that year there is silence until a letter dated February 15, 1815, mentions that "I would actually like to paint the two brides that I drew for our blessed brother Pforr."[2] He actually did paint the picture almost fifteen years later when he wrote to Wenner in 1829 that his further work has brought him to the conclusion that the two brides should represent a pair of loving women, Germania and Italia, encompassing all his feelings as a German in Italy and all the mutual dependence and respect shared by North and South.[3] The painting which he is describing is now in Munich with a very close replica in Dresden.

There is a large drawing in Lübeck[4] which apparently represents the second stage of Overbeck's work on his project. It bears the evidence of having been

1. Jensen, J. C. *Friedrich Overbeck, Die Werke im Behnhaus,* p. 39, cat. no. 13.
2. Ibid.
3. Neue Pinakothek, Neue Staatsgalerie, München, *Meisterwerke der Deutschen Malerei des 19 Jhr.,* 2, 71, cat. no. WAF 755.
4. Op. cit.

traced (via a carbonlike process applied to the back of an initial drawing) and is quite finished. (Overbeck frequently worked by transferring an outline drawing and then finishing it.) However, this drawing shows the two figures seated under a Renaissance arch and is very close in almost all respects (e.g. contours, layout of folds, specificity of the wreathes, etc.) to the Munich painting. In short, as it stands it does not appear to represent Sulamit and Maria. Jensen points out, though, that under the drawing of the arch a group of figures can be detected. There is a priest and a garlanded young man with the facial features of Pforr. Behind them is a view of a city. Here, then, replaced by the arch, was the bridegroom, Pforr, come to claim his Maria. With the exception of the cloth of honor behind the women, we have the same basic composition as in the oil sketch.

When, then, was the oil sketch made? Did Overbeck, sensing the imminence of his friend Pforr's death, make a hurried oil sketch for him to see what the picture would look like? This is conceivable, yet we are tempted to doubt it on the basis of his carefully worded desire "to paint *(malen)* the two brides he had drawn *(gezeichnet)* for Pforr" (1815). Also the cloth of honor and the ledge separating the two brides from the figures behind seem to suggest a certain distance, or displacement, from the actuality of a wedding scene.

It seems logical that the arch was added to the Lübeck drawing at the time Overbeck decided finally to make the picture Wenner had commissioned in 1815. Perhaps he toyed with the idea of using such a Renaissance setting for his *Germania and Italia* before opting for the open wall and ledge. Our oil sketch could have been made, hastily drawn, then painted alla prima at that time to record for his own private memories what was to have been his love gift to his friend Pforr had he lived. This might well explain the similarity of the ledge and church building in the sketch to those in the Munich picture. According to Jensen, the Nazarenes in general do not become interested in the inclusion of patterned and highly decorative elements (like the cloth of honor) in their paintings before the decade of the thirties. But, also according to Jensen, Overbeck's oil sketches do not become really free and loosely painted before the fifties. Hence, we can imagine that this oil sketch might have been made very late in Overbeck's life; that it was purely a memory picture made by an old man regretting and reliving his youth in much the same way as, on his deathbed, he relived his own emotional responses to Pforr's final dying gift of his own *Sulamit and Maria* to him.

FRANZ PFORR
(1788 Frankfurt–1812 Albano)

Early studies with his father, Georg Pforr, a horse painter (characterized by his own contemporaries as a "German Wouverman"). 1801: Kassel, studies with his uncle J. H. Tischbein. 1805: visits Frankfurt; friendship with Passavant. 1803–07: at Vienna Academy; close friendship with Overbeck. 1809: July, founding member of Brotherhood of St. Luke. 1810: to Rome and Cloister San Isidoro. 1811: visits Naples. 1812: July, dies of consumption.

[74.] *St. George Killing the Dragon* (ca. 1810–12)   PLATE 18
Städtische Galerie, Frankfurt

Oil on canvas; 11⅛″ x 8½″; unsigned; Inv. no. SG 419

This painting is neither dated nor signed, but has been placed in Pforr's Roman period because it seems to have more in common with the slightly angular figures and modeling and the medievalized landscape setting of Pforr's *Sulamit and Maria* (Schäfer Collection) than it does with the painterly, late eighteenth-century draftsmanship he learned from his father and uncle Johan Tischbein.

The subject matter of *St. George and The Dragon* seems a logical compromise between Pforr's inclination toward medieval and narrative themes and Overbeck's insistence on religious pictures. The style of the painting demonstrates the clarity, delicacy, and decisiveness of Pforr's mature draftsmanship and his tendency to organize forms in fairly large, simplified patterns of bright colors, in the manner of medieval manuscript painting. (He was a collector of early Northern woodcuts and chronicles.) Unlike Overbeck, Pforr continued to cling to fifteenth-century traditions despite the proximity of high Renaissance exemplars in Rome. Hence, the compact, rounded arcs of the horse's body and the decorative particularization of St. George's armor recall the frescoes of Paolo Uccello. Pforr died at such an early age that we cannot speculate about the eventual path his art would have taken; but the gentle narrative sweetness and the rhythmic vitality of forms in *St. George* indicate the high level of quality he was capable of achieving.

JOHANN ANTON RAMBOUX
(1790 Trier–1866 Cologne)

Early studies with the Benedictine, Abraham zu Florenville. 1812: Paris, studies with David. 1815: Munich. 1817–22 and 1829–41: in Rome; friendship with Nazarenes; collector of Italian primitive paintings. 1843: becomes conservator of Wallraf'schen Sammlung (which in 1861 becomes Wallraf-Richartz Museum). 1862: publication of *Katalog der Gemälde alteritalienischer Meister (1221–1640) in der Sammlung des Conservator J. A. Ramboux.*

[75.] *Rebecca and Elieser at the Well* (1819)   PLATE 21
Stiftung Preussischer Kulturbesitz, Staatliche Museen, Nationalgalerie, Berlin

Oil on panel; 9⅞″ x 12½″; signed on back "Gio: Ant. Ramboux fece nel 1819. Roma. rappresenta il corso nel Tevere apresso la fontana del aqua accettosa"; *Berlin*, p. 172, Inv. nos. A 11 726, NG 1671

While it is clear that Overbeck, Cornelius, and the other Nazarenes depended primarily upon the art of Raphael, Michelangelo, and later Italian masters, it should not be forgotten that much of the initial impetus behind Nazarenism and the writings of Tieck, Wackenroder, Schlegel, and others derived from a late eighteenth-century rediscovery of Gothic art. Ramboux is the only painter of his generation (except Pforr who died young) who, in Italy, held fast to the actual first principles of Nazarene Romanticism. He collected and made copies of Italian primitive pictures and based his small output of original paintings almost wholly upon quattrocento styles.

With the exception of fleeting references to Michelangelo in a few figure poses, like the seated figure on the left which recalls the Sistine prophet Jeremiah, *Rebecca and Elieser at the Well* reminds us of the work of Fra Angelico in its smallness of scale, delicacy of drawing, and use of clear, jewellike colors. Ramboux seems to have a genuine quattrocento involvement with gentle biblical narrative, exotic imagined landscape (although, in this case, the desert's topography is based upon an actual bend in the Tiber River above Rome), and strange, foreign creatures. He brings these together with an obviously sophisticated ability to render space and to articulate figure groupings in a way which charges the whole scene with a kind of power and vitality seemingly beyond its tiny size.

FERDINAND VON RAYSKI
(1806 Pegau, Saxony–1890 Dresden)

1814–16: grows up in the house of Count Friedrich von Beust in Dresden. 1821: enters military service in Royal Cadet Corps, Dresden. 1823: Dresden Academy. 1825–29: second lieutenant in Saxon Grenadier Guard at Ballenstedt. 1831–34: returns to Dresden Academy. Admitted to Saxon Kunstverein. 1834–39: travels to Paris, also visiting Trier, Frankfurt, Munich, Düsseldorf. After 1840: in Dresden, patronized by the most eminent Saxon and Prussian families.

[76.] *Portrait of Count Haubold von Einsiedel* (1855)   PLATE 51
Stiftung Preussischer Kulturbesitz, Staatliche Museen, Nationalgalerie, Berlin

Oil on canvas; 29¼″ x 24⅞″; signed "F. v. R." with emblem of dog's head; *Berlin*, p. 172, Inv. no. A 1 956, NG 1005; Walter, no. 791. Formerly in the collection of Adolf Graf von Einsiedel.

Rayski painted three generations of the Einsiedel family, beginning in 1837 with a portrait of Count Carl von Einsiedel (Walter, no. 447) and ending with a portrait of Helene Sahrer von Sahr, born Countess von Einsiedel (Walter, no. 750), in about 1875. The portrait of Count Haubold von Einsiedel, along with one of his father, Count Alexander von Einsiedel (Walter, no. 560), was painted in 1855, two years after a portrait of his mother, Countess Friederike von Einsiedel, born Baroness Blome (Walter, no. 738). At the time Rayski painted him, Haubold was between nine and ten years old. He died thirteen years later; Rayski painted a memorial image of him (ca. 1868) for the Church of Friedersdorf (Saxony), *Count Haubold von Einsiedel as the Angel at the Grave of Christ* (Walter, no. 29).

Rayski's personal connections with the Einsiedel family seem to have been closer than with any other of his major patrons. His portraits of various members of this family are of a uniformly high order of quality and involvement. The portrait of Haubold is the best of the group and quite possibly Rayski's masterpiece. It is painted with a forceful directness of pose and a manner of paint handling which derives its particular energy from the personality of the sitter, rather than seeming self-generated and pyrotechnical. Graff's style (cf. pl. 2) provided the source for Rayski's brilliant, painterly development of the figure and for the freshness of its flesh tones and grays, while Rayski's knowledge of French art—particularly of Géricault—sponsored the taut, psycho-

127

logically expressive presence which the image finally possesses. Walter lists a second portrait of Haubold from 1857 (Walter, no. 793).

ALFRED RETHEL
(1816 Diepenbend, Aachen–1859 Düsseldorf

1827–29: studies in Aachen under J. B. I. Bastiné. 1829–36: works at Düsseldorf Academy under W. von Schadow. 1836–47: further study at Städelsche Kunstinstitut (Frankfurt) under Philipp Viet. 1840: wins competition for decorations in Rathaussaal in Aachen, does not begin work there until 1847. 1842: visits Dresden. 1844–45: in Italy. 1846: briefly in Berlin. 1847: returns to Aachen. 1851: Aachen frescoes finished. 1851–52: in Dresden again. 1852–53: in Rome. After 1853: severe mental illness.

[77.] *The Harkort Factory on Burg Wetter* (1834)   PLATE 45
DEMAG–AG, Duisburg

Oil on canvas; 17⅛″ x 23⅛″; unsigned

Very little is known about this picture. Its subject matter, like that of Blechen's *Rolling Mill* from the same period, is quite surprising and wholly different from Rethel's better-known historical subjects which carry out the predominantly Nazarene values of his work in general. What pictures like this one demonstrate most clearly is the subcurrent of painterly naturalism that distinguishes Rethel from other second-generation Nazarenes such as Schwind. Schadow was Rethel's first master; and this fact, at least, begins to explain how a picture like that shown here was able to happen. The half-Nazarene, half-naturalist bias of the Düsseldorf Academy during Shadow's reign as director permitted both landscape and history painting to flourish. Not only did both flourish, but a considerable mutual influence and interdependence developed as well, so that Düsseldorf landscape (Schirmer's, for example) is very dramatic, almost histrionic in conception, while Düsseldorf history painting relies (far more than that of Cornelius or Overbeck) on careful oil studies of figures made directly from models rather than generated from pure style. In order to make room for this naturalism (at least in individual figures) Schadow's own work is more open and baroque in its structure than most other Nazarene painting. Particularly in the years prior to his move to Frankfurt and his work with Viet, Rethel followed the naturalist precedents and implications of Schadow's work even more thoroughly than Schadow himself.

In his painting of this imposing new factory complex on what was apparently the site of an old citadel. Rethel found an ideal naturalist vehicle for an imposingly constructed and brilliantly pictorialized "historical landscape." The image of the factory looms as impressively and as romantically as a medieval castle—its sheds and smokestacks ominously punctuating the skyline, its smoke recalling some ancient siege. The factory is set into a deep, theatrical (almost Poussin-like) space. Its details are carefully delineated, but its color is contrasting and resonant against the distant sky. Light is handled very crisply, so that everything remains hard (and Nazarene-like) in its definiteness, while at the same time participating in the dramatic luminarism of the painting as a whole. The image is finally a beautifully wrought, appropriately historiated attempt to deal with one of the increasingly prominent aspects of a modern world which Nazarene art in general studiously avoided confronting.

PHILIPP OTTO RUNGE
(1777 Wolgast–1810 Hamburg)

Early education from Kosegarten. 1793–99: Hamburg; works with Herterich and Hardorff d. Ä; brother Daniel begins art dealership. 1799–1801: at Copenhagen Academy, works with Jens Juel. 1801: May, to Greifswald to visit Friedrich; enters Weimarer Kunstfreunde competition; arrives in Dresden; friendship with Graff, Tieck, and Goethe. 1803: visits Hamburg in November; visit to Weimar. 1804: meeting with Rumohr; spring, marriage to Pauline Bassenge; moves to Hamburg. 1806: January, visited by Overbeck. Summer 1806–April 1807: in Wolgast; publication of engravings of *Four Times of Day*. 1808: summer, begins painting *Morning*, after work on sketches since December 1806. 1808–10: work on *Farbenkugel*, published early 1810.

[78.] *Self-Portrait in a Brown Coat* (ca. 1809–10)   PLATE 4
Hamburger Kunsthalle

Oil on oak panel; 19⅛″ x 18⅞″; unsigned; *Hamburg,* no. 1005

This is the latest of Runge's five self-portraits (if we count *We Three,* destroyed in 1931, which depicted Runge's wife and brother, Daniel, as well). As records of himself through his eight to ten years of making pictures they are no less diffuse and discontinuous than the overall group of paintings produced. They seem to partake of the same essential weakness—that of being sometimes polemical and definition-oriented—while presenting the same strength, an ability to engage acutely, almost challenge, the viewer.

If we allow the fresh paint handling, but nonetheless systematized flat, high-value lighting, and faceted, almost chiseled, modeling of Runge's early painting style to be suggested by Graff's *Portrait of Bause,* we can perhaps determine some of the changes in pictorial intention that evolve during Runge's short career. It should, however, be remembered that Runge for most of his life depended on incisive, sharp contours far more than did Graff.

The portrait shown here has surrendered this dependence on contours for a more atmospheric and less intense light. Highlights and shadows are now stroked over the flesh in a series of curved rhythms, with the result that the artist's own rather fleshy sensuality is effectively rendered. This, combined with the intensity of his eyes and the slightly sardonic expression conveyed by his petulant lips and raised eyebrow, offers the same kind of obtrusive, almost rude, challenge to the viewer that we find in much of Correggio's work. Runge had recently received from his friend Klinkowstrom a copy of Correggio's *Night* (Dresden) and was obviously thinking about that painter (March 1809: *HS, 1,* 173). The image type in his *Self-Portrait* seems directly to reflect another Dresden Correggio, the *Madonna with St. George* where St. George, with his semireligious, semisexual appeal to the viewer, invites us with much the same profile and glance.

129

The development that occurs in the course of Runge's mature art is much the same in type, if not in specific dependencies, as that which happens to Nazarene art in Rome—a gradual surrender of essentially Northern linear modes of expression (in Runge's case informed as well by the hard neoclassicism of the Copenhagen Academy, and the softer eighteenth-century Frenchness of Graff's art) to the swelling forms and basically optical definition of Italian art, whose tendencies toward idealism were held in check by Runge's almost visceral fix on nature.

[79.] *Morning* (large version) (ca. 1808–10)   PLATE 5
Hamburger Kunsthalle

Oil on canvas (segments of whole painting cut apart 1890; remounted, 1927); 60⅞″ x 45⅛″; unsigned; *Hamburg,* no. 1022, see discussion for indication of all preliminary studies for this; and *Hamburg,* no. 1016 for first painted version and its studies.

Runge's initial drawings of the *Four Times of Day* were finished by the end of March 1803 *(HS, 1, 36)*. Stylistically these represent his recent involvement with the flatly separated darks and lights of Copenhagen neoclassicism and his still current interest in the decorative, wiry contour drawings of Flaxman and the botanical specificity and rhythmic aliveness of Dürer's engravings, especially the marginalia in his *Prayerbook for Maximilian,* recently republished. The drawing of *Morning* shows a lily growing up from the bare, cloud-shrouded earth to blossom forth a group of putti kneeling and dancing under the morning star (cf. upper portion of painted version). From the lily's stem, drooping back to the earth (to whom they offer flowers) are four more buds on whose stems sit music-making putti. Despite the smallness of scale, delicate linearity, and pre-ponderantly verbal, rather than pictorial, imagery of the drawings, Runge in-tended for them to become monumental room decorations, working together as four basic ideas within a totality—the structure of a symphony. He dreamed that they were, as Tieck said they were, "the union of mathematics, music, and color, securely described in huge flowers, figures and lines" *(HS, 1, 36)*. It is essentially correct to see the next five years of Runge's art and life as a seeking out, only semiconscious but intuitively driving, of the pictorial and symbolic abilities to make the four little drawings monumental, universal, and many-sided enough to achieve their intended destiny.

130

At the time of his death the search was not yet ended and the final version of his *Morning* remained an aggregate of only partially explored visual ideas and formless, almost too universal to be verbalized, imagistic longings. The conten-tual idea of *Morning* was beginning, birth, newness—interpreted within almost every mythical system known to man. Letters concerning the drawn *Four Times of Day* are replete with biblical imagery of the Creation. The central image in the frame decoration for the 1803 *Morning* is a sunburst containing the Hebrew word, "Jehovah." Combined with this is Runge's desire to bring into being a new art—landscape—in which men can see themselves mirrored in natural phenomena and, through contemplation of the essentially human within plant life, be brought to recognize anew the paradise God made around them and be-come aware that in all men is the image of God *(HS, 1, 24)*. As the artist, Runge, himself becomes the creator, or at least the interpreter, of God's presence on earth at this moment, his picture not only explains the beginning, but is a beginning. Hence the formal relationship between the final painted version shown here and Michelangelo's *Last Judgment*, which to Runge represented the final flowering of the old art, in which men were depicted only as the mirrors of their times.

However, as Runge grew away from Tieck and the neo-Catholicism of Romantic Dresden he found that his two dominant imagistic inclinations—a pantheistic view of nature on the one hand and specifically Christian mystical symbolism on the other—began to draw apart. After 1803 there are no more paintings in which both religious and pantheistic interpretations of a concept are mixed together. What the Child means in the *Rest on the Flight* (1805, Hamburg)—"the Child will be the most lively element of the picture and His own life will be seen to be a new beginning affecting the world in front of Him"[1]— is essentially the significance of the baby in the *Mother and the Source* (1804, destroyed 1931), but the image systems of religion and nature are distinct. The child in *Morning* means this too, in yet the differing image system of Greco-Roman mythology. Mythology in general provided for Runge a way in which both natural phenomena and the existence of the higher spirit which motivates them could be expressed simultaneously.

Given the incredibly inchoate collection of interpretations of the concept of *Morning* which dominated Runge, it is no wonder that the picture itself is so diffuse. Because no one system could contain it, no single pictorial idea could inform it. We have already discussed in the Introduction the success of Runge's large portraits, which derived their impact from the concentration Runge put into the act of seeing and then managed to achieve again with equal intensity during the process of rendering, and we have acknowledged the decorative and synesthetic harmonies of the drawn *Four Times a Day*. Both try to coexist in the large *Morning*, propped up by a certain reliance on other people's ways of making their art successful. (In Runge's letters after 1806, at the time that Tieck is replaced as companion and mentor by the painter Klinkowstrom, we find an ever-increasing tendency to look and think critically about other paintings.) Aurora, who in earlier painted versions of *Morning* is no more than a sculptural caryatid for the lily, becomes finally a real figure. She owes her presence to the Greek sculpture in Dresden that she is drawn from,[2] but gains her vitality and such power as she has an organizing force for the picture from Runge's realization of exactly how much impact Michelangelo's figure of Christ has in both the image and pictorial system of the *Last Judgment*. The children surrounding the baby derive their plasticity and fleshlike, living actuality from Runge's close attention to how Correggio modeled figures to make them seem so human. The specificity of flower types comes both from Runge's own powers of observation and his correspondence and exchange of drawings with the doctor-botanist Gustav Bruckner.

It is the baby, feeling the sun and squirming with joy in the meadow, which

131

1. Letter, 10 May, 1805, in *The Romantic Movement*, Tate Gallery; catalogue entry for the *Rest on the Flight*.
2. Gunnar Berefelt, *Philipp Otto Runge, Zwischen Aufbruch und Opposition*, pls. 100–01.

represents most fully the singularity and power of Runge's own art. As in the *Hulsenbeck Children* (Hamburg), we have that combination of incisive drawing and heightened modeling and color usage which makes almost hyperreal that which Runge has seen with such involvement and intensity that he cannot set it down without exaggeration. In this one small detail where child, flowers, and light are made vital, living parts of the continuing life cycle of nature by the artist's intensity of seeing and believing in what he sees, we sense what Runge perhaps realized too late, that if he painted what he saw was there he could, and did, make it mean what he knew it meant.

The painting was a glorious failure and Runge knew that, asking as he lay dying that his brother Daniel destroy it. But the pieces are there and with them perhaps is the beginning of a knowledge that Friedrich already had—that what one may think or imagine to be components of a spiritual or mythic world are only faint shadows of what one can, and must if he would paint, see in the world of nature.

LUDWIG SCHNORR VON CAROLSFELD
(1788 Königsberg–1853 Vienna)

Early studies with his father Hans Veit Schnorr von Carolsfeld. 1804: moves to Vienna; at Vienna Academy under Füger; acquaintance with pre-Roman Nazarene group, Olivier brothers, and Koch. 1811: brother Julius Schnorr von Carolsfeld comes to Vienna Academy. 1818: Austrian kaiser buys his *Faust* for 2500 gulden. 1821–23: first teacher of Moritz von Schwind. 1834: travels to Munich, Tirol, Switzerland, and Paris. 1835: member of Vienna Academy. 1837: travels to Dresden, Weimar, and North Germany. 1841: assistant curator of Belvedere Gallery, Vienna. 1843: becomes chief curator.

[80.] *Leap from the Rocks* (1833)   PLATE 23
Georg Schäfer Collection, Schweinfurt

Oil on panel; 29⅝″ x 17⅝″; signed lower left with monogram "18 LS 33"; Inv. no. 1935; *KR,* no. 172; *RR,* no. 161 and p. 15

Like Ferdinand Olivier, Ludwig Schnorr was a Nazarene by inclination and association, though he never went to Italy. His early works primarily concern biblical and literary themes, relying usually upon details of costume and/or romanticized, visually onomatopoeic landscapes to infuse his paintings with the inner life of Teutonic fairy tales. *The Leap from the Rocks* was conceived as an illustration for *Der Kränzelbusche* by Friedrich Kind. This poem, with an engraving after Schnorr's original drawing, appeared in *Huldigung der Frauen,* a pocketbook for the year 1825 published by J. F. Castelli. Both the poem and the painting concern the traditional right of the lord of the land to claim as his own the young women of his domain during their first night of marriage—a right which was not revoked in Austria until 1848. The combination of Kind's poem and the complementary imagery of his libretto for Weber's *Der Freischütz* (first performed, Berlin, 1823) provided Schnorr with the impetus to boil down all the Romantic, religious, and hazily republican ideals of his generation into one arch-Nazarene pictorial triumph.

The form of Schnorr's painting represents for us the Northern elements of the

Nazarene aesthetic—Germania, uninformed by the architectonic, spatially conceived monumentality of Italian art. The organizing pictorial force of *The Leap* derives from linear elegance and decorativeness. The vitality of the painting (and its implicitly sexual theme) results primarily from its all-encompassing, centrifugal surface rhythms which move outward from the organic, flowerlike complexities of the maiden's bridal dress. Her chaste, bodiless union with her lover, elegantly circumscribed by long, slow contours, is contrasted with the evil, staccato aliveness of the squire (with sword erect) and his lunging dogs. In the best tradition of Northern narrative no detail is too small to go unelaborated; every branch, weed, and rock surface responds vibrantly to the painting's dominant rhythms. Color, too, has the deep resonance of Northern manuscript illumination and seems to amplify the tone of the narrative very considerably. Schnorr's painting wholeheartedly bears witness to the power and the validity of that which the Nazarenes in Rome wanted to retain as at least half of their art.

CARL SCHUCH
(1846 Vienna–1903 Vienna)

1865–68: student at Vienna Academy under Ludwig Halauska. 1868–69: travels to Italy with Albert Lang. 1870–72: in Munich. 1870: meets Trübner. 1871: meets Leibl. 1873: to Italy, later works with Hagemeister. 1874: travels to Austria, Holland, and Belgium; works with Hagemeister and Trübner. 1875: travels to Italy again. 1874–76: mostly in Munich. 1876–82: in Venice. 1882–94: in Paris. 1894–1903: in Vienna. After 1875: works mostly on still life subjects.

[81.] *Still Life with Leeks* (ca. 1883–84)   PLATE 85
Niedersächsisches Landesmuseum (Städtische Galerie), Hannover

Oil on canvas; 24¼″ x 30⅜″; signed on back "Schuch"; Inv. no. KM 1912/165

My still lifes present me with all the pressure of reality. There is distance, air and the darkness of space. My objects all possess the strongest local color, out of which derives a contradiction, since local color is one thing close up and another, when it appears more distant. It is tone (relative color value) which expresses the latter, since local color is too hard and loud. What is this tone other than the modification that local color undergoes through the coincidence of light and distance? Doesn't tone perhaps have its own force? This is worked out in practice, since that is where one finds answers. Absolute light and absolute dark are the extremes of tone, and both tend to destroy local color and plasticity as well. From this one must conclude that he who wants to paint with greatest strength and plausibility excludes tone necessarily, and, conversely, he who wants to paint tone must necessarily permit ambiguities of plasticity and local color (Wolf, pp. 81–82).

This is a free translation of part of a letter from Schuch to Hagemeister. It verbalizes a basic perceptual and conceptual dilemma of Munich realism and finally proposes that in the "meaning of tones" lies the aesthetic essence of things, rather than in their definite and definable material appearance. Tones, conveyed by cautiously applied patches of brushwork become the trademark of Schuch's art. In order to honor them exclusively he abandoned the tenser combinations of experienced and expressed plasticity and painted flatness that continued to mark the more ambitious and more qualitatively successful efforts of Leibl and Thoma, neither of whom could decide quite so precisely where the limits of what they did finally lay.

MORITZ VON SCHWIND
(1804 Vienna–1871 Niederpöcking am Starnberger See)

1818–21: student of philosophy at Vienna University. 1821–23: studies art with Ludwig Schnorr von Carolsfeld and P. Kraft at Vienna Academy; friendship with Schubert, Grillparzer, and Olivier brothers. 1827: visits Munich. 1828: moves to Munich; briefly studies at Munich Academy under Cornelius. 1832–38: paints frescoes in Tieckzimmer of Munich Residenz (recommended by Cornelius). 1834: returns to Vienna. 1835: March, to Italy—Venice, Padua, Florence (for one day), Ferrara, Bologna, Rome (with Nazarenes and Cornelius), Naples; October, returns to Munich. 1836: frescoes in Munich Festsaalbau and in Schloss Hohenschwangau; returns to Vienna. 1840–44: Karlsruhe. 1844: professor of history painting at Städelsches Kunstinstitut, Frankfurt. 1847: professor at Munich Academy. 1854–55: frescoes in the Wartburg. 1857: travels to London and Manchester. 1866–67: frescoes in Vienna Opera House.

[82.] *Portrait of the Singer Caroline Hetzenecker* (1848)   PLATE 24
Germanisches Nationalmuseum, Nuremberg (on loan from the City Art Collection, Nuremberg)

Oil on canvas; 49⅛″ x 38″; unsigned, marked middle right, "München 1848"; Inv. no. ST. N. GM 704; Weigmann, no. 279

While the bulk of Schwind's art concerns itself with a mythical cast of knights, nymphs, and anchorites, drawn from Nordic saga or Greek, Roman, or medieval legend and history, his portraits (outside of his immediate family and occasional patrons) generally represent the people concerned with keeping that mythology alive—theater people, opera singers, the composer Franz Schubert, and other music makers and poets. Caroline Hetzenecker was a principal singer in the Munich Opera before her marriage and is celebrated frequently in Schwind's art at this time. In a series of eight drawings and watercolors he shows her costumed for her most famous roles (Weigmann, nos. 260–61); then, in another, he depicts all of Munich's music lovers paying homage to her, with Mozart, Glück, and Handel looking on (Weigmann, no. 259). The fact of her marriage was noted by a rather wistful drawing of *Hymen Taking the Singer Caroline Hetzenecker from the Stage* (Weigmann, no. 277) while a final tribute is paid her by his *Symphony,* where she is the lead singer in the predella of what is basically an altarpiece illustrating Beethoven's *Phantasie for Klavier, Orchestra, and Choir* (Weigmann, nos. 283–87).

Schwind, a second generation Nazarene, demonstrates here, as in most of his work, a basic preference for the Nordic rather than Italian pictorial values of the Nazarene aesthetic—a preference which emerges generally in Nazarenism, once the primary impetus of Italian art itself is removed. Like his teacher, Ludwig Schnorr, he relies upon decorative and linear elaboration to bear the burden of pictorialization, sometimes stressing the complexities of narrative, at other times evolving into abstracted rhythmic designs in which contours and color harmonies are mutually interdependent. In this picture his achievement is one of elegance and majesty, phrased by an almost musically articulate series of geometric arcs and angles that weld the portrait image and its attendant attributes into a compelling, simultaneously human and mythical entity.

MAX SLEVOGT
(1868 Landshut, Bavaria–1932 Neukastel, Pfalz)

Childhood in Würzberg. 1885: moves to Munich where he studies at Munich Academy under W. Diez. 1889: travels to Paris. 1889–90: travels to Italy. 1898: travels to Holland. 1890–1900: in Munich regularly. After 1896: illustrator for "Jugend" and "Simplisissimus." 1900–01: in Frankfurt. 1901: moves to Berlin. 1913–14: travels in Egypt. 1914: paints war pictures from the German front lines at the beginning of World War I. 1917: named director of master class at Berlin Academy and lives chiefly at his country house in Neukastel. Member of Berlin, Munich, and Dresden academies.

[83.] *Portrait of Gertraud Fuchs as a Child* (1903) PLATE 102
Staatsgalerie, Stuttgart

Oil on canvas; 30⅞″ x 25⅝″; signed lower right "Slevogt 03"; *Stuttgart*, p. 173, Inv. no. 2579; Imiela, p. 377

The collector, writer, and art historian, Eduard Fuchs (1870–1940), had been a friend of Slevogt's since 1893. In three separate portraits of Fuchs, his wife, and his daughter from 1903 to 1905, Slevogt honored this friendship in what may well be the most successful run of work he ever achieved. Like Corinth in his *Rumpf Family,* Slevogt was driven by the very fact of his friendship to press for unique characterizations and to forge with utmost care and sensitivity the pictorial means for achieving them. Unlike Corinth he did not work with the family as a group, but as three personalities, expressed formally and psychologically in three distinct ways. The composite character of Slevogt's art at this time —its consistent emulation of Manet (an emulation first expressed in paintings of animals from the Frankfurt Zoo in 1900–01), its responses to Liebermann, Corinth, and Edvard Munch—was for once an advantage, since it enabled him to seize immediately upon exemplars capable of providing formal guidelines to aid in the expression of the psychological values he intended in each separate portrait.

For the portrait of Fuchs's young daughter, Gertraud—the first of the three portraits—Slevogt relied directly upon Manet, and the image recalls specifically the best of his (Slevogt's) Frankfurt Zoo pictures from two years before. The flat and vigorously cross-hatched patchiness of his brushwork, the brilliant whites, flesh tones, and bright reds combine to give the sitter a very definitely pre-adult optical (as opposed to psychological) presence, while the fixed stare of the eyes and the delicate, slightly *Jugendstil* nervousness of the drawing of the hair clearly suggests an at least latent femininity. What distinguishes the image from Manet is the slightly forced and unfeeling showiness of Slevogt's brushwork. It possesses a cursive freedom that Slevogt has assumed, more as a claimed artistic right than as a true by-product of his own personal and self-informing sense of artistic significance.

[84.] *Frida Fuchs* (1904)   PLATE 103
Staatsgalerie, Stuttgart

Oil on canvas; 36⅞″ x 29⅝″; signed upper left "Slevogt 04"; *Stuttgart*, pp. 173–74, Inv. no. 2578; Imiela, p. 378

For the portrait of Fuchs's wife Slevogt simply elaborates the feminizing complexity of his drawing with paint (which was already apparent in the *Gertraud*), concentrating on the outstretched fan held across the subject's lap and on the frilly intricacy of the tracery of her dress, as well as on her hair. He makes a notable contrast between the optical lightness of his treatment of the subject's pink dress and a slightly heavier, more modeled rendering of her face. Across the set-back right side of the figure, passages of shadow are diagrammed by clearly marked shifts in tone, and the image as a whole becomes more somber, introspective, and psychologically elaborate than the portrait of Gertraud. The pose of Fuchs's wife in semiprofile (perhaps recalling from a distance the many similar poses of Nanna by Feuerbach) itself initiates and supports an image which abandons the iconic frontality of *Gertraud* and settles back more thoughtfully into a shallow pocket of pictorial space.

Once again Manet's influence is pronounced, but the graphic busyness of Slevogt's paint handling stands in partial (and unresolved) opposition to the bold patches of more densely impasted light and dark tones that recall Manet. Unlike Manet, Slevogt does not move very directly or easily from drawn edges to patches of color- and tone-bearing paint. His transitions never feel natural, either from an illusionistic or from a purely formal standpoint. What one feels in an image like this is the, at times unfortunately tenuous, balancing of purely painterly and purely draftsmanly impulses in Slevogt's work. In this picture the forceful characterization of the subject tends to override demonstrably unsuccessful resolutions of one or another pictorial accent, but Slevogt did not always manage to conceal his formal superficiality this successfully.

[85.] *Eduard Fuchs* (1905)   PLATE 101
Staatsgalerie, Stuttgart

Oil on canvas; 72⅛″ x 28⅛″; signed lower left "Slevogt 1905"; *Stuttgart*, p. 174, Inv. no. 2576; Imiela, p. 378

136

The portrait of Fuchs himself is in many respects the most successful of the group of portraits of the Fuchs family. For this portrait Slevogt has adopted certain elements from the contemporary portraiture of Corinth and Munch, as well as continuing to employ aspects of style that derive generally from Manet. The looming and slightly quivering silhouette of the figure set ambiguously against a rather stark background recalls Munch directly, while the rhythmic echoes of the figure's outer contours into the brushwork of the background make this recollection even more precise. Yet the upper torso of the figure breaks outward from its silhouette and seems to move into the viewer's more immediate physical presence; and, here, the energetic modeling of black, earth, and flesh tones definitely suggests the influence of Corinth. However, Slevogt's brushwork itself finally avoids the compelling energy of Corinth's, stressing instead a kind of surly optical removal, presumably more in keeping with the formal discipline of Manet, or at least of that part of Manet which Slevogt was able to understand. This quality of removal is, oddly enough, more apparent in Slevogt's painting of Fuchs's face than it is, for example, in the area of the lower hands and arms, where a truly Corinth-like urgency momentarily appears. The whole of Slevogt's image finally focuses on the movement of the hands, and particularly on the left hand as it probes for a manuscript which it seems about to present to the viewer. What Slevogt has done is to make physically present that which Fuchs literally produced—namely, his writings—while his personality withdraws into what is for the period a conventionally "psychological" image of human frailty and self-consciousness.

[86.] *Portrait of a Woman* (1905)   PLATE 104
Bremen Kunsthalle

Oil on canvas; 56⅞" x 36⅞"; signed lower right "Slevogt 1905"; Inv. no. 45; Imiela, p. 378

This portrait, tentatively identified by Imiela as Dr. Grete Ring, attempts to combine several of the separate qualities of Slevogt's portraits of the Fuchs family. Like the *Eduard Fuchs* it features a Munch-like, all-enclosing, and rather nervous silhouette, and it cuts off the figure at roughly knee level. Like the *Frida Fuchs* it dwells in a painterly fashion on the textural intricacies and delicacies of the subject's costume—here a gray fur jacket and a veil drawn down across her face. But, unlike the Fuch's portraits, this one concentrates on the rendering of close color values of blacks, blues, and grays in a way which recalls Liebermann in portraits like the *Bürgermeister Petersen*. More than any other of Slevogt's paintings shown here, this portrait displays the undeniable attractiveness of his most characteristic work and its ability to use a wistful, physically appealing sitter, stylishly dressed, as an armature for the display of his truly considerable, if secondhand, painterly finesse. Without being either totally superficial or honestly self-critical, Slevogt contents himself with evoking a kind of monumental charm.

CARL RUDOLF SOHN
(1845 Düsseldorf–1908 Düsseldorf)

A member of the artistically eminent Sohn family of Düsseldorf. His father,   137
Karl Ferdinand Sohn, was a prominent local academician and a favorite teacher of Feuerbach's. Carl Rudolf studied painting primarily with his cousin (and brother-in-law), Wilhelm Sohn, at the Düsseldorf Academy and later privately, after having spent several years (1863–66) preparing to be an engineer at the Polytechnikum in Karlsruhe. He traveled extensively in Italy and visited London and Paris—finally receiving portrait commissions from the English royal family, as well as from various members of the French and German nobility. He married Else Rethel in 1873.[1]

---

1. Biographical information from *Katalog der Düsseldorfer Malerschule,* currently in preparation by Dr. Irene Markowitz.

[87.] *Portrait of Else Sohn-Rethel* (1873)   PLATE 66
Kunstmuseum, Düsseldorf

Oil on canvas; 42⅞" x 34"; signed lower right "Sohn jun. 73"; Inv. no. 4370

Else Sohn-Rethel was the wife of the artist and the only daughter of the painter, Alfred Rethel. She was for a time a singer in the Niederrheinische Musikfestspiele and, along with her mother, an enthusiastic patronness of contemporary Düsseldorf painting. Begun shortly before her marriage to Carl Sohn, this portrait was based initially on a portrait photograph. It was completed after the wedding with the sitter actually posing in the studio. The portrait was praised enthusiastically by local critics when it first appeared, and it stands as one of the very best of Sohn's pictures.

The qualities of the portrait derive far less from its originality than from its sensitive management of a period portrait style which is half-Düsseldorf and half-French in essence. The pose clearly recalls earlier Düsseldorf portraiture—Leutze's *Herr Lottner* for example—but the aristocratic bearing of Leutze's figure type has been deflated, at least slightly, as a result of influences from France. The contemporary portraiture of Carolus-Duran appears to have been instrumental in modifying precedents like Leutze's and in encouraging Sohn to hold fast to a wider range of seemingly real appearances (in particular those yielded so graphically by photography) and to rely less on the support of more traditional portrait conventions. With its free reference to Ingres, Courbet, Manet, and photography, Carolus-Duran's style was a very attractive alternative to the norms that had prevailed for roughly three decades in Düsseldorf.

Sohn tried in this portrait of his wife to combine a Düsseldorf formality of pose (and attendant somber richness of coloration) with a contemporary Parisian comprehensiveness of vision and flexibility of accent. The image which results is unquestionably convincing in the sense it makes of this combination. The portrait head is incredibly delicate and present. The figure, clad in a tightly corseted black dress, is imposingly shaped and quietly responsive to the basic axes and shapes of the background against which it appears. It is almost Degas-like in its total effect and not unlike Degas in the elements of style it stresses in achieving its effect.

CARL SPITZWEG
(1808 Munich–1885 Munich)

138

Originally a pharmacist by profession. 1833: begins to study drawing and painting with C. H. Hanson in Munich. Thereafter largely self-taught; makes many copies of seventeenth-century Dutch pictures. 1840: travels to Italy. 1849: visits Prague and influenced by J. Návratil and J. Mánes. 1851: visits Paris; most impressed by works of N. Diaz and J. Constable. After 1852: generally in Munich. Friends include Schwind. Many secondary artists form a circle around Spitzweg and emulate his work. 1860: copies an early painting by E. Isabey, *Women Swimming at Dieppe,* while it was on exhibition in Munich (for this copy see Berlin, p. 206, inv. no. NG 1025). 1868: honorary member of Munich Academy.

[88.] *In Peacetime* (1856)   PLATE 64
Städtische Kunsthalle, Mannheim

Oil on canvas; 8⅝″ x 19⅞″; signed lower left with monogram; Inv. no. 136; Roennefahrt, WVZ no. 789

Both of Spitzweg's paintings shown here are variants of subjects which the artist treated many times in slightly altered forms. Like many other of his most autographic subjects, they present lone figures seen in isolation in a natural setting. In one or another treatment of each subject anecdotal content is alternately expressed in quite literal terms or, as in the two paintings shown here, given a more generalized expression.

The figure of the sentry in time of peace is one of Spitzweg's most typical vehicles for his characteristically mild, essentially sympathetic poking of fun at the *comédie humaine* of small, provincial, Central European towns in the middle of the nineteenth century. In many of his portrayals of this subject he illustrates the slightly comic boredom and general "unpreparedness" of this presumably watchful figure; but in the Mannheim picture he stresses the almost flaglike dignity and heraldry of the sentry's formal pose against the ruined battlement of some ancient fortification, behind which hangs the rather less dignified (if equally flaglike) detail of a clothesline, billowing with laundry set out to dry in the sun and wind. As an image expressing at once traditional military decorousness and at the same time the old-fashionedness (and the seeming remoteness) of war, Spitzweg's picture is movingly understated.

In strictly pictorial terms the painting seems very naturalistic, both in its graphic rendering of details and in its painterly (and contrast-oriented) treatment of bright, outdoor light and color. Yet this naturalness is clearly as much the result of stylistic borrowings from slightly earlier sources in France as it is based on real observation. This does not, however, compromise the undeniable pictorial conviction of Spitzweg (at least in this picture). The silhouetted setup of the figure, towering above the battlement and making, with it, a truly monumental image in a very small painting, is Spitzweg's personal achievement and it is very impressive.

[89.] *Sunday Afternoon* (1873)   PLATE 65
Georg Schäfer Collection, Schweinfurt

Oil on wood; 8⅝″ x 11⅞″; signed lower left with monogram; Inv. no. 62225315; Roennefahrt, WVZ no. 1280

This is one of the last versions of Spitzweg's figure of the village parson strolling through his parish. Earlier versions frequently show the parson witnessing one or more of his parishioners, engaged either straightforwardly or slightly humorously in some form of daily routine. The wandering, sympathetic, and all-observing parson frequently seems to be a kind of autographic figural substitute for Spitzweg himself. In the Schäfer picture the parson (and the artist) appear on the threshold of old age. Somehow Spitzweg's image of the parson moving alone along the path toward the dark of the forest conveys in universally comprehensible terms (nearly as compelling as Friedrich's) the acquired wisdom of old age and the resigned acceptance of the approach of death.

The inviting softness and quiet of Spitzweg's setup of the landscape and his rich treatment of interpenetrating zones of sunlight and shadow are instrumental in generating the psychological warmth of the painting's late afternoon mood. The delicate, softly stroked lightness of his painterly touch and the now quite unconventional naturalist conviction of the pictorial language of his artistic maturity combine to produce an image that seems perfectly just in its calibration of visual means to both formally and psychologically meaningful ends.

HANS THOMA
(1839 Bernau–1924 Karlsruhe)

Early studies as lithographer in Basel; jewelry and watchcase painter in Furtwangen. 1858: Karlsruhe Kunstschule, studies under Descoudres, Schirmer, and Canon; spends summer in Bernau with his family. 1867: moves to Düsseldorf Academy. 1868: spring, to Paris with Otto Scholderer; autumn, teaches at Karlsruhe Kunstschule. 1870: winter, to Munich; friendship with Leibl circle, Victor Müller, and Böcklin. 1874: winter, to Italy; meets Marées in Rome. 1876: autumn, in Frankfurt; shares atelier with Steinhausen; paints frescoes in Frankfurt and Schweinfurt. 1877: marries Cella Bertender, takes permanent residence in Frankfurt. 1890: reputation expands as a result of Munich Kunstverein Exhibition. 1899: director of Karlsruhe Gallery, professor at Kunstschule. 1909: Thoma museum in Karlsruhe opened for his seventieth birthday. 1909: publication of *Im Herbst des Lebens*. 1919: publication of *Im Winter des Lebens*. 1824: Thoma retrospective in Basel and Zürich shortly before his death. Various trips to Italy: 1874, 1880, long stay in Rome; 1886, visits Hildebrand in Florence; 1892, Venice; 1897, general travel in Italy again.

[90.] *Head of a Woman* (1862)   PLATE 72
Kunstmuseum, Düsseldorf

Oil on herringbone canvas, doubled; 20″ x 16⅛″; signed lower right with monogram "H Th 1862/Karlsruhe in der/Kunstschule gemalt" (signature was added later and the background was apparently retouched); *Düsseldorf*, no. 4182; Thode, p. 6

Thoma's years at the Karlsruhe Kunstschule were, in general, typical of any mid-century German academic study. One of his teachers was J. W. Schirmer, a Schadow student and painter of somewhat Blechen-like landscapes who had already taught Böcklin in Düsseldorf. Another teacher, more influential according to Thoma, was Hans Canon, who first introduced to the students at the Kunstschule the basically old-master technique of modeling by laying lights over a dark ground. It was in his work that Thoma apparently first sensed the conflict between style and naturalistic inclinations that informs so much of his own later work.

Almost all of the studies of heads made by Thoma in the painting class at the Kunstschule work by building a bust portrait up in light tones on a darkish, neutral ground. Rarely are the sitters' clothes articulated; instead their usually dark silhouettes are employed to enhance the plasticity of the heads themselves. Much of this plasticity derives from Thoma's work at copying casts, his success-

140

ful education in academic modeling. This study, however, is far more human, more psychologically aware than many of them and owes much of its immediacy and actuality to Thoma's acute observations of his sitter and his careful rendering of what he saw. Unlike other studies from this time, he has kept to a minimum his tendency, borrowed from Canon's work, to systematize modeling into a series of patterns. We are reminded, by the still evident reliance on academic techniques, by a rather pearly type of coloration, and by its stark aptness of observation, of Böcklin's early portrait of his wife, Angelica (1863, Berlin).

[91.] *Portrait of the Painter Wilhelm Steinhausen* (1869)   PLATE 74
Staatliche Kunsthalle, Karlsruhe

Oil on canvas; 30⅝″ x 41⅝″; monogram upper right "H Th 1869"; Inv. no. 1486; Thode, p. 23

This portrait was painted almost a year after Thoma and Scholderer were in Paris. While there are distinctly French references in other of Thoma's works from this period (cf. *In the Sunlight*, Karlsruhe [Thode, p. 21], and the *Wedding Party*, Frankfurt [Thode, p. 20]) few of them so successfully combine the type of pictorial grace learned from the French with Thoma's own highly individualized sense of layout and his incisive observation. This is probably one of the best pictures that he ever painted. As in his early studies, he relies on a neutral background to provide an impetus toward plasticity in the figure. But now the figure's decorative shape is as important as its relief and, as in much later pictures, Thoma uses the leaves and the very linear shape of the chair to provide a frame for the intricacies of its contours. The paint handling is simultaneously broad and loose (according to Steinhausen, Thoma worked with a palette knife[1]) and incredibly soft, seemingly more haze than substance. It is not the rather raucous building material that Courbet interpreted it to be; nor, despite its restriction to a group of values within one basic hue, the slightly fussy substance with which the Barbizon painters worked. In short, Thoma's Frenchness here reaches out beyond the circle of people he admits to being influenced by ("Millet, Rousseau, Corot and so forth, and above all . . . the stormy revolutionary Courbet" [*Im Herbst des Lebens*, p. 36]). The soft modeling and restriction of hues, the abraded edges slightly haloed with light, and the poignancy of the silhouette remind us of the work of Fantin-Latour, especially of his 1867 portrait of Manet (Chicago Art Institute). It is during this period that Fantin was very influential among the Impressionists, and it is clear that Scholderer knew him, at least by 1870, when he was included as one of the group in Fantin's *Studio in the Batignolles Quarter* (Louvre).

141

[92.] *The Rhine near Laufenberg* (1870)   PLATE 75
Stiftung Preussischer Kulturbesitz, Staatliche Museen, Nationalgalerie, Berlin

Oil on canvas; 22¾″ x 18⅜″; monogram lower right "H Th 70"; *Berlin*, p. 211, Inv. nos. A 1 100, NG 1172; Thode, p. 27; cf. Thode, p. 209 for later (1883) view of Laufenberg.

This is one of a group of four views of southern Rhine towns made shortly

1. *Hans Thoma und Sein Kreis* (Karlsruhe, 1961), cat. no. 8.

before Thoma went to Munich. In its size and steep vertical layout, due primarily to the viewer's position high on a hill overlooking the river and medieval town, it is a pendant to the view of Rhinefelden (Thode, pp. 26–29).

Thoma refers to himself at one point as a born realist. "I will paint nothing but what I myself have seen, yes, what I have lived; that which I (can) see before me is beautiful enough" *(Im Herbst des Lebens,* p. 34). However, he does not mean by this the type of realist ambitions pursued by Courbet, but rather a much more universal, albeit distinctly fuzzy, Friedrich-like conception that reality derives simultaneously from the visual world and from the inner spiritual life of the artist. "It is not the subject that gives the picture artistic worth, but rather it is perception, the sum of demonstrable intuitions that speak through the work" *(Herbst,* p. 32).

Given feelings such as these, we are not surprised by the frequently Romantic —in a Dresden sense—cast of his landscapes. Although we feel that every building in Laufenberg is accurately counted and described and that there is a hill overlooking the town exactly where Thoma says there is, we sense an almost insurmountable distance between the two closely knit, communing figures and the urban setting which they observe and discuss. In the manner of Friedrich the figures are seen as closed silhouettes—somewhat more incidental to be sure, but no less chained by their humanity. Sunlight sparkles across the rooftops and sharply edges the figures as it does in the best of Carus's work, and the whole has an eerie, nonatmospheric, and dreamlike presence.

[93.] *Self-Portrait* (1871)   PLATE 73
Hamburger Kunsthalle

Oil on canvas; 42⅛″ x 31″; monogram lower left "H Th 1871"; *Hamburg,* no. 1544; Thode, p. 35

Thoma's self-portrait, the earliest of the seven he was to paint, presents us with a different aspect of his work than either of the two other portraits shown here. While the *Head of a Woman* presents itself as an unusually talented, youthful exercise in painting and the *Steinhausen* seems to gain its success from Thoma's obvious harmony and empathy with his sitter, this self-portrait, like all of them, appears to be a rather polemical presentation of himself, a statement of what being an artist means, in the same context as Böcklin's many views of himself. Although Thoma painted no more self-portraits after 1899, both his books present much the same aphoristic, very centralized and structured self-image that we find in the paintings.

142

With the exception of his rather staring, intense eyes and his carefully rendered right hand—the essential implements of his art that are described throughout the self-portraits (cf. Thode, p. 424, for his 1899 *Self-Portrait* in Frankfurt, where his right hand is bent and tense, the hand of an old, weakening man)—the image is rather stenographic and flat within closed contours, against an indefinite landscape background. We are reminded of photographs from the 1860s and 1870s and of the relentlessly neutral backgrounds behind much portraiture in both France and Germany during the sixties. At the same time, this type of close-to-the surface, nondescriptive foliage and sky background anticipates the overtly decorative backdrops which Böcklin, Marées, and Thoma himself were to employ effectively in their later portraits.

The Rhine near Säckingen (1873) PLATE 76
Stiftung Preussischer Kulturbesitz, Staatliche Museen, Nationalgalerie, Berlin

Oil on canvas; 25⅞" x 45"; signed lower right "Hans Thoma 1873"; *Berlin,* p. 212, Inv. nos. A 1 851, NG 1031; Thode, p. 62; cf. Thode, pp. 29, 62, 68, 178, 198, 320, for other views of Säckingen which Thoma often visited. *The Rhinetal near Säckingen* (Thode, p. 198) is a virtual duplication of the picture shown here, with a large tree added on the left and the family group replaced by three dryly silhouetted, almost Millet- (or Seurat-)like figures and three cows.

In the three years that have passed since his *View of Laufenberg* Thoma has softened the quality of his brushwork and hazed his edgy drawing, thereby achieving somewhat more atmospheric, hence believable, landscape effects; but he is still more involved with the poetic than the realistic qualities of the scene before him. The foreground, carpeted with lush, white flowers is inaccessible to the viewer, placing him at a properly contemplative distance. The figures are not necessarily germane to this particular moment in time, but universal—closely related to Millet's peasants. They could very easily be intended to suggest a flight into Egypt, in any one of four centuries' concern with that particular theme.

Rather than relying on the Romanticism of Dresden painting, or referring to the type of visual empiricism current in French Impressionism, Thoma here seems to be working in sympathy with the pastoral quietude of the Barbizon painters. We are reminded of several aspects of the work of Daubigny, especially his broadly extended, horizontal formats and his loosely brushed, tonal paint handling, shot through with sudden accents of primary colors to provide figural emphasis and a further degree of visual animation.

[95.] *The Weed Sower* (1888) PLATE 77
Städtische Galerie, Frankfurt

Oil on paper; 30" x 38⅞"; monogram lower left "H Th 88"; Inv. no. SG 95; Thode, p. 281; cf. Thode, pp. 288, 337, 347, 490, for variants.

The Weed Sower presents us with an excellent example of Thoma's late, proto-*Jugendstil* decorative manner. As in his frescoes and large religious pictures, there is a compressed middle ground of space, while foreground articulation and background design, even the incisively drawn contours of the figures themselves, serve to emphasize the picture's inherently two-dimensional, decorative qualities. We are reminded of the arborlike settings and rigorously wall-respecting design of Marées's frescoes. At the same time the vitality of the twisted, linear rhythms recalls the mythic works of Moritz von Schwind, which Thoma would have known in Munich.

As an image, *The Weed Sower* represents the somewhat theosophical confluence of Christian imagery and Greco-Roman mythology in Thoma's late work. The same lithe, angularly moving figure will appear again in 1890 as the devil tempting Christ (Thode, p. 327) and in 1907 as one of two rain gods symbolizing November (Thode, p. 490). As a sower of weeds he is almost always painted at approximately the same chronological moment as the figure of a single bowman or a group of nymphs, implying some kind of nonverbal family relationship. Apparently, for Thoma, he represents a pantheistic allegory of

143

temptation, or the planting of evil (cf. Thode, p. 337, where the image is in fact entitled *The Evil Sower*).

WILHELM TRÜBNER
(1851 Heidelberg–1917 Karlsruhe)

1867–68: art school in Karlsruhe on the advice of Feuerbach. 1869: to Munich, enrolls in Munich Academy; sees Leibl's and Courbet's work in International Exhibition. 1869–70: to Stuttgart to study with Hans Canon. 1870: returns to Munich and studies with W. von Diez. Meets Schuch. 1871: summer, with Schuch in Bernried; Leibl visits for several days. 1872: back in Munich, meets Thoma and other members of circle around Leibl. Shares studio with Thoma in summer; travels to Italy with Schuch in the fall. 1873: travels to Holland with Schuch. 1875–90: regularly in Munich. 1879 and 1889: visits Paris. 1884–85: London. 1895: moves via Heidelberg to Frankfurt to teach at Städelsche Kunstinstitut. 1903–17: professor at Karlsruhe Academy. 1917: named to position in Berlin Academy, but dies before taking it up.

[96.] *Boat Landing on the Herreninsel* (1874)   PLATE 78
Staatliche Kunsthalle, Karlsruhe

Oil on canvas; 16⅝″ x 22⅝″; signed lower right "W. Trübner"; Inv. no. 2006; Wolf, p. 186, mentioned

In this early landscape Trübner makes an extremely successful resolution of qualities gleaned from his two current exemplars, Leibl and Thoma. The latter's influence predominates at this point, leading Trübner to a pure, landscape subject, related in type to Thoma's Rhein and Main landscapes of 1870–74. But, if the overall rendering of the scene recalls Thoma both in aspect and in the brightness of its color values, the more ordered quality of Trübner's brushwork reflects Leibl.

What is uniquely Trübner's in the picture is the impulse toward the forceful design of individual shapes. Despite the painterly breadth of the brushwork, every landscape element is sharply, almost starkly defined. The character of Trübner's shapes is tougher and less decorative than that of Thoma's, but it is comparably two-dimensional in impact. It refuses to yield its surface tautness in favor of any truly atmospheric development of color. Near and distant elements are equally definite in their shapes. Yet, the color remains somehow fresh and sensuous in spite of this, perhaps as a result of the novel practice of painting landscape out-of-doors at this early stage of Trübner's career. Shapes, too, have a more unpredictable character than Trübner will permit later in his career. The meandering track of the boat landing is unquestionably one of the most spontaneous and convincing passages Trübner ever achieved.

[97.] *Lady in Gray* (1876)   PLATE 79
Museum Folkwang, Essen

Oil on canvas; 42½″ x 37¼″; signed lower left "W. Trübner"; *Essen,* no. 198, Inv. no. G 188; Wolf, p. 189

As Thoma's influence predominates in the *Boat Landing,* Leibl's comes to the

144

fore in the *Lady in Gray* and in most other of Trübner's figure paintings from the 1870s. The impression of Leibl's *Frau Gedon* (Munich) which Trübner first saw in the International Exhibition of 1869 remained firmly fixed in his mind; and in this picture it contributes directly to the substantial success he achieves. However, as in the *Boat Landing*, Trübner is enormously concerned with both general and internal shapes in his image. His brushstrokes seem arranged around preestablished units of design rather than conveying, like Leibl's (or Schuch's), a direct response to observed color values. This is not to say that Trübner is inattentive to color values, but, rather, to suggest that he tends to schematize (and to generalize) them in order to keep his brushwork essentially consistent in appearance and responsive to the demands of his design. Without actual drawing and also without much definite illusionistic emphasis on the textures of his sitter's costume, Trübner implies both with his systematized brushstrokes. There is a definite tour de force aspect in his development of this brushstroke system and in his ability to keep it intact, while simultaneously seeming to express what he sees. Compared to the discipline of Leibl's contemporary "hard style," Trübner's systematized brushwork supports a similarly bright range of colors and a comparable desire to achieve predictable refinement. Yet, there exists a busyness and a kind of self-conscious haughtiness in Trübner's work which derives from a growing confidence in theoretical, rather than aesthetic, justifications for what he does.

Superficial appearances notwithstanding, there seems relatively little direct relationship between Trübner's work from the 1870s and that of Manet. In conversations during the mid-1880s Corinth found Trübner generally ignorant about Manet. However, Trübner certainly knew something of Manet's work, even before his first visit to Paris in 1879. He had seen it, at least in passing, in the International Exhibition of 1869 and in later exhibitions in the Munich Glaspalast. He must also have heard it discussed by Leibl and Thoma; but he seems almost to have avoided confronting it directly, perhaps because he feared that it threatened (through its greater sensuousness) the purity of his own system of painting.

[98.] *Frauenchiemsee Landscape* (ca. 1890)   PLATE 80
Von der Heydt-Museum, Wuppertal

Oil on canvas; 20¾″ x 26⅜″; signed lower right "W. Trübner"; Inv. no. G 80; not mentioned in Wolf

145

This is one of a group of landscapes made in the Chiemsee area between 1890 and 1893 (see Beringer, pls. 58–63). Beringer's plate 58 shows the same motif as the Wuppertal picture seen from a different direction. The landscapes of this period make pictorial sense of the prevailing painterly harshness of Trübner's mature style. In pictures such as the *Frauenchiemsee Landscape* the truly aesthetic instincts of the earlier *Boat Landing* appear once again in conjunction with a more extended palette. Shapes retain (and perhaps even increase) their firmness of definition, but the variegated textures and tones of landscape force Trübner to stretch his system of painting to encompass a somewhat wider range of descriptive effects than usual.

On the basis of pictures like this, one can understand Liebermann's continuing appreciation of Trübner's art. Somehow it remained modern and alive almost in spite of itself. High-value colors become increasingly prevalent in Trübner's later work; a stentorian clarity (and a kind of airlessness) of vision prevails. Intervals between color values are jarring, almost metallic, in their impact, while the design of basic pictured shapes becomes angular and at times almost intentionally ugly—particularly when compared to the proto-*Jugendstil* rhythms of Thoma's late style. Trübner's pictures are increasingly flat in the last three decades of his life, but they are flat for the same optical reasons as those of the mature Liebermann.

FRITZ VON UHDE
(1848 Wolkenburg, Saxony–1911 Munich)

1866: briefly studies at Dresden Academy. 1867–78: military service. Field action during Franco-Prussian War (occupied the studio of the French painter Charles Jacques for one night). Later stationed in Dresden, Borna, and Leipzig. Achieves rank of brigade adjutant. After 1871: studies painting with L. A. Schuster. 1876: travels to Vienna to study with H. Makart. 1877–79: lives in Munich, studies with K. von Piloty, W. von Diez, and W. von Lindenschmidt at Munich Academy. Meets F. von Lenbach and advised to study Dutch painting in Alte Pinakothek. 1879–80: moves to Paris on the advice of M. von Munkácsy. Meets Liebermann. 1882: in Holland (Zandvoort) working under Liebermann's influence. 1880–1911: generally in Munich. 1893: one of the founding members of the Munich Secession.

[99.] *Young Woman at the Window* (ca. 1891)   PLATE 99
Städtische Galerie, Frankfurt

Oil on canvas; 32¼″ x 26¼″; signed lower left "F. v. Uhde"; Inv. no. SG 632; Rosenhagen, p. 110

As has been demonstrated many times, the lone figure, posed looking out of a window, is one of the archetypal subjects of nineteenth-century painting. Uhde's version of the subject is one of the last, but it recalls, in its comparative simplicity and directness, Friedrich's of 1815 (Nationalgalerie, Berlin) which, whether Uhde knew it or not, was to all intents and purposes the first. Uhde, like Friedrich uses the middle ground window to divide the picture in both two and three dimensions (and to provide an interior frame), but he does not reinforce axial symmetry by his placement of the figure. As a result, his image as a whole becomes less discomforting and his expression of psychological isolation (or estrangement) less cogently abstract. The "meaning" of Uhde's image is, by Friedrich's standards, presented very literally in terms which are, for the period, distinctly social realist, albeit politely so. The unoccupied chair and sewing machine are quite clearly the, perhaps commercial, perhaps housewifely, bonds which alienate the female figure from a purer and freer existence in nature, which stands just beyond her window and by implication beyond her grasp. Her alienation is as practical and definite in its roots and causes as that of Friedrich's figure is spiritual and intentionally universal in its significance. Uhde's image is finally sentimental where Friedrich's objectifies a category of pure feeling. In a later variant of this picture (Rosenhagen, p. 173) Uhde added yet another layer of specifically sentimental meaning to the image by recasting the figure as an abandoned mother, bent over, crying at her sewing table with her young daughter beside her.

Pictorially, the image is one of the more convincingly straightforward of Uhde's generically "Impressionist" works. While too clever and too self-certain in its overall design, the painting reflects, in its careful attention to color values in the interior of the room and in the broadly brushed, brightly colored landscape beyond, the salutary influence of Liebermann. At the same time it contains definite reminiscences of earlier German naturalist painting, such as Carus's *On the Elbe near Dresden,* in its use of the figure as a pictorial transition between interior and outdoor light.

[100.] *The Artist's Daughters in the Garden* (1901)   PLATE 100
Städtische Galerie, Frankfurt

Oil on canvas; 54⅞" x 60⅝"; signed lower right "F. v. Uhde 1901"; Inv. no. SG 81; Rosenhagen, p. 238

The case for Uhde as an important painter (rather than simply a maker of large-scale, sentimental illustrations) can best be argued on the basis of his numerous (roughly fifteen) paintings of his family—usually of his daughters. These paintings increase in their quality and frequency during the last decade and a half of Uhde's life, although the earliest of them were painted in the late 1880s. In the Frankfurt picture from 1901 the daughters (three of them) appear almost fully grown and in a garden setting with the family dog. The prototypes for this picture are numerous—that of Monet's *Woman in a Garden* (Paris, Louvre) is probably the most important, but those of Liebermann (such as the *Terrace of the Restaurant Jacob* or the *Papageienallee*) were probably more direct in their influence upon Uhde. In the closeness of Uhde's viewpoint and the resulting large scale of foreground figures (set in half-shadow) one is reminded of Corinth as well.

What is most impressive about Uhde in paintings like this is his ability, after years of relatively eyeless and mindless technical fluency and cleverness, to confront himself with truly challenging pictorial situations. The odd, slightly clumsy nature of the shapes of his foreground figures, the difficult intervals of space between foreground and background which result from his viewpoint, and the richness of effects of interacting color and light all achieve their pictorial realization in a truly personalized and affecting way. Brushstrokes are alternately coarse and delicate and they succeed generally in remaining true to Uhde's perceptions, rather than stressing virtuosity per se. The final image is optically less strict than comparable Liebermanns (and less concise) and it is less physically urgent than comparable Corinths. However, it is ambitious by any standards, and its qualities are sufficient to make one lament the very real talent that was denied a direct voice in so much of Uhde's work.

147

FRIEDRICH WASMANN
(1808 Hamburg–1886 Meran, Tirol)

1824–28: Dresden Academy, studies with Hans Naeke. 1829: summer, to Munich via Lübeck and Harz Mountains; November, enrolls in Munich

Academy. 1830: August, in Meran. 1831: travels in southern Tirol. 1832–35: in Rome; good weather spent mostly in the *campagna,* Tivoli, Olevana, Subiaco, etc., and on coast, often with Hamburg painter, Janssen. 1835: April, conversion to Catholicism, induced by Overbeck; July returns to Meran; November, to Munich until 1839. October 1839–1843: Meran and Bozen. Summer 1843–46: Hamburg. (Winter 1845: in Munich and Meran.) 1846: June, marries Emilie Kramer; August, to Munich, then permanent residence in Meran.

[101.] *Etschtal with Two Children on a Hill* (1831)   PLATE 31
Niedersächisches Landesmuseum (Landesgalerie), Hannover

Oil on paper mounted on panel; 8⅛″ x 14¼″; signed and dated on back "Friedrich Wasmann Etschtal, 1831"; Inv. no. PNM 575; Nathan, no. 264. There is an oil sketch in the Georg Schäfer Collection *(FR,* no. 278), another in Hamburg. There is a chalk drawing for the children and a further large charcoal drawing also in Hamburg.

Besides the various sketches for this oil, Wasmann made from it a large charcoal layout (Hamburg) for a genre painting which apparently never materialized. His ambitions for both are implicit in the changes he made between one early oil sketch (Schäfer) and the completed version shown here. There are three children in the Schäfer sketch, two talking together, the third gazing at the viewer who is invited visually into the scene by the accessibility of a broad, open area in front of the rocky hill. The male figure is a gentle guardian for the children and a bent, softly arced shape enclosed within the area of the large rock. Wasmann's paint handling is loose and sure, relying on the paint surface and essential rightness of moves made by his brush to describe what he saw.

The larger painting shown here was changed to a more static format, dependent as much on careful compositional organization as on the rendering of nature. Apparently Wasmann, after two years in Dresden (1826–28) was impressed enough by the imagistic potential of his sketch that he felt within himself the possibility of producing a Dresden-type "picture-of-the-life-of-the-earth." Hence, in what seemed to be the pictorial manner of Friedrich, he brought the massive, rocky shape of the hill close to the foreground and made it inaccessible to the viewer. The children were depicted as lone, isolated silhouettes. The old man, who had been a comfortable part of the original setting, was turned profile to the viewer and made jagged and tense. He was clothed in a hat, as Friedrich's men almost always are to complement their already evident disjunction from nature. To enhance his imagery Wasmann borrowed from the styles of Carus and Dahl the mannerism of lining edges with light to emphasize foreground silhouettes and their differing atmospheric intensity from the background.

While the picture fails to evoke much of the emotional response that is called forth by Friedrich's nature emblems, we are enchanted visually by its clarity of color, the transparency of the sunlit leaves in the foreground and the soft blue haze in the mountain valleys. We appreciate Wasmann's simultaneous rendering of atmospheric distance and the acutely observed flowers and rock textures nearby. It is further development of these aspects of his style and not his slightly self-conscious aspirations toward meaningful imagery which makes the best of his later landscapes as high in quality as they are.

148

[102.] *Garden of Flowers in Meran* (ca. 1840)   PLATE 32
Hamburger Kunsthalle

Oil on paper mounted on cardboard; 16″ x 13⅝″; unsigned; *Hamburg,* no. 1399; Nathan, no. 248

The painting shown here is a rerun about ten years later, of a small painting made about the same time as the *Etschtal.* The earlier canvas (Nathan, no. 132) is almost bare of painted surface texture and is geometrically conceived; its hard, blue sky and red roofs remind us of Nazarene landscapes. The woman and two children facing the viewer in the foreground are seemingly stenographic notations, oddly out of scale and inconceivably distant—emblematic rather than described attendants in the garden. A border at the painting's base serves to remove the picture almost completely from a realm of description into a realm of ideality. We are reminded of Olivier's landscape in *Jesus with his Apostles.*

The late picture shown here feels closely dependent on reality. Though Wasmann reused his earlier subject, he worked by establishing himself anew on the balcony (perhaps a few feet to the left) and painting what he saw. The woman and the dog, perhaps, are leftovers, added without having been seen; all else is immediate and freshly rendered. Ten years and the differing demands of a sketch (or purely visual rendering) from those of a composed picture, have wrought quite a change in Wasmann's style. No longer does his brush tend to dwell only on small details, counting the leaves of a bush or dotting a rock with separate spots of color. Instead his hand moves freely, less in the manner of a precise draftsman. Here, as in the finest of his oil sketches of mountain landscapes, we sense an "Impressionistic," almost Liebermann-like (cf. *Beach at Scheveningen)* handling of paint. Although his brushstrokes and the whole scale of the painting are small, it is the flowing liquidity of the paint itself which is being used to shape images, build roofs and towers, and render contours of hills and valleys when they occur. There is an unmistakable one-to-one relationship between the visual sensations received by the painter's eye and the physical moves required to set them down in paint. The mind as an interpreter and image maker is at rest.

[103.] *Portrait of Frau Maria Lun (Bust of a Young Lady)* (1841)   PLATE 29
Niedersächsisches Landesmuseum (Landesgalerie), Hannover

Oil on canvas; 12⅛″ x 9⅝″; signed lower right "Wasmañ f. 1841"; Inv. no. PNM 574; Nathan no. G 36. See Nathan nos. G 44 and G 45 for pendant portraits of Alois Lun (Maria's husband) and his second wife Rosa Maria.

Alois Lun was a wine merchant in Bozen. His wife Maria died in November 1840, so this portrait of her is a memory picture, perhaps started as her sickness became obviously grave, perhaps painted completely from cameos or other image records after her death. The fern she holds presumably symbolizes death; but Wasmann has made the point of her absence from our world more poignant by his arrangement of the contours of her face. Rather than seeking a closed, smooth outline, as was his usual habit, he permitted a jarring disjunction between the contours of her chin and of her hair. In order to complete visually the implicit oval of her face we must imagine her turning away from us, into the non-world of the picture space. The halo of pentimenti surrounding her head indicates that Wasmann worked long and hard to place it exactly.

Wasmann characterized his portrait style as "a type of old-German manner" (Nathan, p. 22), which this portrait, in its large-scale presentation of the figure and its rich pictorial embellishment, exemplifies. However, there is little attention to actual facts of facial structure under the even lighting and undifferentiated paint surface; nor are there any of the stresses on physical individualities that we would find in the best of fifteenth- and sixteenth-century German portraits. Wasmann's hard, brittle line reminds us less of old German drawings than of Cornelius's incisive pen draftsmanship or the geometricizing pencil lines still evident under the lightly brushed paint surface of Overbeck's *Italia and Germania*. Even the casual sweep of the paint arabesque used to fudge the problem of making Maria Lun's hand actually emerge from her sleeve seems related to Overbeck's sketch style. Further, Wasmann has used, behind Maria Lun, the flat-sided pitched-roof buildings and towers of a Tyrolean monastery in the same way as Overbeck used the schematized rural pre-Renaissance church to signify Italia's Catholic homeland. Many of Wasmann's genre pictures owe their inspiration directly to Overbeck and overtly exhibit the same type of hardness and lack of conviction that is implicit in this portrait. On the whole, Wasmann's old-German manner seems less dependent on any real confrontation with fifteenth- and sixteenth-century German pictures than on the way Overbeck interpreted and idealized that style.

[104.] *Dr. Adolf Wasmann* (1843)   PLATE 27
Hamburger Kunsthalle

Oil on mahogany panel; 13⅛" x 10⅞"; signed lower left "Wasmañ f. 1843"; *Hamburg*, no. 1395; Nathan, no. G 69

[105.] *Frau Caroline Luise Mathilde Wasmann* (ca. 1843)   PLATE 28
Hamburger Kunsthalle

Oil on mahogany panel; 13⅛" x 10⅞"; unsigned; *Hamburg*, no. 1396; Nathan no. G 70; pendant to above

These two portraits of Wasmann's brother Adolf and his wife indicate clearly that neither old-Germanness nor Overbeck define the full scope of Wasmann's pictorial vocabulary. In painting these urbane, sophisticated city dwellers, he shows himself aware of more complicated society portrait traditions which are modified to suit his own brand of pictorial naïveté and his inclinations toward ornamentation. The use of emblems—a canary for Frau Wasmann; the cigar, pictures of flowers and botanical specimen in a jar for her doctor-husband —is not relinquished. The setting is no longer the backdrop landscape of Meran, but, inside, looking out on the parks and skyline of urban Hamburg. However, like the landscapes, neither the space within the room nor its extension out through the window is actually made tangible; instead a decorative, simplified shorthand of already tested pictorial effects is employed. We are left with the feeling that much of both pictures was put together during the sitters' absence, relying on already two-dimensional images and ideas. Within Wasmann's collection of oil studies and sketches are several views of windows which, based on the process of seeing, almost always succeed in describing realistically the transition from the shallow space within a room to the endless vistas outside. Working from sketches like these and from equally available conventions of posing and dressing sitters (in the case of Dr. Wasmann the pose is almost a copy, in reverse, of his Meran portrait of Johann Ringler [See Nathan, no. G 30]), the painter could almost completely bypass concentrated observation and build a framework of decorative embellishment within which small moves toward human characterization can be made very expressive. Only the sardonic half-smile of Adolf Wasmann and the disconcerting disjuncture between his plastically conceived head and flat, schematic body outlines lend real life to the portrait; but they succeed in communicating extreme vitality. The portrait of his wife also receives its communicative impact from basically the same small concessions to visual appearance. Wasmann has again relied on a carefully structured opposition between his rendering of the sitter's body and her face. The face is a series of ovals, bare of shadow, in which the insistent drawing of the eyes can be counted on to command instant attention. In comparison, her dress has been described by a system of repetitive modules, each carrying about the same number of loose, liquidly painted stripes and all resolving into a nicely articulated group of fan shapes sitting close to the surface of the picture. Similar modules, the braids in her hair, are used to frame her face, emphasizing its severe simplicity and living separateness from the decorative elements of fabric and setting that bear the burden of what a society portrait should be.

[106.] *Mary Krämer* (1845)   PLATE 30
Hamburger Kunsthalle

Oil on oak panel; 8¾″ x 7¼″; signed lower right "Wasmañ f. 1845"; *Hamburg,* no. 2550; Nathan, no. G 76

Wasmann's small, stark oil sketch of his wife's mother provides a visual relief from the decorative complexities of his other portraits and an indication of the powerful and humane talent that was too often obscured by the trappings of his successful portrait business. His drawing style has relaxed enough that edges do not circumscribe, but enhance, the pictorial qualities of his form and facial structure exists as flesh over bone. Frau Krämer's folded hands and pensive, rounded face, highlighted within the ripples and curves of blackness that enclose her, communicate a moving humanness, sincerely described even though the image itself is not necessarily spontaneously generated.

151

While the neutrality of the background and the simple poignancy of the model's silhouette seem to anticipate a coming mode in European portraiture (cf. Thoma's *Wilhelm Steinhausen*), they seem to depend for pictorial assistance on a currently successful new image-making medium—the daguerreotype, which would have been common and widely discussed in Hamburg by the time of Wasmann's 1843–46 stay there. Static, closed poses were demanded by the camera's fifteen-second exposure time, while its limited photographic depth of field made it impossible to portray both sitter and background clearly. Frau Krämer is motionless. Her edges are eroded by the light that then passes around her solid body to illumine the blank background. The broad-value painting of her black cloak and dress and the indistinct, slightly unfocused shadows on her face are further reminiscences of Daguerre's images. In this portrait, Wasmann shows himself to be quite modern and independent in his responsiveness to and grasp of the visual qualities of the new medium of photography and their applicability to the age-old art of painting.

PLATE LIST

(in order according to arrangement of plates in catalogue)

Plate		*Cat. no.*
I.	COVER: Carus, Carl Gustav. *On the Elbe near Dresden* (1827) Kunstmuseum Düsseldorf, 11⅝″ x 8⅞″	9
II.	FRONTISPIECE: Feuerbach, Anselm. *Iphigenia* (1871) Staatsgalerie, Stuttgart, 77″ x 56″	28
1.	Hetsch, Philipp Friedrich von. *Allegory of Washington* (1793) Georg Schäfer Collection, Schweinfurt, 43⅝″ x 35⅛″	41
2.	Graff, Anton. *Portrait of Johann Adolf Freiherr von Thielmann in Saxon Husar Uniform with the Order of St. Heinrich* (ca. 1797) Germanisches Nationalmuseum, Nurnberg, 80″ x 45⅔″	38
3.	*Portrait of the Printmaker Bause* (ca. 1807–08) Bremen Kunsthalle, 28⅔″ x 22¾″	39
4.	Runge, Philipp Otto. *Self-Portrait in a Brown Coat* (ca. 1809–10) Hamburger Kunsthalle, 19⅛″ x 18⅞″	78
5.	*Morning* (large version) (ca. 1808–10) Hamburger Kunsthalle, 60⅞″ x 45⅛″	79
6.	Friedrich, Caspar David. *Woman in the Morning Light* (ca. 1809) Museum Folkwang, Essen, 8¾″ x 12″	29
7.	*The Lone Tree* (1823) Stiftung Preussischer Kulturbesitz, Staatliche Museen, National-galerie, Berlin (hereafter Berlin), 22″ x 28⅜″	31
8.	*Moonrise on the Sea* (1823) Berlin, 22″ x 28⅜″	32
9.	*Riverbank in Fog* (ca. 1816–20) Wallraf-Richartz Museum, Cologne, 8¾″ x 13⅜″	30
10.	*Man and Woman Contemplating the Moon* (ca. 1820–24) Berlin, 13⅝″ x 17⅜″	33
11.	*Neubrandenburg Burning at Sunset* (ca. 1834) Hamburger Kunsthalle, 28⅞″ x 40½″	34
12.	Kobell, Wilhelm von. *Horses in the Isar near Munich* (1815) Georg Schäfer Collection, Schweinfurt, 8⅞″ x 12⅜″	43
13.	*Landscape with Hunters near Schorndorf* (1823) Museum Folkwang, Essen, 17⅝″ x 25⅛″	44
14.	Koch, Joseph Anton. *Waterfall by Subiaco* (1813) Berlin, 23¼″ x 27¼″	46
15.	*Mountain Landscape* (1796) Wallraf-Richartz Museum, Cologne, 44″ x 64½″	45
16.	*Grotta Ferrata* (ca. 1834) Niedersächsches Landesmuseum (Landesgalerie), Hannover (here-after Hannover), 30¾″ x 41⅝″	47
17.	*Macbeth and the Witches* (ca. 1834) Von der Heydt-Museum, Wuppertal, 14⅝″ x 21¾″	48

18. Pforr, Franz. *St. George Killing the Dragon* (ca. 1810–12)
    Städtische Galerie, Frankfurt, 11⅛″ x 8½″ — 74
19. Overbeck, Friedrich Johann. *Italia and Germania* (ca. 1811–69)
    Georg Schäfer Collection, Schweinfurt, 8¾″ x 10¼″ — 73
20. Cornelius, Peter von. *The Five Wise and the Five Foolish Virgins*
    (ca. 1813–19)
    Kunstmuseum, Düsseldorf, 45½″ x 61″ — 18
21. Ramboux, Johann Anton. *Rebecca and Elieser at the Well* (1819)
    Berlin, 9⅞″ x 12½″ — 75
22. Olivier, Ferdinand. *Jesus and His Apostles* (ca. 1840)
    Georg Schäfer Collection, Schweinfurt, 9⅞″ x 11⅞″ — 72
23. Schnorr von Carolsfeld, Ludwig. *Leap from the Rocks* (1833)
    Georg Schäfer Collection, Schweinfurt, 29⅝″ x 17⅝″ — 80
24. Schwind, Moritz von. *Portrait of the Singer Caroline Hetzenecker* (1848)
    Germanisches Nationalmuseum, Nuremberg (on loan from the
    City Art Collection, Nuremberg), 49⅛″ x 38″ — 82
25. Leutze, Emanuel Gottlieb. *Frau Oberst Lottner* (ca. 1845)
    Staatsgalerie, Stuttgart, 22″ x 18⅞″ — 54
26.   *Herr Lottner* (1852)
    Kunstmuseum, Düsseldorf, 52⅜″ x 40″ — 55
27. Wasmann, Friedrich. *Dr. Adolph Wasmann* (1843)
    Hamburger Kunsthalle, 13⅛″ x 10⅞″ — 104
28.   *Frau Caroline Luise Mathilde Wasmann* (ca. 1843)
    Hamburger Kunsthalle, 13⅛″ x 10⅞″ — 105
29.   *Portrait of Frau Maria Lun (Bust of a Young Lady)* (1841)
    Hannover, 12⅛″ x 9⅝″ — 103
30.   *Mary Krämer* (1845)
    Hamburger Kunsthalle, 8¾″ x 7¼″ — 106
31.   *Etschtal with Two Children on a Hill* (1831)
    Hannover, 8⅛″ x 14¼″ — 101
32.   *Garden of Flowers in Meran* (ca. 1840)
    Hamburger Kunsthalle, 16″ x 13⅝″ — 102
33. Gensler, Johan Jacob. *Beach near Blankenese* (1842)
    Hamburger Kunsthalle, 13¾″ x 19¾″ — 36
34. Carus, Carl Gustav. *Bacharach on the Rhine* (1836)
    Georg Schäfer Collection, Schweinfurt, 40⅝″ x 20⅜″ — 10
35.   *Balcony in the Moonlight* (ca. 1836–43)
    Georg Schäfer Collection, Schweinfurt, 40″ x 20⅞″ — 11
36. Dahl, Johann Christian Clausen. *Cloud Study* (1834)
    Berlin, 10″ x 11⅛″ — 19
37.   *The Copenhagen Harbor by Moonlight* (1837)
    Georg Schäfer Collection, Schweinfurt, 21⅝″ x 28½″ — 20
38. Gille, Christian Friedrich. *The Brühlsche Terrace in Dresden* (1862)
    Hannover, 13⅜″ x 21⅛″ — 37
39. Gärtner, Eduard. *The New Guardhouse* (1833)
    Berlin, 18⅞″ x 30⅞″ — 35

154

40. Hummel, Johann Erdmann. *The Granite Dish in the Pleasure Garden, Berlin* (ca. 1832)
Berlin, 26⅜" x 35⅝" — 42

41. Blechen, Karl. *The Interior of the Palm House on the Pfaueninsel* (1832)
Berlin, 25⅝" x 22⅜" — 3

42. *View of Rooftops and Gardens* (ca. 1828)
Berlin, 8" x 10" — 1

43. *A Bay near Naples* (ca. 1829)
Städtische Kunsthalle, Mannheim, 11¼" x 17" — 2

44. *Rolling Mill near Neustadt-Eberswalde* (ca. 1834)
Berlin, 10" x 13⅛" — 4

45. Rethel, Alfred. *The Harkort Factory on Burg Wetter* (1834)
DEMAG-AG, Duisburg, 17⅛" x 23⅛" — 77

46. Menzel, Adolf von. *The Room with a Balcony* (1845)
Berlin, 23¼" x 18¾" — 67

47. *View of a Factory Fire* (ca. 1854)
Private Collection, Germany, 8¾" x 13¼" — 68

48. *King Wilhelm I's Farewell to the Army on July 31, 1870* (1871)
Berlin, 25¼" x 31¼" — 70

49. *Théâtre du Gymnase in Paris* (1856)
Berlin, 18⅜" x 24¾" — 69

50. *The Wall of the Studio* (1872)
Hamburger Kunsthalle, 44⅜" x 31¾" — 71

51. Rayski, Ferdinand von. *Portrait of Count Haubold von Einsiedel* (1855)
Berlin, 29¼" x 24⅞" — 76

52. Feuerbach, Anselm. *Youthful Self-Portrait* (ca. 1852–54)
Staatliche Kunsthalle, Karlsruhe, 16⅞" x 13⅛" — 24

53. *Nanna* (1861)
Wallraf-Richartz Museum, Cologne, 29⅜" x 22⅛" — 25

54. *Portrait of the Artist's Stepmother* (1867)
Kurpfälzisches Museum, Heidelberg, 42⅜" x 33" — 27

55. *Paolo and Francesca da Rimini* (1864)
Städtische Kunsthalle, Mannheim, 30⅜" x 23⅛" — 26

56. Böcklin, Arnold. *The Artist with His Wife* (ca. 1863–64)
Berlin, 25¼" x 20" — 5

57. *Blue Venus* (ca. 1869)
Hessiches Landesmuseum, Darmstadt (on loan from the Bundesrepublik, Deutschland), 54⅞" x 31⅝" — 6

58. *Wedding Trip* (1875)
Städtische Galerie, Frankfurt (on loan from the Bundesrepublik, Deutschland), 28⅞" x 21" — 8

59. *Self-Portrait with Death as the Fiddler* (1872)
Berlin, 30" x 24⅜" — 7

60. Marées, Hans von. *Self-Portrait with Hildebrand and Grant* (1873)
Von der Heydt-Museum, Wuppertal, 32" x 32⅜" — 64

61. *Foraging Soldiers* (1862)
Von der Heydt-Museum, Wuppertal, 21⅛" x 29⅝" — 63

155

62. *Orange Picker* (1873)
Berlin, 79⅛″ x 39⅛″ 65
63. *Boys Bathing* (ca. 1874)
Von der Heydt-Museum, Wuppertal, 32″ x 40″ 66
64. Spitzweg, Carl. *In Peacetime* (1856)
Städtische Kunsthalle, Mannheim, 8⅝″ x 19⅞″ 88
65. *Sunday Afternoon* (1873)
Georg Schäfer Collection, Schweinfurt, 8⅝″ x 11⅞″ 89
66. Sohn, Carl. *Else Sohn-Rethel* (1873)
Kunstmuseum, Düsseldorf, 42⅞″ x 34″ 87
67. Leibl, Wilhelm. *The Painter Eduard Fischer* (1875)
Wallraf-Richartz Museum, Cologne, 17⅝″ x 26⅝″ 49
68. *The Wife of the Bürgermeister of Kutterling* (1892)
Georg Schäfer Collection, Schweinfurt, 26″ x 19¾″ 51
69. *Countess Rosine Treuberg* (1878)
Hamburger Kunsthalle, 41⅝″ x 32⅞″ 50
70. *The Description of the Hunt* (1893)
Wallraf-Richartz Museum, Cologne, 29⅜″ x 34⅝″ 52
71. *Kitchen in Kutterling* (1898)
Wallraf-Richartz Museum, Cologne, 33⅝″ x 25¾″ 53
72. Thoma, Hans. *Head of a Woman* (1862)
Kunstmuseum, Düsseldorf, 20″ x 16⅛″ 90
73. *Self-Portrait* (1871)
Hamburger Kunsthalle, 42⅛″ x 31″ 93
74. *Portrait of the Painter Wilhelm Steinhausen* (1869)
Staatliche Kunsthalle, Karlsruhe, 30⅝″ x 41⅝″ 91
75. *The Rhine near Laufenberg* (1870)
Berlin, 22¾″ x 18⅜″ 92
76. *The Rhine near Säckingen* (1873)
Berlin, 25⅞″ x 45″ 94
77. *The Weed Sower* (1888)
Städtische Galerie, Frankfurt, 30″ x 38⅞″ 95
78. Trübner, Wilhelm. *Boat Landing on the Herreninsel* (1874)
Staatliche Kunsthalle, Karlsruhe, 16⅝″ x 22⅝″ 96
79. *Lady in Gray* (1876)
Museum Folkwang, Essen, 42½″ x 37¼″ 97
80. *Frauenchiemsee Landscape* (ca. 1890)
Von der Heydt-Museum, Wuppertal, 20¾″ x 26⅜″ 98
81. Hagemeister, Karl. *White Poppies* (1881)
Hannover, 31⅝″ x 46¾″ 40
82. Eysen, Louis. *Still Life with Apples and Quinces* (ca. 1869–70)
Städtische Galerie, Frankfurt, 9⅞″ x 13⅜″ 21
83. *White House on a Hill* (ca. 1887)
Städtische Galerie, Frankfurt, 13¼″ x 21⅜″ 23
84. *Flower Still Life with Delft Vase and Brass Ware* (ca. 1882)
Staatliche Kunsthalle, Karlsruhe, 22⅝″ x 17¼″ 22
85. Schuch, Carl. *Still Life with Leeks* (ca. 1883–84)
Hannover, 24¼″ x 30⅜″ 81

86. Liebermann, Max. *The Bleaching Ground* (1882)
   Wallraf-Richartz Museum, Cologne, 43⅝″ x 69¼″   56

87.   *Papageienallee, Amsterdam* (1902)
   Bremen Kunsthalle, 35⅛″ x 29″   58

88.   *Terrace in the Restaurant Jacob, Nienstedten* (ca. 1902)
   Hamburger Kunsthalle, 28″ x 40″   59

89.   *Beach at Scheveningen* (ca. 1908)
   Von der Heydt-Museum, Wuppertal, 26⅛″ x 31⅞″   62

90.   *Bürgermeister Petersen* (1891)
   Hamburger Kunsthalle, 82⅜″ x 47⅝″   57

91.   *Self-Portrait* (1908)
   Saarland Museum, Saarbrücken, 38⅞″ x 30⅜″   61

92.   *Portrait of Freiherrn Alfred von Berger* (1905)
   Hamburger Kunsthalle, 44⅞″ x 34⅜″   60

93. Corinth, Lovis. *Self-Portrait with Image of Death* (1896)
   Städtische Galerie (Im Lenbach Haus), Munich, 27⅛″ x 35⅛″   14

94.   *Portrait of the Artist's Father* (1888)
   Private Collection, 46½″ x 39⅜″   12

95.   *Susanna in the Bath* (1890)
   Museum Folkwang, Essen, 63⅝″ x 44⅜″   13

96.   *Portrait of the Painter Eckmann* (1897)
   Hamburger Kunsthalle, 44″ x 22″   15

97.   *Recumbent Nude* (1899)
   Bremen Kunsthalle, 30″ x 48″   16

98.   *The Family of the Painter Fritz Rumpf* (1901)
   Berlin, 45⅛″ x 56″   17

99. Uhde, Fritz von. *Young Woman at the Window* (ca. 1891)
   Städtische Galerie, Frankfurt, 32¼″ x 26¼″   99

100.   *The Artist's Daughters in the Garden* (1901)
   Städtische Galerie, Frankfurt, 54⅞″ x 60⅝″   100

101. Slevogt, Max. *Eduard Fuchs* (1905)
   Staatsgalerie, Stuttgart, 72⅛″ x 28⅛″   85

102.   *Portrait of Gertraud Fuchs as a Child* (1903)
   Staatsgalerie, Stuttgart, 30⅞″ x 25⅝″   83

103.   *Frida Fuchs* (1904)
   Staatsgalerie, Stuttgart, 36⅞″ x 29⅝″   84

104.   *Portrait of a Woman* (1905)
   Bremen Kunsthalle, 56⅞″ x 36⅞″   86

157

PLATES

1. Hetsch: *Allegory of Washington*, 1793. 43⅝″ x 35⅛″
    Georg Schäfer Collection, Schweinfurt   Cat. no. 41

2. Graff: *Portrait of Johann Adolf Freiherr von Thielmann*, ca. 1797. 80″ x 45⅔″
Germanisches Nationalmuseum, Nuremberg   Cat. no. 38

3. Graff: *Portrait of the Printmaker Bause,* ca. 1807–08. 28⅔″ x 22¾″
   Bremen Kunsthalle   Cat. no. 39

4. Runge: *Self-Portrait in a Brown Coat,* ca. 1809–10. 19⅛″ x 18⅞″
   Hamburger Kunsthalle   Cat. no. 78

5. Runge: *The Morning* (large version), ca. 1808–10. 60⅞″ x 45⅛″
   Hamburger Kunsthalle   Cat. no. 79

6. Friedrich: *Woman in the Morning Light,* ca. 1809. 8¾″ x 12″
Museum Folkwang, Essen   Cat. no. 29

7.   Friedrich: *The Lone Tree*, 1823. 22″ x 28⅜″
        Nationalgalerie, Berlin   Cat. no. 31

8.   Friedrich: *Moonrise on the Sea*, 1823. 22″ x 28⅜″
        Nationalgalerie, Berlin   Cat. no. 32

9.   Friedrich: *Riverbank in Fog,* ca. 1816–20. 8¾″ x 13⅜″
     Wallraf-Richartz Museum, Cologne   Cat. no. 30

10.   Friedrich: *Man and Woman Contemplating the Moon,* ca. 1820–24. 13⅝″ x 17⅜″
      Nationalgalerie, Berlin   Cat. no. 33

11.   Friedrich: *Neubrandenburg Burning at Sunset,* ca. 1834. 28⅞″ x 40½″
      Hamburger Kunsthalle   Cat. no. 34

12.   Kobell: *Horses in the Isar near Munich*, 1815. 8⅞" x 12⅜"
Georg Schäfer Collection, Schweinfurt   Cat. no. 43

13.   Kobell: *Landscape with Hunters near Schorndorf*, 1823. 17⅝" x 25⅛"
Museum Folkwang, Essen   Cat. no. 44

14. Koch: *Waterfall by Subiaco,* 1813. 23¼″ x 27¼″
Nationalgalerie, Berlin   Cat. no. 46

15. Koch: *Mountain Landscape,* 1796. 44″ x 64½″
Wallraf-Richartz Museum, Cologne   Cat. no. 45

16.   Koch: *Grotta Ferrata*, ca. 1834. 30¾″ x 41⅝″
Niedersächsisches Landesmuseum, Hannover   Cat. no. 47

17.   Koch: *Macbeth and the Witches*, ca. 1834. 14⅝″ x 21¾″
Von der Heydt-Museum, Wuppertal   Cat. no 48

18. Pforr: *St. George Killing the Dragon,* ca. 1810–12. 11⅛" x 8½"
       Städtische Galerie, Frankfurt   Cat. no. 74

19.   Overbeck: *Italia and Germania,* ca. 1811–69. 8¾″ x 10¼″
George Schäfer Collection, Schweinfurt   Cat. no. 73

20. Cornelius: *The Five Wise and Five Foolish Virgins,* ca. 1813–19. 45½" x 61"
Kunstmuseum, Düsseldorf   Cat. no. 18

21. Ramboux: *Rebecca and Elieser at the Well,* 1819. 9⅞″ x 12½″
Nationalgalerie, Berlin   Cat. no. 75

22. Olivier: *Jesus and His Apostles,* ca. 1840. 9⅞″ x 11⅞″
George Schäfer Collection, Schweinfurt   Cat. no. 72

23. Schnorr von Carolsfeld: *Leap from the Rocks,* 1833. 29⅝″ x 17⅝″
     Georg Schäfer Collection, Schweinfurt   Cat. no. 80

24. Schwind: *Portrait of the Singer Caroline Hetzenecker*, 1848. 49⅛″ x 38″
Germanisches Nationalmuseum, Nuremberg (on loan from the City Art
Collection, Nuremberg)   Cat. no. 82

25. Leutze: *Frau Oberst Lottner,* ca. 1845. 22″ x 18⅞″
Staatsgalerie, Stuttgart   Cat. no. 54

26. Leutze: *Herr Lottner,* 1852. 52⅜″ x 40″
Kunstmuseum, Düsseldorf   Cat. no. 55

27. Wasmann: *Dr. Adolph Wasmann*, 1843.
13⅛″ x 10⅞″
Hamburger Kunsthalle   Cat. no. 104

28. Wasmann: *Frau Caroline Luise Mathilde Wasmann*,
ca. 1843. 13⅛″ x 10⅞″
Hamburger Kunsthalle   Cat. no. 105

29. Wasmann: *Portrait of Frau Maria Lun (Bust of a
Young Lady)*, 1841. 12⅛″ x 9⅝″
Niedersächsisches Landesmuseum,
Hannover   Cat. no. 103

30. Wasmann: *Mary Krämer*, 1845, 8¾″ x 7¼″
Hamburger Kunsthalle   Cat. no. 106

31. Wasmann: *Etschtal with Two Children on a Hill*, 1831. 8⅛" x 14¼"
     Niedersächsisches Landesmuseum, Hannover   Cat. no. 101

32. Wasmann: *Garden of Flowers in Meran*, ca. 1840. 16″ x 13⅝″
Hamburger Kunsthalle
Cat. no. 102

33. Gensler: *Beach near Blankenese*, 1842. 13¾″ x 19¾″
Hamburger Kunsthalle
Cat. no. 36

34.   Carus: *Bacharach on the Rhine*, 1836. 40⅝″ x 20⅜″
Georg Schäfer Collection, Schweinfurt   Cat. no. 10

35. Carus: *Balcony in the Moonlight,* ca. 1836–43. 40″ x 20⅞″
Georg Schäfer Collection, Schweinfurt   Cat. no. 11

36. Dahl: *Cloud Study*, 1834. 10″ x 11⅛″
    Nationalgalerie, Berlin   Cat. no. 19

37.   Dahl: *The Copenhagen Harbor in the Moonlight*, 1837. 21⅝″ x 28½″
Georg Schäfer Collection, Schweinfurt   Cat. no. 20

38.   Gille: *The Brühlsche Terrace in Dresden*, 1862. 13⅜″ x 21⅛″
Niedersächsisches Landesmuseum, Hannover   Cat. no. 37

39. Gärtner: *The New Guardhouse*, 1833. 18⅞″ x 30⅞″
      Nationalgalerie, Berlin   Cat. no. 35

40. Hummel: *The Granite Dish in the Pleasure Garden, Berlin*, ca. 1832. 26⅜″ x 35⅝″
      Nationalgalerie, Berlin   Cat. no. 42

41.   Blechen: *The Interior of the Palm House on the Pfaueninsel,* 1832. 25⅝″ x 22⅜″
Nationalgalerie, Berlin   Cat. no. 3

42. Blechen: *View of Rooftops and Gardens,* ca. 1828. 8″ x 10″
    Nationalgalerie, Berlin   Cat. no. 1

43. Blechen: *A Bay near Naples,* ca. 1829. 11¼″ x 17″
    Städtische Kunsthalle, Mannheim   Cat. no. 2

44. Blechen: *Rolling Mill near Neustadt-Eberswalde,* ca. 1834. 10″ x 13⅛″
Nationalgalerie, Berlin   Cat. no. 4

45. Rethel: *The Harkort Factory on Burg Wetter,* 1834. 17⅛″ x 23⅛″
DEMAG-AG, Duisburg   Cat. no. 77

46.   Menzel: *The Room with a Balcony*, 1845. 23¼" x 18¾"
       Nationalgalerie, Berlin   Cat. no. 67

47. Menzel: *View of a Factory Fire,* ca. 1854. 8¾″ x 13¼″
Private Collection, Germany   Cat. no. 68

48.   Menzel: *King Wilhelm I's Farewell to the Army on July 31, 1870*, 1871. 25¼″ x 31¼″
       Nationalgalerie, Berlin   Cat. no. 70

49.   Menzel: *Théâtre du Gymnase in Paris*, 1856. 18⅜″ x 24¾″
       Nationalgalerie, Berlin   Cat. no. 69

50.   Menzel: *The Wall of the Studio,* 1872. 44⅜″ x 31¾″
Hamburger Kunsthalle   Cat. no. 71

51. Rayski: *Portrait of Count Haubold von Einsiedel,* 1855. 29¼″ x 24⅞″
     Nationalgalerie, Berlin   Cat. no. 76

52. Feuerbach: *Youthful Self-Portrait*, ca. 1852–54. 16⅞″ x 13⅛″
Staatliche Kunsthalle, Karlsruhe   Cat. no. 24

53. Feuerbach: *Nanna*, 1861. 29⅜" x 22⅛"
    Wallraf-Richartz Museum, Cologne   Cat. no. 25

54. Feuerbach: *Portrait of the Artist's Stepmother,* 1867. 42⅜″ x 33″
Kurpfälzisches Museum, Heidelberg   Cat. no. 27

55. Feuerbach: *Paolo and Francesca da Rimini,* 1864. 30⅜" x 23⅛"
Städtische Kunsthalle, Mannheim   Cat. no. 26

56. Böcklin: *The Artist with His Wife*, ca. 1863–64. 25¼″ x 20″
Nationalgalerie, Berlin   Cat. no. 5

57. Böcklin: *Blue Venus,* ca. 1869. 54⅞″ x 31⅝″
    Hessiches Landesmuseum, Darmstadt (on loan from the Bundesrepublik, Deutschland)
    Cat. no. 6

58.   Böcklin: *Wedding Trip*, 1875. 28⅞″ x 21″
     Städtische Galerie, Frankfurt (on loan from the Bundesrepublik, Deutschland)   Cat. no. 8

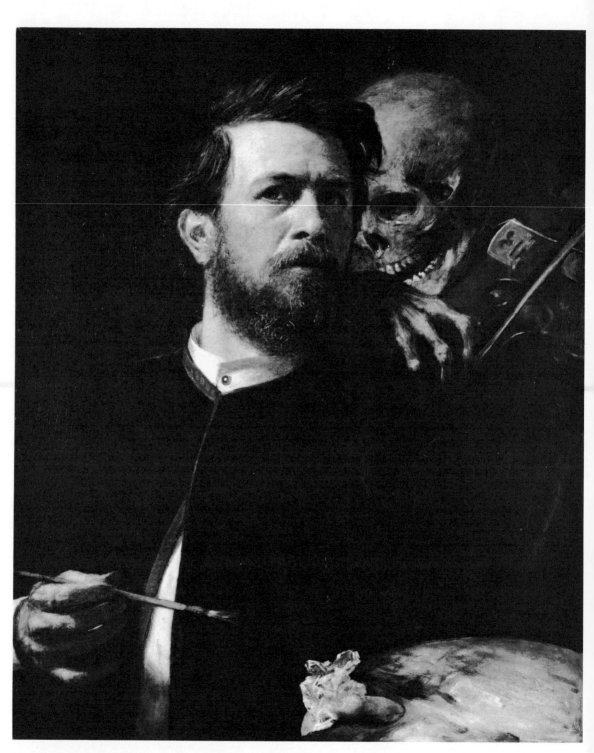

59.   Böcklin: *Self-Portrait with Death as the Fiddler*, 1872. 30" x 24⅜"
      Nationalgalerie, Berlin   Cat. no. 7

60.   Marées: *Self-Portrait with Hildebrand and Grant*, 1873. 32″ x 32⅜″
Von der Heydt-Museum, Wuppertal   Cat. no. 64

61. Marées: *Foraging Soldiers*, 1862. 21⅛″ x 29⅝″
     Von der Heydt-Museum, Wuppertal   Cat. no. 63

63. Marées: *Boys Bathing*, ca. 1874. 32″ x 40″
     Von der Heydt-Museum, Wuppertal   Cat. no. 66

62.   Marées: *Orange Picker*, 1873. 79⅛″ x 39⅛″
Nationalgalerie, Berlin   Cat. no. 65

64. Spitzweg: *In Peacetime*. 1856. 8⅝″ x 19⅞″
       Städtische Kunsthalle, Mannheim   Cat. no. 88

65. Spitzweg: *Sunday Afternoon*, 1873. 8⅝″ x 11⅞″
       Georg Schäfer Collection, Schweinfurt   Cat. no. 89

66.   Sohn: *Else Sohn-Rethel*, 1873. 42⅞″ x 34″
Kunstmuseum Düsseldorf   Cat. no. 87

67. Leibl: *The Painter Eduard Fisher,* 1875.
17⅝″ x 26⅝″
Wallraf-Richartz Museum,
Cologne   Cat. no. 49

68. Leibl: *The Wife of the Bürgermeister of
Kutterling,* 1892. 26″ x 19¾″
Georg Schäfer Collection,
Schweinfurt   Cat. no. 51

69.   Leibl: *Countess Rosine Treuberg*, 1878. 41⅝″ x 32⅞″
Hamburger Kunsthalle   Cat. no 50

70. Leibl: *The Description of the Hunt*, 1893. 29⅜″ x 34⅝″
Wallraf-Richartz Museum, Cologne   Cat. no. 52

71. Leibl: *Kitchen in Kutterling*, 1898. 33⅝″ x 25¾″
Wallraf-Richartz Museum, Cologne   Cat. no. 53

72. Thoma: *Head of a Woman*, 1862. 20″ x 16⅛″
Kunstmuseum, Düsseldorf   Cat. no 90

73. Thoma: *Self-Portrait*, 1871. 42⅛″ x 31″
Hamburger Kunsthalle   Cat. no. 93

74. Thoma: *Portrait of the Painter Wilhelm Steinhausen*, 1869. 30⅝″ x 41⅝″
Staatliche Kunsthalle, Karlsruhe   Cat. no. 91

75. Thoma: *The Rhine near Laufenberg*, 1870. 22¾" x 18⅜"
Nationalgalerie, Berlin Cat. no. 92

76. Thoma: *The Rhine near Säckingen*, 1873. 25⅞″ x 45″
Nationalgalerie, Berlin   Cat. no. 94

77. Thoma: *The Weed Sower*, 1888. 30″ x 38⅞″
Städtische Galerie, Frankfurt   Cat. no. 95

78. Trübner: *Boat Landing on the Herreninsel*, 1874. 16⅝″ x 22⅝″
Staatliche Kunsthalle, Karlsruhe   Cat. no. 96

79. Trübner: *Lady in Gray*, 1876. 42½″ x 37¼″
Museum Folkwang, Essen   Cat. no. 97

80. Trübner: *Frauenchiemsee Landscape,* ca. 1890. 20¾″ x 26⅜″
Von der Heydt-Museum, Wuppertal   Cat. no. 98

81. Hagemeister: *White Poppies,* 1881. 31⅝" x 46¾"
Niedersächsisches Landesmuseum, Hannover   Cat. no. 40

82. Eysen: *Still Life with Apples and Quinces*, ca. 1869–70. 9⅞″ x 13⅜″
    Städtische Galerie, Frankfurt   Cat. no. 21

83. Eysen: *White House on a Hill*, ca. 1887. 13¼″ x 21⅜″
    Städtische Galerie, Frankfurt   Cat. no. 23

84. Eysen: *Flower Still Life with Delft Vase and Brass Ware,* ca. 1882. 22⅝" x 17¼"
Staatliche Kunsthalle,
Karlsruhe   Cat. no. 22

85. Schuch: *Still Life with Leeks,* ca. 1883–84.
24¼" x 30⅜"
Niedersächsisches Landesmuseum,
Hannover   Cat. no. 81

86.   Liebermann: *The Bleaching Ground*, 1882. 43⅝″ x 69¼″
Wallraf-Richartz Museum, Cologne   Cat. no. 56

87. Liebermann: *Papageienallee, Amsterdam*, 1902. 35⅛″ x 29″
Bremen Kunsthalle   Cat. no. 58

88. Liebermann: *Terrace in the Restaurant Jacob, Nienstedten*, ca. 1902. 28" x 40"
    Hamburger Kunsthalle   Cat. no. 59

89. Liebermann: *Beach at Scheveningen*, ca. 1908. 26⅛" x 31⅞"
    Von der Heydt-Museum, Wuppertal   Cat. no. 62

90. Liebermann: *Bürgermeister Petersen*, 1891. 82⅜″ x 47⅝″
Hamburger Kunsthalle   Cat. no. 57

91. Liebermann: *Self-Portrait*, 1908.
   38⅞″ x 30⅜″
   Saarland Museum,
   Saarbrücken   Cat. no. 61

92. Liebermann: *Portrait of Freiherrn Alfred
   von Berger*, 1905. 44⅞″ x 34⅜″
      Hamburger Kunsthalle   Cat. no. 60

93. Corinth: *Self-Portrait with Image of Death*, 1896. 27⅛″ x 35⅛″
Städtische Galerie (Im Lenbach Haus), Munich   Cat. no. 14

94. Corinth: *Portrait of the Artist's Father*, 1888. 46½″ x 39⅜″
Private Collection   Cat. no. 12

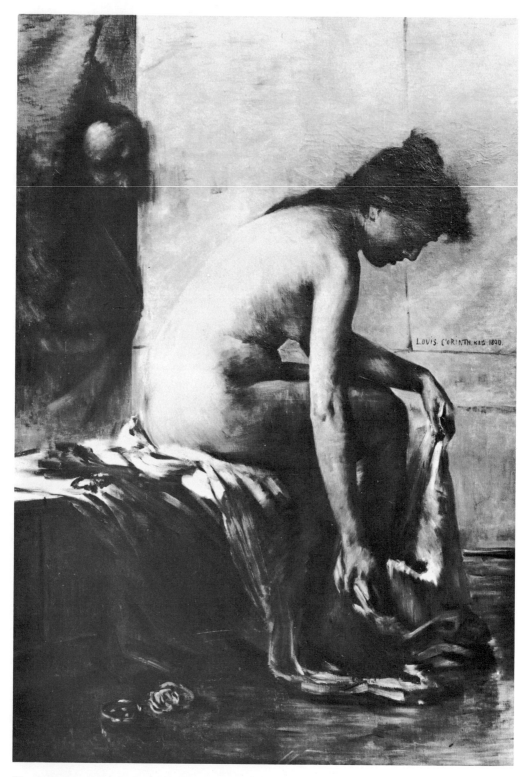

95. Corinth: *Susanna in the Bath*, 1890. 63⅝″ x 44⅜″
     Museum Folkwang, Essen   Cat. no 13

OTTO·HICKMANN·AETATIS·SUAE·XXXIII·LOVIS·CORINTH·PINXIT·ANNO·1897

96.   Corinth: *Portrait of the Painter Eckmann,* 1897. 44″ x 22″
Hamburger Kunsthalle   Cat. no. 15

97.   Corinth: *Recumbent Nude,* 1899. 30″ x 48″
      Bremen Kunsthalle   Cat. no. 16

98.   Corinth. *The Family of the Painter Fritz Rumpf*, 1901. 45⅛" x 56"
Nationalgalerie, Berlin   Cat. no. 17

99.   Uhde: *Young Woman at the Window*, ca. 1891. 32¼″ x 26¼″
      Städtische Galerie, Frankfurt   Cat. no. 99

100.   Uhde: *The Artist's Daughters in the Garden*, 1901. 54⅞″ x 60⅝″
Städtische Galerie, Frankfurt   Cat. no. 100

101. Slevogt: *Eduard Fuchs*, 1905. 72⅛″ 28⅛″
Staatsgalerie, Stuttgart   Cat. no. 85

102. Slevogt: *Portrait of Gertraud*
      Fuchs as a Child, 1903.
      30⅞″ x 25⅝″
        Staatsgalerie, Stuttgart
        Cat. no. 83

103. Slevogt: *Frida Fuchs,* 1904.
      36⅞″ x 29⅝″
        Staatsgalerie, Stuttgart
        Cat. no. 84

104. Slevogt: *Portrait of a Woman*, 1905. 56⅞" x 36⅞"
Bremen Kunsthalle   Cat. no. 86

BIBLIOGRAPHY

This bibliography is limited to works directly cited in the text of the catalogue, to other basic studies which the authors have found especially helpful, and to works in English. For more extended bibliographies see those books below which are marked with an asterisk.

Allgeyer, Julius. *Anselm Feuerbach.* Edited by Carl Neumann. 2 vols. Berlin and Leipzig, 1904.

Andree, Rolf. *Katalog der Gemälde des 19. Jahrhunderts im Wallraf-Richartz Museum.* Cologne, 1964.

*Andrews, Keith. *The Nazarenes: A Brotherhood of German Painters in Rome.* Oxford, 1964.

Berckenhagen, Ekhart. *Anton Graff: Leben und Werk.* Berlin, 1967.

Berefelt, Gunnar. *Philipp Otto Runge: Zwischen Aufbruch und Opposition 1777–1802.* Stockholm and Uppsala, 1961.

Berend-Corinth, Charlotte. *Die Gemälde von Lovis Corinth.* Introduction by Hans Konrad Röthel. Munich, 1958.

Beringer, Josef August. *Trübner: eine Auswahl aus dem Lebenswerk des Meisters.* Stuttgart and Berlin, 1921.

Berlin Nationalgalerie. *Verzeichnis der Vereinigten Kunstsammlungen Nationalgalerie (Preussischer Kulturbesitz) Galerie des 20. Jahrhunderts (Land Berlin).* Berlin, 1968.

Bisanz, Rudolf M. *German Romanticism and Philipp Otto Runge.* Dekalb, Ill., to be published in 1970.

Börsch-Supan, Helmut. *Die Bildgestaltung bei Caspar David Friedrich.* Munich, 1960.

Carus, Carl Gustav. *Friedrich der Landschaftsmaler.* Dresden, 1841; facsimile. Berlin, 1944.

Düsseldorf, Kunstmuseum. See Kunstmuseum, Düsseldorf.

Einem, Herbert von. *Caspar David Friedrich.* 3d ed. Berlin, 1950.

Essen, Museum Folkwang. See Museum Folkwang, Essen.

Ettlinger, L. D. *Caspar David Friedrich.* London, 1967.

German Library of Information. *Caspar David Friedrich, his Life and Work.* New York, 1940.

Goethe, Johann Wolfgang von. *Theory of Colors.* Translated by Charles Lock Eastlake. London, 1840; facsimile. London, 1967.

Grundy, J. B. C. *Tieck and Runge: A Study in the Relationship of Literature and Art in the Romantic Period, with Especial Reference to "Franz Sternbald".* Strasbourg, 1930.

Holt, Elizabeth Gilmore. *From the Classicists to the Impressionists: A Documentary History of Art and Architecture in the 19th Century.* New York, 1966.

Imiela, Hans-Jürgen. *Max Slevogt.* Karlsruhe, 1968.

Jensen, J. C. *Friedrich Overbeck: Die Werke im Behnhaus.* Museumsheft 4. Lübeck, 1963.

Justi, Ludwig. *Deutsche Malkunst im Neunzehnten Jahrhundert: Eine Führer durch die Nationalgalerie.* Berlin, 1921.

*Kaiser, Konrad, et al. *Der Frühe Realismus in Deutschland: Gemälde und Zeichnungen aus der Sammlung Georg Schäfer, Schweinfurt.* Nuremberg, 1967.

*———. *Klassizismus und Romantik in Deutschland: Gemälde und Zeichnungen aus der Sammlung Georg Schäfer, Schweinfurt.* Nuremberg, 1966.

*———. *Romantik und Realismus in Österreich: Gemälde und Zeichnungen aus der Sammlung Georg Schäfer, Schweinfurt.* Vienna, 1968.

Karlsruhe, Staatliche Kunsthalle. See Staatliche Kunsthalle, Karlsruhe.

Krafft, Eva Maria, and Schümann, Carl-Wolfgang. *Katalog der Meister des 19. Jahrhunderts in der Hamburger Kunsthalle.* Hamburg, 1969.

Kuhn, Alfred. *Peter Cornelius und die Geistigen Strömungen seiner Zeit.* Berlin, 1921.

Kunstmuseum, Düsseldorf. *Sammlungs-Katalogue.* Düsseldorf, 1959, 1962. *Katalogue der Düsseldorfer Malerschule.* Forthcoming (with same ref. nos.).

Lutterotti, Otto R. von. *Joseph Anton Koch mit Werkverzeichnis und Briefen des Künstlers.* Berlin, 1940.

Mann, Golo. *The History of Germany since 1789.* Translated by Marian Jackson. London, 1968.

Marées, Hans von. *Briefe.* Munich, 1923.

Meier-Graefe, Julius. *The Development of Modern Art, Being a Contribution to a New System of Aesthetics.* 2 vols. New York, 1908; *Entwicklungsgeschichte der Modernen Kunst* 2d German ed. 3 vols. Munich, 1927.

———. *Hans von Marées.* 2 vols. Munich and Leipzig, 1910.

Museum Folkwang, Essen. *Gemälde—19. und 20. Jahrhundert.* Essen, 1963.

Nathan, Peter. *Friedrich Wasmann: sein Leben und sein Werk.* Munich, 1954.

Nochlin, Linda. *Realism and Tradition in Art 1848–1900.* Sources and Documents in the History of Art. Englewood Cliffs, N.J., 1966.

*Novotny, Fritz. *Painting and Sculpture in Europe 1780–1880.* Pelican History of Art. Baltimore, Md., 1960.

Oldenbourg, Rudolf, and Uhde-Bernays, Hermann. *Die Münchner Malerei im Neunzehnten Jahrhundert.* Munich, 1922.

Pauli, Gustav. *Max Liebermann: des Meisters Gemälde.* Klassiker der Kunst. Stuttgart and Leipzig, 1911.

Prause, Marianne. *Carl Gustav Carus als Maler.* Dissertation, Cologne, 1963; republished. Berlin, 1968.

Rave, Paul Ortwin. *Deutsche Malerei des 19. Jahrhunderts.* Berlin, 1945.

———. *Karl Blechen: Leben Würdigungen, Werk.* Berlin, 1940.

Roennefahrt, Günther. *Carl Spitzweg: Beschreibendes Verzeichnis seiner Gemälde, Ölstudien und Aquarelle.* Munich, 1960.

Rosenhagen, Hans. *Uhde: des Meisters Gemälde.* Klassiker der Kunst. Stuttgart and Leipzig, 1908.

Runge, Philipp Otto. *Hinterlassene Schriften (herausgegeben von dessen ältestem Bruder).* 2 vols. Hamburg, 1841; facsimile. Göttingen, 1965.

Scheffler, Karl. *Menzel: der Mensch, das Werk.* 2d ed. Munich, 1955.

Schmid, Heinrich, Anton. *Arnold Böcklin: eine Auswahl der Hervorragendsten Werke des Künstlers.* 4 vols. Munich, 1892–1901.

Staatliche Kunsthalle, Karlsruhe. *Anselm Feuerbach.* Karlsruhe, 1961.

———. *Hans Thoma und sein Kreis.* Karlsruhe, 1961.

Staatsgalerie, Stuttgart. *Katalog der Staatsgalerie Stuttgart: Neue Meister.* Stuttgart, 1968.

Tate Gallery, London. *The Romantic Movement.* London, 1959.

Thode, Henry. *Thoma: des Meisters Gemälde.* Klassiker der Kunst. Stuttgart and Leipzig, 1909.

Thoma, Hans. *Im Herbste des Lebens.* Munich, 1909.

Wachtmann, Hans Günther. *Von der Heydt–Museum, Wuppertal—Verzeichnis der Gemälde und Skulpturen* (without page or catalogue reference numbers, so no citation in text above. Wuppertal, 1968.

Waldmann, Emil. *Wilhelm Leibl: eine Darstellung seiner Kunst, Gesamtverzeichnis seiner Gemälde.* Berlin, 1930.

Walter, Maräuschlein. *Ferdinand von Rayski: sein Leben und sein Werk.* Bielefeld and Leipzig, 1943.

Weigmann, Otto. *Schwind: des Meisters Werke.* Klassiker der Kunst. Stuttgart and Leipzig, 1906.

*Wichmann, Siegfried. *Realismus und Impressionismus in Deutschland: Bemerkungen zur Freilichtmalerei des 19. und Beginnenden 20. Jahrhunderts.* Stuttgart, 1964.

Wolf, Georg Jacob. *Leibl und sein Kreis.* Munich, 1923.

Zimmermann, Werner. *Der Maler Louis Eysen.* Frankfurt, 1963.